HEAR *us*
ROAR

LIONESS EDITION

KMD
BOOKS

CONTENTS

KAREN WEAVER
INTRODUCTION

'Stealth is the sacred art of entering the faith of your heart and leaving behind the noise of your mind.'

When the *Lioness* book called me to create it, I envisioned bringing together extraordinary women – and men – who are roaring in this world, sharing their stories of stealth and faith. I wanted readers to truly grasp the essence of these two intertwined forces. This book embodies exactly that.

Oh, my goodness – the stories that have come into this book are nothing short of powerful. Stealth is about moving with quiet determination, taking action without the need for validation and allowing your results to speak for themselves. Faith is the unwavering trust in your journey, even when the path isn't clear. Both require belief, persistence and an unshakable commitment to something greater than us. These principles align beautifully with the teachings of Napoleon Hill, which many of our contributors – Napoleon Hill Institute coaches and devoted students – live and breathe especially our chief lioness, Cliona O'Hara, CEO of the Napoleon Hill Institute.

Each co-author embodies the very essence of stealth and faith, guiding themselves, and through sharing their story, countless individuals to embrace their power and step boldly into their dreams.

But this book is more than just one philosophy. It also holds stories from individuals who have tapped into their own infinite intelligence, sharing what stealth and faith have meant in their lives. I am so proud of this second instalment. I never imagined we could match the impact of book one, *Hear Us Roar Lion Edition, Courage and Perseverance*, but this book shines just as brightly in its own way. It is a beacon of inspiration.

I wholeheartedly believe that when the right story reaches the right heart and mind, it changes lives. It awakens something within. That is my calling – to help awaken those who are ready. Within these pages, you may not connect with every story, but I urge you to embrace what speaks to you. If something resonates, it's for a reason – it's a call to action.

We, the storytellers, are here to walk beside you on this journey, offering our experiences so you may learn, heal, ignite your own power and awaken to new possibilities. Stories connect us. They heal, educate, empower and remind us of our shared humanity. And right now, the world needs connection more than ever.

To all the incredible co-authors who have courageously shared their truths – thank you. Your bravery will be rewarded in ways you may not yet see. And to you, the reader – I hope this book serves as a guiding light. Read it with an open heart, receive its message as it was intended, and if it touches you, pass it on.

This is love in motion. This is *Hear Us Roar: Lioness – Stealth and Faith*.

May this book serve you well,

With love, Karen x

CLIONA O'HARA
UNVEILING YOUR MASTERPIECE TO THE WORLD

Stealth and faith, though two seemingly different concepts, are intricately woven together in the journey of transformation and success. Stealth operates in silence, strategy and patience, while Faith thrives on belief, expectation and an unwavering knowing that what is unseen will soon become reality. Together, they form the foundation upon which dreams are built and fulfilled.

THE POWER OF FAITH

Faith is a force that transcends logic; a superpower that everyone has access to. It is the bedrock of personal transformation, the catalyst for moving from limitation to abundance, from despair to joy, from the ordinary to the extraordinary. But faith does not exist in a vacuum, it requires intentional action, an alignment of the mind and action with a willingness to surrender doubt and worry.

Indeed,   are the greatest adversaries of faith. They creep in when we allow past experiences, limiting beliefs and external opinions to dictate our potential. But here's the truth, faith is a decision. It is an unwavering decision to believe in the invisible and lean into the aid of unseen power potential and support from infinite intelligence. Faith says I am able to do so even when I do not have proof of the outcome. Faith is an emotion of trusting in unseen forces that orchestrate our success. It is the courage to walk forward even when you cannot see the entire path.

Consider the words of Napoleon Hill and Andrew Carnegie, in the book who understood that faith is an applied principle, not just an abstract idea. "Faith encourages all that is right. Fear encourages all that is wrong." This profound truth reveals the opposing forces at play; faith builds and uplifts us, while fear can only destroy and suppress our dreams. Most importantly, faith attracts, while fear repels.

STEALTH IS THE SILENT STRATEGY OF SUCCESS

While faith is the internal force that drives belief and expectation, stealth is the external strategy that ensures execution and longevity. Stealth is about moving with precision, acting with wisdom and making decisions that do not require external validation or applause. It is about strategic patience, knowing when to act and when to remain silent.

Stealth is often misunderstood. Some associate it with secrecy or deception, but in reality, it is a form of wisdom. It is the ability to protect your energy, your vision and your purpose from external interference. Too often, people share their dreams with those who do not understand or support them, only to have their faith weakened by scepticism and negativity. Stealth allows you to build in silence, to cultivate your strength without unnecessary exposure.

A perfect example of stealth in action is found in nature. Consider the eagle, a creature of unparalleled vision and strength. Before it soars, it observes. Before it strikes, it calculates. It does not announce its intentions, it simply moves with certainty and precision. Similarly, those who master stealth understand the importance of timing and discretion. They do not seek validation, they seek results.

THE SYNERGY OF STEALTH AND FAITH

Every child who gets up and starts walking has faith that if they fall, they will get back up again. We're born with faith, but we still have to take the first step.

Faith without action won't achieve results, but action without wisdom is reckless. This is where stealth and faith merge. Faith gives you the confidence to move forward, while stealth ensures you move wisely. Faith tells you your dreams are valid, while stealth ensures they are protected.

Imagine a sculptor working on a masterpiece. In the early stages, the work may appear rough, unrecognisable to the untrained eye. If the sculptor were to seek approval at this stage, they might encounter criticism that could shake their confidence, but the sculptor, wise in stealth and firm in faith, continues in silence. They know what they are building, even if others do not see it yet. And everyone is in awe when the masterpiece is finally revealed.

The same principle applies to life and success. There are seasons for sharing and seasons for building in silence. There are moments when faith must be loudly declared and moments when it must be quietly cultivated. Understanding this balance is the key to achieving greatness.

OVERCOMING FEAR AND DOUBT

Fear is the shadow that seeks to extinguish faith. It thrives on uncertainty and magnifies perceived challenges. But like the 'six ghosts of fear' Napoleon Hill speaks of, fear is merely an illusion. It has no true substance until we give it substance.

So how does we overcome fear and doubt? Through practice. Faith, like a muscle, must be exercised daily. It is strengthened through repetition, through unwavering belief in oneself and the greater forces at play. Every time you choose faith over fear, you reprogram your mind. Every time you act in stealth rather than seeking external validation, you reclaim your power.

A practical way to overcome doubt is through affirmations and visualisations. Speak your faith into existence. Declare it boldly. Visualise your success as if it has already happened. Act as if the reality you desire is already yours. This is not wishful thinkin, this is the very essence of creation. Faith and action together create tangible results.

THE ROLE OF DECISION IN FAITH AND STEALTH

Success is not by accident; it is a series of decisions made with a belief in a positive outcome. Every great leader, visionary and changemaker has had to make a pivotal decisions - to trust in the unseen, to move in faith and to operate in stealth until the right moment.

Consider historical leaders who have changed the course of history - Nelson Mandela, Mahatma Gandhi, Mother Teresa. Each of them had unwavering faith in their mission, yet they also moved with strategic precision. They did not waste their energy convincing those who could not see their vision. Instead, they acted in stealth, building momentum until their impact became undeniable.

This is the formula: **Decision > Faith > Stealth > Execution > Manifestation.**

When you decide, you activate faith. When you move in faith, you employ stealth. When you execute wisely, you manifest success. This cycle repeats until you reach your ultimate goal.

PRACTICAL APPLICATIONS OF STEALTH AND FAITH

1. **Set Clear Intentions:** Know what you want and decide that it is already yours.
2. **Guard Your Vision:** Share your dreams selectively. Not everyone needs to know your plans.

3. **Strengthen Your Faith Daily:** Read, listen and engage with content that reinforces your belief.

4. **Act Without Hesitation:** Move when intuition and wisdom align.

5. **Stay Resilient in the Face of Doubt:** Understand that fear is an illusion meant to test your commitment.

6. **Embrace Patience:** Success is a process; trust in divine timing.

7. **Celebrate in Silence:** Let your results speak for you.

Stealth and faith are the silent architects of success. When mastered together, they create an unstoppable force. Faith gives you the vision; stealth ensures its execution. Faith gives you the courage to dream, while stealth gives you the wisdom to build.

If you find yourself in a place of doubt, remember this: every great achievement was once just a thought, an idea held together by faith and protected by stealth. Your dreams are no different. Believe, move wisely and watch as the unseen becomes reality.

You are the sculptor of your destiny. Move in faith. Build in stealth. And when the time is right, unveil your masterpiece to the world.

ABOUT CLIONA

Introducing Cliona O'Hara, CEO of the Napoleon Hill Institute! Cliona is an experienced entrepreneur, philanthropist and thought leader in the area of personal development.

As CEO of the Napoleon Hill Institute official coaching division, she is one of the worlds foremost female authorities on personal achievement.

She is also a sought after personal development coach and speaker, with a particular focus and definite goal to share the Laws of Attraction to the masses.

In her late twenties Cliona came to the USA as an immigrant and began her inner self discovery journey, immersing herself in the realm of self-development and human potential, devoting herself to daily study, drawing her inspiration from the timeless teachings of Napoleon Hill and then Bob Proctor.

Taking this knowledge and applying the teachings in her life, honing her skills and expertise in the personal development industry and establishing herself as a prominent figure in the field.

Through her drive, Cliona rapidly rose through the ranks alongside the legendary Bob Proctor, becoming VP of sales and senior inner circle coach within the Proctor Gallagher Institute.

Following the passing of her mentor, Cliona found a calling to revisit the foundational teachings of Napoleon Hill and with her fifteen years of being a student of his work, embarked on her new endeavour of being CEO of The Napoleon Hill Institute.

She is also the mother of three, she has gone from poverty to wealth, health and happiness, has since become a permanent resident and has manifested the life of her dreams.

Cliona is now on a mission to teach, share and educate billions of lives and to help them achieve their goals and dreams using the principles that transformed her own life.

In addition to her work as a CEO, Cliona also serves as a mentor for young entrepreneurs through her involvement with Project Uprise which serves those who have escaped human trafficking, a well as mentoring young ladies from her former secondary school in Northern Ireland, St Cecilias.

Cliona's goal is to provide practical advice and guidance that will enable people to unlock their full potential and success.

Through her work, Cliona is inspiring a new generation of success seekers to learn the success Laws of Attraction through Napoleon Hill's work – *Think and Grow Rich, Laws of Success, Outwitting the Devil* and much more.

Join Cliona O'Hara on a journey of transformation and discover the success power within you! You can contact and follow Cliona on:

IG –@clionaohara

FB – Cliona O'Hara

LinkedIn – Cliona O'Hara

X – Cliona O'Hara

YouTube – @clionaohara

AMY MOSSER
ROOM AT THE TOP

I have been on this Earth for 18,989 days.
   That means I have:
- Made 18,989 mistakes.
- Doubted myself 18,989 times.
- Shrunk back into silence 18,989 times.
- Lowered my visibility 18,989 times.
- Fallen down 18,989 times.
- Ignored my intuition 18,989 times.
- But I have also:
- Risen up 18,989 times.
- Forgiven myself and others 18,989 times.
- Belly-laughed 18,989 times.
- Stepped out in faith 18,989 times.
- Said 'I love you' 18,989 times.
- Believed in miracles 18,989 times.

I am an authentic human being who refuses to give up – on myself, my family or my calling. I am real, raw and overflowing with gratitude. My daughter says I raised her with 'delusional confidence' and my son Charlie credits his resilience and perseverance to me. But what I know for sure is this; *everything happens* for *you, not* to *you*.

Some of my greatest lessons came during the hardest times of my life. I've silenced my voice, shrunk back into the shadows and doubted myself, like so many women do. But over and over again, God has called me to rise. He has reminded me that my voice matters – not just for me, but for the lives I am meant to impact.

One of those pivotal moments came when I was called to be a real-life Charlie's Angel. It was a time when I had dimmed my light and let fear silence me. But when my son needed me most, I realised I couldn't stay in the back row any longer.

Charlie's story began like any other little boy's – full of laughter, milestones and dreams. But everything changed one day when he was just two and a half years old. He was in his car seat when my then-husband heard a terrible gasp. Looking in the rearview mirror, he saw Charlie's complexion turn ashen. My husband pulled over, grabbed Charlie from his seat and ran into the foyer of a nearby restaurant, screaming for help.

As he laid Charlie on a bench, people appeared – strangers who began to pray over him. My husband didn't see them come in and didn't notice when they left, but their presence was undeniable. Later, when he told me the story, I knew they were angels sent to remind us that God was with us, even in the darkest moments.

That was just the beginning of our journey. Months of tests, hospitals and unanswered questions finally led us to a diagnosis – Lennox-Gastaut syndrome (LGS); a rare and severe form of epilepsy. The doctors told us to expect developmental delays, hundreds of seizures a day and a future of helmets, wheelchairs and endless medications. They gave us a 4% chance he would ever be seizure and disability free.

It was devastating, but I refused to accept that this was Charlie's story. Even as I sat in a hospital in Minnesota surrounded by children with the same diagnosis, I clung to the belief that this was not the end.

One night, overwhelmed by grief and fear, I found myself crawling down a dark hospital hallway. When I hit the wall at the end, I crumbled. I cried out to God, and in that brokenness, I heard His voice:

'Stand up. Your child will be healed. Your child will be a miracle.'

In that moment, I chose to believe. I visualised Charlie thriving. I whispered dreams into his ears every night, imagining a world where he played baseball, made friends and lived a full, beautiful life. Even as the odds were stacked against us, I held onto faith.

And then, the miracle happened. The seizures stopped. The lesions on his brain disappeared. The little boy doctors said might never walk was now running bases. By the time Charlie was eight, his doctors took him off all his medications, calling him a miracle.

Watching Charlie heal and thrive taught me the power of perseverance and faith. Those lessons carried me through my own journey of starting over.

Years later, I found myself at another crossroads. My marriage was over. I had built a successful life with my then-husband, but I knew staying wasn't an option. Walking away meant leaving behind financial security, the home we had built and nearly everything I had worked for. I had $100,000 to my name – far less than the life we had shared – but I also had faith.

God had shown me through Charlie's healing that miracles were real. And He had always reminded me to trust His plan, even when I couldn't see the next step. When I left, I didn't have a road map, but I had His voice whispering; *'Build people, not buildings. Serve bigger.'*

Starting over wasn't easy. The odds were stacked against me again. But just as I had seen the vision of Charlie's healing before it happened, I saw the vision for my life. I knew I could rebuild, not because I had all the answers, but because I had faith and perseverance.

I leaned into my intuition, which I now know is God's voice guiding me. As women, we so often ignore that voice. We silence our intuition, dismiss our own knowing and shrink back. I had done it before. But this time, I chose to listen.

Over the years, that choice has led me to build multiple businesses into the top 4% of their industries. Not because it was easy, but because I refused to stop. I refused to let fear, doubt or the opinions of others write my story. Just as I had prayed over Charlie's life, I prayed over my businesses, my calling and my purpose.

There were moments of exhaustion, tears and uncertainty, but God showed up every single time. Each success, each step forward, wasn't just about business, it was about honouring the calling on my life to help others to rise.

The lessons I've learned through Charlie's story and my own journey are woven together by one truth; faith can move mountains. Whether it's fighting for your child's life or rebuilding your own, the power of belief is transformational.

Today, I watch my son lead his teammates with determination and heart and I'm reminded of the little boy I held through sleepless nights. His story, and mine, are living proof that miracles happen when you believe, listen to God's voice and refuse to give up.

So, I ask you; *What's your 4% dream?* What is the vision in your heart that feels impossible? What is the calling you've been afraid to step into?

I'm here to tell you – it's possible. Your dreams are possible. Your miracle is possible. But you have to rise. You have to trust your intuition, lean into faith and take the first step.

There is room for you at the top. You were created for greatness. Trust the whispers of your intuition, as they are God's voice calling you higher. Turn up the volume on your voice, take a deep breath and get ready – because together, we're going up.

ABOUT AMY

I made the decision to live unapologetically authentic at the age of nineteen, created my own lane and never looked back. As a serial entrepreneur since the age of twenty-two, I have built and sold several businesses and hundreds of millions of dollars in real estate. I have also mentored and coached thousands of people to rediscover their true potential and greatness and scale six and seven-figure businesses.

My success is due to my incredible mindset. From a young age, I envisioned myself being an entrepreneur and building and selling businesses. My grit and perseverance along with my incredible relational and listening skills are keys to success. A multimillion-dollar producer and coach for the last twenty years, I bring a joyous and fun approach to kicking ass and creating a beautiful life. I have owned a 90,000 square-foot gym, retail golf franchises, numerous real estate investments, and built successful businesses in real estate, coaching and social selling.

Amy Mosser
Woods Bros Realty
402-730-6818

MOLLY LUNN KROEKER
THE POWER WITHIN

I'll be honest, stealth is not a word that comes up frequently for me in my everyday conversations, but boy, it is a word that is incredibly powerful when you finally realise what it means.

I should explain a little bit about who I am; a middle child in the prime of my life … absolutely in love with life; in love with my incredible husband of thirty-one years, my kids, my family and with how I was raised. It is such a magical place to be when you are crazily and madly in love with your life … and that is where I am.

I'm a child of God, with a huge heart. I love people. I'm a hugger. I am a 'look you in the eyes' kinda girl. I want to hear your story. I want to hear what makes you unique. I want to sit at your feet and just listen. I love *seeing* people. I love *hearing* people, and I love knowing that they feel seen and heard.

Indeed, that is one of my greatest gifts; to ensure people feel *seen and heard*. That is who I am to my core. I am an adventurer, a traveller and I have joy in my life at all times. I was put on this Earth with the most positive mental attitude and I'm probably one of the most optimistic people you'll ever meet.

With a very science-based background, I have to admit letting stealth and faith into my life has taken years of work. I love the word stealth because it's about getting out of your head and into your heart. I would say I did not do this well for the first fifty years of my life and that's probably why the word stealth never came up for me. But looking to the next fifty years, there has been a dramatic shift in consciousness for me. That's exactly what stealth is for me. *Now*, it's something I enter into every day, because to get out of my head and get into my heart has become such an easy and effortless way to live; it's about being in a state of flow. And when you're in this flow state, you are open to receive. So to me, *stealth* means creating a state of flow and allowing myself to be open to receive.

So having thought briefly about *stealth*, I'd like to spend a little time here talking about *faith*. Faith is something I've always known. I grew up in a religious, church-oriented family; we were at church every Sunday. We would go to youth group on Wednesday nights, and it was something we loved doing. To be honest, when you're broke, church is free, so it covered all the necessities. But because of this, faith was always something that I *knew*. *Faith* in a religious sense, I think, is about the Bible and Jesus. For someone like me who was raised in the church, faith meant you had a belief that there was someone or something else outside of your control.

But let's look at faith in a more spiritual sense, about what faith means to me now in this latter half of my life; how it will look for my next fifty years. I now understand that *faith* is a voluntary state of mind. It is how you can create everything you desire. It is a change in consciousness. Your consciousness is all about the thoughts you have; the love, your desires, the belief that you have consented to – all of this creates faith. It's about trust. For me, it is faith that moves you from needing something, which is about a scarcity and desperation mindset, to wanting something and trusting you will receive it. And it's okay to want something. You can just want something because you want it. In *spiritual faith*, you are taken from believing, to a *knowing*.

It's like when you land in the Midwest (USA) in the middle of a snowstorm or blizzard, and you *believe* you know where your car is parked at the airport in uncovered parking in the middle of a snowstorm, versus you *know* where your car is parked. It's a huge difference. Faith truly is an inner knowing.

Things really start to happen in life when you take stealth, moving from your head to your heart, and then you apply faith.   The amazing thing is you can't explain it. I've been raised in a very scientific world being a sports medicine physical therapist – a place where things have to be proven. You have to show great research to get reimbursed for physical therapy services by insurance companies. You can't just say, 'I have faith that this treatment will work.' They're just not going to pay you for that. So, faith to me, often feels like the opposite of science.

It's the law of duality. I've moved away from that scientific space, to a new way of feeling, I have an inner *knowing* of what is going to happen and the next step to take. When you have faith, you have a strong emotion (energy in motion). So, when I have faith that something is going to happen, I take that energy in motion, with a deep knowingness, and then I know the *how* will simply unfold. Put the *how* on hold because it will come when you have faith, and it will feel like a miracle. But really, it's not a miracle, it's just a *knowingness*.

It's an intuitive sense, and we all have that same level of intuition. But often what happens, and what I did for the first fifty years of my life, is that we push past that intuitiveness because it can be hard to spend some time in quiet reflection and truly listen to yourself. But when you do, your intuition is so strong. My intuition was not strong because I used to be in sync with what other people thought of me and what I was doing.

When you have true faith, you will experience a change in consciousness. Your consciousness is what you think and what you desire, what you love and what you believe. When you fully understand that and bring faith into the mix, that is when you will start to see results in your outer world. It can only happen with faith. You need to see your wish fulfilled as if it has already happened. Your faith comes into action when you live life as if your wishes have come true.

When you intuitively decide to go within and listen to your gut, I love to call it *a tug*. Some people call it the Holy spirit and I love that, but you can feel *a tug*, when you decide the opinions of others really don't matter. When you can act on your own opinion, that's when there's a faith in your *knowingness*.

This is how I perceive stealth and faith, and how they are used in my life. Early on in life, I had some religious faith, but I did not have the spiritual sense of faith that I have now. An example of this in my life was when my nephew was diagnosed with Lennox-Gastaut syndrome and my mum with breast cancer for the first time, all within a few weeks. My 'human' very quickly got in the way and I was angry. I was mad because I wanted to be there for both my mum and my nephew, and be present and not miss treatments or doctor's appointments. And I'm the medical person in my family, so there was some frustration there.

But I'll never forget seeing a rainbow as we headed off to the hospital to see my nephew (who lived in another state). It's hard to explain, but on the trip to see my nephew, all the different family members (my sister's husband, his family, my family, my parents) all saw the rainbow, despite travelling in from different directions. We all saw it! It was the sign I needed to fully feel my faith. And in that moment, *I just knew,* that both of these people I loved very much, would be healed. I didn't know how it was going to happen. I just had a *knowingness* that it would. And when you have a knowingness, the fear leaves. There is no room for fear. Fear and faith cannot exist together. I believe it's completely impossible. And that is the first time I remember truly experiencing *faith*.

In more recent times, my faith kicked in when I raced Ironman. I was a good athlete, but not anything exceptional. I wasn't going to a D1 college on an athletic scholarship, but I was good enough, and let's say, I did stand out in athletics. It was something that got me recognition when I was younger and that feeling stayed with me for the next few decades. I remember being an average athlete until I committed to my first triathlon. I was thirty-two years old. I had just run the San Diego Marathon, and decided I wanted to run a sprint triathlon, which is really the shortest distance out there. It doesn't take very long to do – it's a quick race, usually 750 metres of swimming, 14 miles biking and a 5km run. I did it with a toddler, a baby and my husband cheering me on … and I made it on the podium. For the first time in my life, I felt like I had finally found the thing I was really good at. I played tennis, basketball, volleyball, all those things and ran track, but this was the thing that came easily to me. It created a journey over the next twenty years of me racing all kinds of distances.

But the best, for me, was the Half Iron Man distance. This means swimming 1.2 miles, biking 56 miles, and running a 13.1 mile race, a half marathon. This was the distance I was good at and always felt good to me. I raced all kinds of distances over those twenty years and I had my eye on Ironman for several years (I always thought I would do Ironman when I was forty), but because of our kids' busy lives and travelling out of state for athletic events, as well as working full-time, it didn't happen. I made all the excuses. I would train and run in some shorter races, but it just didn't happen until I finally made a decision to actually register for Ironman, despite this being after a horrible Half Iron Man where it rained the entire time and my husband has a video of me saying, 'I will never do that again. I will never do Ironman.'

That was in October and, like the pain of having a baby, you forget. In February, I signed up to do Ironman. I made the decision to train and to start sharing my intention with other people. What actually happened is that I had faith, *a knowing*, that this was it. This was going to be my Ironman race, something I had wanted for twelve years. I would listen to affirmations at night of recordings I had made, telling myself how great a sleep I was getting, how I was rested, how I was strong, how I had a fiercely strong and lean body, how I had an incredible strength in my mindset. I really developed that faith 'muscle'. It must move into form.

There was a knowingness. There was never a moment that I felt it would not happen. And this comes from a girl that doesn't like to swim in lakes.

For all my racing years, whenever I had to swim in a lake, I was terrified. But for that Ironman race, I had such a knowingness, it didn't even phase me. In fact, what played over in my head was a magical humming of people cheering ... I could audibly hear it in my head as I swam, which made that 2.4 mile swim go lightning fast.

I had so much faith that I would finish, I would even get emotional talking about it. People would ask me and I would burst into tears because I had such a profound faith that it was already done. I never once wondered; *What if I don't finish? What if I don't make it in the time cut off?* My faith allowed me to finish the race and finish it well. One of the toughest Ironmans out there in the world, is Wisconsin. It's notoriously hilly, and I did it like a champ. I finished, thank goodness, because my twenty-two-year-old daughter ran 13 miles with me. But never once did I question not finishing.

At the risk of repeating myself here, the biggest thing I want you to know about faith, is that it is truly *a knowingness.* It's not something that can be measured or recorded by some device, it's just something that comes from within. It's in that quiet voice that says, *Yes, you can.* It's that whisper that says, *You've got this.* It's a quiet confidence that exudes and, suddenly, you will see the amazing results in your reality.

I hope this chapter of my experience with faith, helps you to identify where you have stealth and faith in your own life, because at the end of the day, we all have it, it's just about slowing down enough to recognise the powerful you within.

ABOUT MOLLY

From healing bodies to transforming lives, Molly, has always been driven by a passion for impact. Beginning her journey as a sports medicine physical therapist, she dedicated years to helping others regain their strength and overcome painful limitations in their bodies. When she saw the power of entrepreneurship, she pivoted, building a social marketing empire that rose to the top 1%—proving that success is not just about skill, but about vision, belief, and inspired and relentless action.

Now, as a sought-after speaker, mentor, and coach, she is on a mission to empower women worldwide, helping them step into abundance, healing, and worthiness and experience a radical transformation. Happily married for 31 years, she and her husband have raised two incredible children, Sam (25) and Sophie (22), who inspire her daily. Whether on stage, in business, or through personal connection, she is committed to guiding women to break free from limitations and embrace the limitless life they were meant to live.

LINDA LOVELESS
MY JOURNEY TO
THE CROWN

I was called to the dressing room at the department store I worked to alter a gown for a customer. After introducing myself as *the alteration lady* and asking how I could be of service, I proceeded to sit on the floor and began pinning her gown. I asked her, 'Where are you wearing this beautiful gown?' She said, 'I'm being recognised on stage in front of thousands of people as a top achiever in my company.' 'Wow,' I replied. After a moment of silence, she looked down at me and asked, 'Honey, what are you doing down there on that floor?' After taking a deep breath, I looked up at her with tears running down my face and thought to myself – *I don't know what I'm doing down here on this floor.* No-one had ever asked me that before. *What did she see in me?* I thought. I had always been very quiet and reserved, very much an introvert and felt invisible most of my life. I was raised in a large family, second to the oldest of seven children, my dad was a pastor and there were a lot of unspoken expectations. I felt loved, but not really seen or heard. She literally picked me up off that floor and invited me to her studio to be her model for her training that evening. That was a huge inflection moment that began *my journey to the crown.*

I was in my teens when my uncle Russ, my mum's brother, sent a letter to Mum. He wrote something special about each one of us kids; for me he wrote, 'Linda needs to reclaim her crown.' *What does that mean?* I thought.

Twenty years later, I'm married, sitting on the floor in our first apartment, cutting out a pattern watching the first annual Mrs America pageant on TV. I said to myself, *I'm going to do that some day.*

Another twenty years later, I found myself on stage as a pageant contestant in the Mrs Kansas pageant. Until that moment, I had completely forgotten what I had said to myself twenty years earlier. I have since learned the power of our thoughts and to be mindful of what we think about; good, bad or indifferent.

Leading up to the pageant, I had made the decision to step out in faith and start my own business as a designer/dressmaker/image consultant, to be more available to my three small children. Desperate to put food on the table for my family, I found myself burning the midnight oil, night after night. As a result of completing a huge project I submitted for a big annual event in Kansas City, I received a lot of media attention that booked me out for two years – solid. One evening, I sat at my sewing machine exhausted, burned out and crying. (One thing I knew for sure was I didn't want to be sitting in this same place five years from now.) I remember having a conversation with God, asking the question, *Is this all there is? There must be more to life than this, I know I'm made for more!*

Shortly after, a woman called to have her gown altered after she had lost a significant amount of weight in her fifties, to do a beauty pageant. She inspired me, and at age forty, I decided to enter the Mrs Kansas pageant. That was my debut out of the basement.

While preparing for the pageant at the local modeling agency, I was invited to a private business reception and introduced to a skin care line. After trying it, I immediately saw and felt a difference in my skin and was curious to understand why it was so different from what I was currently using. After learning more and meeting other beautiful, sharp women who had built their businesses with this product, I saw hope through them of something more! And so, my journey to the crown continued.

I was hungry to learn and showed up to everything, building my belief in the products, the company, the industry and finally … in myself. My business was a personal development course, and the pageant was a target date to help me work toward my personal goals of becoming my best self. I was first runner up for the first two years and ended up winning on my third try, competing against twenty-three-year-olds who were my daughter's age. This was a huge accomplishment that I had worked so hard toward. So why was I feeling unsettled; a holy discontent? It felt like the behind the sewing machine moment again. I thought to myself, *How dare I let a judge decide whether I am good enough or not?* I realised this wasn't it, and so the journey to the crown continued.

I made the decision to open my pageant coaching business alongside my skin care business to share my experience and expertise and to help guide women on *their* journey to the crown. I was thrilled that all my girls were recognised in the top five and/or won the pageant year after year! I loved seeing their transformation, as well as mine, as we worked together to uncover their unique beauty that set them apart from all the other beautiful young ladies on the stage. I felt fulfilled and my business was flourishing!

I received a call from my mum to tell me Dad was in the hospital and was not doing well, and that I needed to hop on a plane as soon as I could to Sacramento. I walked into his hospital room and was greeted by his strongest voice. 'Well hello, Mrs Kansas!' Dad had a revolving door of people coming through to share the impact he made in their lives as a pastor. I said, 'Dad, your crown is so much bigger than mine,' and with that, he squeezed my hand and said, 'Linda, take them all to the top with you.' Those words made a huge impact on me and still I am reminded of those words today.

In that moment, I realised as Dad was taking his last breath, that *today matters!* This moment matters! We don't know if we have tomorrow. I asked myself the question, *What am I doing, who am I being, that is leaving a legacy that will impact generations not yet born?* I saw clearly that day the gift I had been given (my behind-the-sewing-machine moment) to have built a sustainable business that prepared me for this moment, allowing me the freedom and peace of mind to be here fully present for the important things in life. The month Dad passed, we achieved the top level in my business. I looked up and said, 'Thank you, Dad!' I know he had a huge hand in orchestrating that! The gift that keeps on giving!

It has now been twenty years since I was promoted to the top level of my business, and thankfully, it continues to sustain through the highs and lows of life. The last four years have been interesting to say the least. My husband was diagnosed with Parkinson's which impacted me more than I realised.

My sister, my best friend, was diagnosed with breast cancer so I flew to Sacramento to help her get moved into her new home after she retired from her thirty-year career as a high school counsellor, to be closer to Mum in Sacramento from Long Beach.

It was an interesting time. Because of the pandemic, I was not allowed in the hospital with her. I dropped her off the morning of New Year's Eve 2020 and picked her up later that afternoon – it was an in and out procedure. As I was preparing her for bed that evening, she blacked out. I called 911 and she was taken back to the hospital. The next morning, I checked in on Mum and she looked as pale as my sister did the night before. I took mum to the ER and again, was not allowed to go in with her. Three days later, I picked my sister up from the hospital to get her settled while her daughter arrived from New York to care for her, so that I could care for mum after learning her diagnoses of stage four colon cancer. I was reminded again of the gift in building a sustainable business that took care of me. Because I took care of it early on, I was able to be with Mum for the three months before she passed on 15 March 2021. My sister was in remission and doing well. In 2022, I ended up very sick myself, with long-COVID while on a road trip to Florida from Kansas. It was a very scary time for me.

On 5 April 2022, I received a call from my niece saying her mum was in the hospital again. I asked if she needed me to fly out there; she got very quiet as she looked at her mum for direction. My sister evidently nodded her head – YES. I later found out she was trying to protect me (because that's what sisters do). I did not realise how sick she really was until I walked into her home the next day and was shocked to see her hooked up to oxygen and didn't have the energy to walk across the room on her own. I had no idea! Fifteen days later, she was gone. I cherish those fifteen days with her. Before she passed, I told her I would carry on the work we talked and dreamed about doing together. I told her, 'When you're ready to guide, direct and download, just give me a sign, I'll be ready.' I have had so many signs, through butterflies, hummingbirds and dragonflies. In fact, just recently, as I was walking through Central Park, a dragonfly landed on my cheek and gave me a gentle kiss. I said, 'Thanks, sis. I love you and I know you are here with me.'

How many of you feel like you are down there on that floor and know in your heart there's more? My hope is that sharing my story will inspire women to collectively rise up, to be strong powerful voices for those who have felt invisible to embrace their quiet power. Step out in faith, walk in your beauty and greatness and discover your unique superpowers. Be visible, be seen and heard, feel loved, valued and safe to speak on big stages and platforms all over the world. Together we are creating a movement of one million women millionaires globally who are changing and impacting the world by sharing their powerful stories of hope and their *journey to the Crown* in honour of my mum, my sister and so many more women who no longer have a voice.

We know the true reward is in the journey to the crown! En-JOY the journey!

ABOUT LINDA

Linda Loveless lives in Shawnee Kansas, is a Mom of three adult children, Nana to three beautiful grandchildren, two step-grandchildren and one great-grand, married for 49 years. She has built a successful Global Health and Wellness business over the past 29 years and as a top leader has developed top leaders globally. Among her many entrepreneurial accomplishments Linda is an inspirational speaker, mentor, coach, trainer, skin care educator, makeup artist, award winning dress designer, image consultant, style coach, modeling instructor, pageant coach, Certified Color1 Consultant, Self-Talk Trainer, StrengthScope Practitioner and Certified Napoleon Hill Institute Coach. Linda was Mrs. Kansas America in 1999.

She currently works with successful women entrepreneurs who are challenged with being all things to everyone, who find themselves stuck, stressed out and pushing themselves to the point of burnout.

She helps them reclaim their life by identifying their unique superpowers, what lights them up, who they are at their highest and best. Accomplishing this means more clarity in what and where they choose to spend their time and energy. They discover a renewed sense of fulfillment in themselves that generates more joy, passion and purpose in their business and life.

Connect with Linda on FB, IG or Website lindaloveless.arbonne.com

CHRISTINA WESTERGAARD LARSEN
MY JOURNEY INTO THE HEART
AND OUT OF THE NOISE

THE MOMENT YOU REALISE YOU WERE NEVER A SHEEP

There is a moment in life when everything changes.

At first, you don't question things. You follow what you've been taught. You walk like the people around you, talk like them, think like them. You believe their rules, their limitations, their fears.

You shape yourself to fit in. You lower your voice when it's too loud, you shrink your dreams when they seem too big. You convince yourself that this is just how life is.

Until one day, you hear the roar.

Orison Swett Marden, in his powerful writings on success and self-discovery, tells the story of a lion cub raised among sheep. From the moment it was born, it only knew one world – the world of the sheep. It followed them, moved like them, made itself small to fit in.

It never questioned why it looked different, why its reflection in the water didn't match the others.

Why would it? It had never seen anything else.

It had spent its whole life grazing, never knowing it was meant to hunt.

It had spent its whole life following, never knowing it was meant to lead.

But one day, everything changed.

One day, the cub heard a roar echo through the valley. It stopped, ears twitching, body frozen. It had never heard anything like it before – deep, powerful, commanding. It shook something inside its soul.

Something forgotten.

The sheep panicked. 'Run!' they cried. 'A lion is coming!' But the cub didn't run.

Something about the roar felt familiar.

Something about it didn't feel like danger –it felt like home.

The sound stirred something inside its bones. A feeling of power, of fire, of something far greater than the life it had been living.

And in that moment, the cub realised the truth.

It was never a sheep.

It had always been a lion.

And suddenly, everything made sense.

The restless feeling. The quiet frustration. The way it never truly fit in with the flock, no matter how hard it tried. The way it longed for more without understanding why.

It wasn't because it was broken.

It wasn't because something was wrong with it.

It was because it was trying to be something it was never meant to be.

For years, I lived as the sheep version of myself– shrinking, doubting, believing I wasn't enough. I believed the limits that had been placed on me, the fears that had been spoken over me.

I thought if I blended in enough, I would finally feel like I belonged.

But then, one day, I heard a roar.

And I remembered.

I remembered who I was before the world told me who I should be.

I remembered that the restlessness in my soul wasn't something to be ignored – it was my true self trying to wake up.

This is my story.

The story of how I stopped listening to the noise of my mind, of the world, of the people who tried to keep me small – and stepped fully into the faith of my heart.

It's the story of how I built the lioness inside me and learned the secret art of stealth - moving in faith before seeing proof.

And if you feel like a lion trapped among sheep, this is your story too.

FINDING EVIDENCE OF FAITH

My grandmother was a light.

She had an energy that could make you forget your worries just by being in the same room. She laughed like no one was watching, and when she laughed too hard when we played games, she would cry out, 'I'm gonna pee!' That was her. Unfiltered joy.

She made the world feel safe.

She made the world feel magical.

And then, one day, she was gone.

I was only six years old, too young to fully understand what death meant. But I understood what absence felt like. The silence in the house, the heaviness in the air.

I remember I ran inside her house and noticed the face of the adults and then ran into her room, and there she was, lying in bed. But something was different. Something was missing.

Her body was there, but she was gone. The warmth, the laughter, the light – vanished. What remained was only a reflection of who she had been, an empty vessel where her soul once lived.

After she passed away my mum always told me that my grandmother was the brightest star in the sky.

And I believed her.

But I wanted to see it for myself.

So I did what children do best – I searched for evidence.

I would stand outside, staring at the sky, whispering, 'If you're still here, show me.'And one day, I found a feather.

It landed right in front of me.

It felt like a message, a sign that she was still with me. That she hadn't left me alone.

That was the moment I first felt faith.

Faith wasn't something I was taught – it was something I discovered.

On my discovery even as a child, I knew I was meant for something more.

But as I grew older I stopped believing in myself and started feeling like I wasn't enough.

But my mum's voice was always in the back of my mind:

*You can focus on the cup that is half empty, or you can focus on the cup that is half full. The choice is yours.*And that's what I took with me when I started shaping my own future.

Her thinking became the starting point of my stealth mode.

THE BLACK SHEEP: LOSING MYSELF IN THE NOISE

Before I discovered the power of stealth, before I heard my inner roar, I remember a childhood where I felt like the black sheep.

I always felt like I was different.

I thought deeply about things other people ignored. I saw life through a lens that others didn't understand. And so, I hid it.

At school, I became the clown. Why? Because if I made fun of myself first, I thought no-one else could do it.

But they still did.

They called me fat. They laughed at me. They bullied me. The worst day was when a guy hit me in the stomach – the very place that already held all my insecurities.

But I took it. I took it on the chin. I pretended it didn't hurt. Even though it did.

It did more than hurt – it scarred me.

It made me question myself. *Am I good enough? Why can't I be like everyone else?*For years, I let those doubts control me.

I became a small version of myself.

A sheep.

DON'T HIDE YOUR SCARS

Every scar tells a story.

For years, I tried to hide mine.

I covered up the wounds from my past, thinking they made me weak. I thought if people saw the battles I had fought, they would see me as damaged.

One of my deepest scars was the day my confidence was broken in an instant.

I was in seventh grade, standing in front of my class, about to speak.

I wasn't nervous. I had never been afraid of speaking before. I actually enjoyed it.

But that day changed everything.

As soon as I started talking, a guy in the class laughed – not just a small chuckle, but a loud, uncontrollable, gut-wrenching laugh.

He laughed so hard that the whole class joined in.

At that moment, I felt my face burn, my stomach drop and my entire body freeze.

Something inside me broke.

I didn't realise it at the time, but that was the day I became a sheep.

That was the day I started shrinking.

That was the day I started believing that my voice wasn't meant to be heard.

From that day forward, I avoided standing in front of people.

I did everything I could to make myself small, to disappear into the background.

I carried that fear with me for years, and no matter how much I wanted to step up, there was always a voice in my head whispering:

*What if they laugh at you again?*And that voice kept me in chains.

But here's the thing about lions – they aren't born knowing they are lions.

Sometimes, they have to remember.

I didn't want to live in fear forever. So I did the work.

I faced my fears through hypnosis, deep mindset work, and pushing myself into discomfort.

I learned that fear is nothing but a cage – and cages are meant to be broken.

And one day, I heard my roar again.

I stood in front of people.

I spoke.

I owned my voice.

And guess what?

Nobody laughed.

In fact, they listened.

They felt my words.

They connected with my truth.

They saw the **lion** in me – because I finally saw it in myself.

That's when I realised:

FEAR IS THE BIGGEST LIAR IN THE WORLD.

The moment you let it control you, you become a **sheep.**

You start **hiding your power, your voice, your truth.**

But when you face it? That's when the lion inside you wakes up.

That's when you reclaim your roar.

So don't let your scars silence you.

Wear them like armor.

Stand tall.

Use your voice.

Because the world doesn't need more sheep.

It needs more lions.

And the only way to become one: Face the fear and ROAR.

When we face fear, we turn away from the darkness and are led into the light.

'The beauty of experiencing the darkness is that we learn to appreciate the light.'
– Christina

And in that light, we are given a choice.

THE ROAR THAT CHANGED EVERYTHING

There comes a moment when you can no longer ignore it, the restlessness inside you, the feeling that you are meant for **something more.**

For years, I tried to silence that feeling. I told myself I needed more experience, more knowledge, more permission. I convinced myself that if I played it safe, if I followed the rules, success would eventually find me.

But deep down, I knew that was a lie.

I saw it clearly for the first time when I was training to become a hypnosis psychotherapist.

I was surrounded by people who had spent years chasing credentials – coaches, therapists, experts with stacks of certifications. They had done everything 'right'. But most of them were struggling. They weren't getting the results they wanted. They weren't winning.

And that made me question everything.

If knowledge alone was the key to success, why were so many people stuck?

Why did some people break through while others spent years spinning their wheels?

That's when I found Bob Proctor, and in my eyes, he was the lion king of personal development.

He knew the secret. I could see it in the way he spoke, in the way he carried himself. He had the roar of someone who had figured it out.

And at that moment, I made a decision.

I wasn't going to just study his work —I was going to meet him.

And in 2020, I did.

That was the moment everything changed.

BURNING THE BOATS

Bob Proctor taught me something no certification ever had:

Success is not about what you know. Success is about who you become.

So I made a decision: I was going all in.

I wasn't going to 'try' anymore. I wasn't going to dip my toe in the water. I was going to burn my boats.

No backup plan. No safety net.

I invested everything I had into myself.

I started studying one hour a day, every single day – just like Earl Nightingale taught.

'If you commit to studying your craft for one hour a day, in five years, you will lead your field.' So I did.

I absorbed, I applied, I became the person who deserved the life I wanted.

And then in 2019, I made the boldest decision of my life.

I walked into my parents' house, heart pounding, adrenaline surging through my veins.

'I just spent everything in my bank account,' I told them.

They stared at me.

'I don't know how, but I'm going to work with this guy in the personal development industry, and I will make one million before I turn thirty.'

The words felt surreal coming out of my mouth, but I knew.

It wasn't just a goal. It wasn't wishful thinking.

It was a decision.

At that moment, my bank account was nearly empty. Logically, it made no sense.

But I wasn't operating on logic. I was operating on faith.

For six months, I went all in.

I studied relentlessly.

I applied everything I learned.

I **acted as if success was already mine.**

And after six months I started working with him, and after eighteen months, I made my first million – doing what I love.

Here's the truth:

Faith is not a feeling. Faith is moving before the evidence appears. So we have to make decisions from faith. And that decision? That was the roar that changed my life forever.

FINDING MY TRUE HOME

But the story doesn't end there.

In 2023, after years of studying, working and building, I found something that felt like home.

I found The Napoleon Hill Institute.

This wasn't just another opportunity.

This was the source.

Everything I had learned – the power of the mind, the principles of success, the faith-based action that changes everything – all of it traced back to Napoleon Hill's teachings.

I had spent years searching for the missing link, and now I had stepped into the legacy of success itself.

I wasn't just learning about success anymore.

I was embodying it.

And that's when I heard my roar.

THE COST OF BECOMING A LIONESS

People don't tell you this part.

They don't tell you that becoming your true self requires loss.

That growth isn't just about gaining – it's about letting go.

That stepping into your power means stepping away from the people who don't want to see you rise.

For me, this was one of the hardest lessons to learn.

I had to say goodbye to a lot of people.

Not because I stopped loving them. But because they wanted me to stay small. They wanted me to stay in the role I had always played; the version of me they were comfortable with.

The version of me who didn't challenge the status quo, who didn't make waves.

Jim Rohn once said,

'You are the average of the five people you spend the most time with.' And I had to face the truth – if I wanted to become the lioness I knew I was meant to be, I couldn't keep surrounding myself with sheep.

As my mum always says, the people around you should be like sunrays, lifting you, energising you, nourishing your dreams.

If they are draining you, doubting you, feeding you negativity – run.

Because negativity is like poison. It won't just slow you down, it will steal years from your life.

'A negative environment can steal seven years of your life.' Seven years.

That's how much time you waste in the wrong energy, in the wrong circles, in the wrong environments.

I refused to let that happen to me.

So I ran toward the people who saw my potential. The ones who challenged me to rise. The ones who made me feel like anything was possible.

And that's when my life truly changed.

Free
For the first time I feel seen
I feel seen for who I truly AM
For who I remembered I could become
She was here all along
But she was hidden
Under all of these layers
Of the distrust of others
Because they never saw her
Therefore they never woke her up
They only saw a shadow
Of what she could be
They never remembered who she was
Now you remind her
You see her for who she is becoming
You see her for who she have always been
Because you remind her
You wake up the sleeping lion
That has been here all along
For the first time
She is reminded of who she is becoming
And for the first time
She feels at home
Finally …

She is free to be who she always felt she could be
Once as a child she believed
But somehow she forgot
And turned into something she was not
Now she woke up
She remembered
Now she arrived
She finally found home
For the first time
She is finally home
And she is free
I AM free
Free to be ME

AWAKEN THE LION WITHIN YOU

This is it.

This is the moment you've been waiting for – the moment you finally wake up.

You have felt it your entire life, haven't you? That deep, restless pull inside of you. That knowing that you were meant for more. That feeling that no matter how much you try to fit in, something inside you refuses to stay small.

Because you were never meant to be small.

You were never meant to walk in the shadows, to follow the crowd, to lower your voice just to make others comfortable.

You were meant to ROAR.

But somewhere along the way, the world told you to be quiet.

To be *realistic*.

To stop *dreaming so big.*

To stop *believing in yourself.*

And maybe you listened. Maybe you started hiding your true self.

Maybe you began to question whether you were crazy for thinking you were destined for something greater.

Maybe you started believing that the fire inside you was a burden instead of a gift.

And so, you silenced it.

But I know something about you.

I know that no matter how much you've tried to dim your own light, no matter how much you've tried to ignore the roar inside you…

It never truly went away.

Because the roar is who you are.

It is your spirit calling you home.

Home to the power you were born with.

Home to the faith you once had.

Home to the unstoppable force within you.

And now, you stand at a crossroads.

You can continue living as a sheep – shrinking, doubting, following, waiting for permission. You can keep telling yourself *someday* while watching others take the risks, make the moves, and create the lives they desire.

Or …

You can ROAR.

You can step into your power. You can stop waiting, stop hesitating, stop letting fear dictate your future.

Because deep inside, you are not a follower.

You are not a victim.

You are not small.

You are a lion.

You were born to lead, to rise, to walk in faith, to own your destiny.

But let me be clear – this won't be easy.

There will be moments when doubt creeps in.

Moments when the people around you won't believe in you.

Moments when your old self screams for comfort, begging you to stay in the familiar.

And in those moments, you must ROAR LOUDER THAN YOUR FEAR.

Because here's the truth:

No one is coming to save you.

If you don't take control of your mind, your faith, your future, someone else will.

And they will use you to build their dream while yours fades away.

This world doesn't need another person waiting for the perfect time.

The world needs leaders.

The world needs lions.

The world needs you.

And it's not enough to just know this – it's time to ACT.

Because knowledge without action is just another wasted roar.

'The lion is not the biggest, the fastest, or the strongest in the jungle. But it is the king. Why? Because it believes it is.' This is your moment to believe.

No more waiting for a sign – THIS is your sign.

No more asking for permission – you don't need it.

No more making excuses – it's time to move.

The question is:

Will you?

Will you be the lion who forgets its power and continues to follow the sheep?

Or will you hear the roar inside you, step out of the noise, and become who you were always meant to be?

Because if you don't roar, the world will never know your voice.

And that would be the greatest tragedy of all.

'A lion that does not roar will be mistaken for a sheep.' So roar.

Not just for yourself.
But for the people who are waiting for you to lead.
For the version of you that has been silenced for too long.
For the life you were BORN to live.
This is your moment.
The world is waiting to hear your roar.

ABOUT CHRISTINA

Christina Westerggaard Larsen is a global certified Napoleon Hill Institute coach, hypnosis psychotherapist, and master NLP practitioner – with more certifications than she can count, but what truly sets her apart is her lived experience of transformation.

As the leader of the Danish division of the Napoleon Hill Institute, she helps conscious achievers break past limitations and apply the principles of *Think and Grow Rich* to create wealth, purpose, and lasting success.

Having coached over 1,500 individuals worldwide, Christina teaches how to reprogram the subconscious mind, eliminate self-doubt, and turn ambition into achievement. Her journey – from playing small to owning her roar – proves that when faith and action align, transformation is inevitable.

Rooted in the teachings of Napoleon Hill and Bob Proctor, she is committed to helping others move with faith before seeing proof and create a life beyond limitations.

LERATO SITHOLE
THE STEALTH OF LOVE
& LONGING

My life, much like that of a lioness, has been marked by silent endurance, watchful patience and calculated movements toward survival and strength.

My name is Lerato Sithole, a name that means *love*. My parents were teenagers when they discovered I was growing inside my mother's womb. They named me Lerato, meaning love, and in that name, I carried both a blessing and a longing. The lioness loves fiercely, but she also knows solitude. From the very beginning, I understood that love was not something always present, but something to be pursued, protected and preserved in stealth.

My mother, a young nurse, walked a path that took her nearly 400 km away from me. Her absence was not a rejection but a sacrifice, much like the lioness who ventures far to provide for her cubs. She would visit occasionally, her presence like a warm sun after a long winter. But I never saw her leave. She would slip away in stealth, sparing us both the agony of parting.

As for my father, he was more of a shadow than a presence. The lioness does not waste time mourning what does not serve her survival, but I felt his absence like a whisper in the wind. I knew him only through my grandmother, his mother, who adored me and filled the void with her love. I never heard his voice call my name. Even when I saw him once, sitting in a car with my mother, he did not reach for me, and I did not reach for him. We were strangers connected by blood but divided by silence.

Yet, I learned early that love is not always loud – it can be quiet, sacrificial and steadfast, even from a distance. It moves unseen, like the steady watch of a lioness who protects her young from the shadows.

THE WATCHFUL EYES OF THE LIONESS

The lioness does not announce herself – she watches, waits and learns before making her move. I grew up under the care of my aunt, my mother's older sister. I was given what I needed to survive; a home, a Catholic education and the knowledge that my mother was working to build a future for me, even if she was not always present.

Despite my longing for my mother, I observed her strength. She ensured that my birthdays were celebrated with cakes and new clothes. She sent me to a prestigious Catholic school – a rare privilege for a black child in apartheid South Africa. She was preparing me for a world that did not always welcome people like us, yet she moved through it with silent determination, making a way where there was none.

Stealth taught me resilience. Watching my mother, my aunt and my grandmother, I learned that love is not just about presence, it is about endurance. It is about waiting for the right moment to act, about knowing when to be still and when to strike. It is about standing strong even when the world seems to be against you.

THE HUNT FOR IDENTITY

A lioness must know who she is before she can lead her pride. My hunt for identity began early.

My mother returned when I was sixteen, and for the first time, we lived together. It was a new and unfamiliar dynamic. We had spent years apart and now we had to learn each other's ways. I was a teenager searching for my place in the world and she was a mother trying to reclaim the daughter, who she had provided for, but not raised. It was a reunion filled with both excitement and unspoken tension.

At the same time, my grandmother, my mother's mother, moved in with us. She was deeply rooted in tradition, while I had begun embracing a Christian faith that challenged some of those traditions. Our home became a quiet battlefield, where faith and culture collided and my mother found herself caught between the two of us.

It was during this time that I realised that my journey was not just about belonging, it was about defining myself. Like a lioness learning the rhythm of the hunt, I knew I had to carve my own path, moving with stealth and faith toward the life I was meant to live.

THE SILENT ROAR OF PAIN

Every lioness faces trials that test her strength. My greatest came when I lost my four-year-old son, Khensile. His name meant 'Great Gratitude', and he was just that; a source of boundless joy. But his life was cut short in a car accident, and the impact shattered me.

The pain was unbearable, a weight so heavy, I often wished I could remove it for just a moment, set it down and breathe. But grief does not work that way. It clings, relentless and unshakable.

Yet, in my sorrow, I found growth. The lioness mourns in solitude, but she does not lose her will to survive. My husband, Solly, and I became fiercely protective of our remaining children, drawing them close as we navigated the grief together. I did not ask God, *Why me?* because, *If not me, then who?* I knew I was not the first to lose a child, and I would not be the last. Instead, I whispered a vow into the night: *I would seek the purpose hidden within this pain.*

THE STEALTH OF BECOMING

I grew up being very quiet and shy, an observer rather than a speaker. I recall many times when my aunt, who both needed and deserved a break, would send me to visit my maternal grandmother in the rural areas. There, I was surrounded by the vastness of nature, which both fascinated and terrified me. I was scared of every insect and animal that crawled upon the earth, and my uncle, my mother's eldest brother, became my 'protector' every night.

It is only in adulthood that I realised how much God truly protected me from my uncle's so-called 'protection'. His actions, though they never moved beyond him kissing and holding me, left a lingering unease in my spirit. At the time, I did not know anything about faith, but looking back, I now see the hand of God shielding me, even in my innocence. It was through this realisation that my trust in God deepened, and my faith became the foundation upon which I built my life.

Born in July, I do not follow zodiac signs, but I have always liked the idea of being a Leo. Over time, I came to embrace the lioness in me; the bold, strong, protective and strategic being that I am. It was this character that shaped my leadership, allowing me to lead with authenticity and unwavering conviction.

During my quiet and shy years, I remember vividly how I would think very deeply and dream very big. The first thing I longed for was a family; a home where both a mother and a father were present and loving. The second thing I dreamed of was *success*, even though I had never seen it, never experienced it and had no reference for what it would look like. In a country where the system was never designed for black people to thrive, I dared to dream anyway.

Everything I dreamed about has come to pass and I am still witnessing some of those dreams manifesting before my eyes. It was at the age of sixteen that I decided to break free from the constraints of my quiet and shy nature. I was tired of feeling invisible, of sitting in class knowing the answers yet never daring to raise my hand. One day, I went home, stood in front of a mirror, and spoke to myself: *From now on, I will speak up.*

Even if I am wrong, even if I become a laughing stock, I will speak up.

From that moment, I gained my confidence, bit by bit. That decision to speak up became one of the most defining moments of my life. The confidence I cultivated carried me through the toughest of situations, and when others were afraid to confront uncomfortable truths, I was willing to step forward.

I became an advocate for those who could not speak for themselves. I defended the rights of others, challenged injustices and used my voice to empower those who felt unheard. This courage to speak, to stand firm in my convictions, became the bedrock of my leadership style. It won me the hearts of many, not because I sought approval, but because I led with truth and conviction.

Stealth and faith have been my constant companions. Like the lioness, I learned to move strategically, to observe before acting, to trust my instincts and to walk with confidence, even in uncertainty. I came to understand that faith is not just about believing, it is about acting, speaking and moving in alignment with that belief.

The quiet girl who once feared the sound of her own voice grew into a leader whose words carried weight and power. I have faced trials that threatened to silence me, but faith has always been my anchor. Even in moments of fear, even when I felt unqualified or unworthy, I leaned into the divine strength that guided me.

Stealth is not about hiding; it is about moving with purpose, with wisdom, with strategy. Faith is not just about hoping; it is about knowing, deep within, that even when the path is unclear, God has already gone ahead to make a way.

And so, I continue to walk this journey, not as a timid girl afraid to speak, but as a lioness who understands the power of her voice, the depth of her faith and the limitless potential of a life led with both stealth and trust in God.

THE STEALTH OF TRANSFORMATION

A lioness does not merely adapt, she transforms her environment, moving through seasons of growth, sometimes pausing in the shadows, sometimes leaping forward with conviction. My transformation has been a journey of faith, resilience and a deep calling to serve.

At the height of my corporate career as a partner at Deloitte, I had achieved financial success, leading a profitable business. Yet, despite my accomplishments, an inner void lingered. I took a three-month sabbatical, a defining period of self-discovery. I embarked on a holistic detox – physically, emotionally and spiritually – stripping away external accolades to uncover my deeper purpose.

During this time, I reconnected with *Think and Grow Rich* by Napoleon Hill, a book that had long influenced me. While my faith remained rooted in the Bible, Hill's principles offered a structured approach to integrating faith with success. This book became more than a guide, it was a catalyst for transformation. I introduced these teachings to my children, having them write chapter reviews to instill a mindset of personal growth.

As my transformation deepened, an unexpected opportunity arose. In 2021, during the lockdown, I stumbled upon an invitation from the Napoleon Hill Foundation to share personal journeys. I submitted my story, reflecting on my dual role as a mother of five and a high-achieving career woman. This led to an invitation to participate in the documentary *Mom's Rising: A Think and Grow Rich Movie*.

During discussions with the film's director, Scott Cervine, I realised I was the only African in the project. This revelation ignited a fire within me. Why was Africa missing from such a powerful movement? Why had *Think and Grow Rich* not been adapted for the African context? That moment planted a seed, and over the next eighteen months, I worked diligently to secure the rights to bring *Think and Grow Rich Africa* to life.

What had started as a personal journey of transformation, now evolved into a mission to uplift others across the continent. Africa's greatest wealth, I realised, is not in its land or resources, but in the untapped potential of its people. This became my calling, not just to lead within the corporate world, but to inspire a paradigm shift in mindset, empowerment and self-belief.

Like a lioness preparing her cubs for the hunt, I incorporated these principles into my leadership style. I mentored young professionals and coached executives, emphasising intentional thinking, persistence and faith. I witnessed people flourish, becoming high-performing individuals, simply by shifting their mindset.

Transformation, like stealth, often begins quietly. Change does not always announce itself with great fanfare; it starts as a whisper, a feeling of misalignment, a nudge toward something greater. Faith is the courage to follow that whisper, to step into the unknown with the conviction that a greater purpose awaits.

I moved forward with faith, embracing the same principles that had sustained me throughout my career; endurance, strategy and the courage to take risks. My advocacy for fairness and opportunity had always been a cornerstone of my work, but now it held deeper significance. I was determined to awaken the sleeping lion within every African who had been told they were not enough.

Transformation requires patience. A lioness does not rush into the hunt. She observes, calculates and waits for the perfect moment. My journey has been no different. Years of expertise, wisdom and strategic positioning had prepared me for this moment. Now, it was time to leap.

Faith has carried me through every trial, setback and moment of doubt. It has been my shield, my guide, my foundation. The lioness in me walks forward, unshaken, knowing that every step is divinely ordered, every challenge holds a lesson and every victory is already written.

And so, I continue moving in stealth, leading with faith, transforming with purpose.

THE TRIALS OF A CAREER LIONESS

My career has been filled with challenges. South Africa's history of apartheid automatically placed obstacles in my path but I was determined to prove that success is not defined by colour. I endured being called names, denied opportunities and forced to work harder than my white colleagues to prove my worth.

There were times I was falsely investigated for misconduct yet vindicated. I was once denied company housing benefits because of my race, but I fought and secured the same privileges as my white colleagues. I was falsely accused, and my login credentials were misused for fraud. Yet again, I was proven innocent because, by God's grace, I was out of town at the time of the fraudulent transactions.

In my career, at the age of twenty-seven, I was given my first flight as a reward after being falsely accused but later proven right. I faced a superior who expected 'favours' for my promotion, and when I refused, attempted to physically intimidate me. I kept my faith and pressed on, knowing my success was destined beyond the trials I faced.

As I grew in my career, I was privileged to travel globally, build wealth and establish a fulfilling life. But the seasons of my career eventually revealed that my time in the corporate world had come to an end. Despite my contributions, my leadership was undermined and my legacy as a coach was being erased. However, those moments of rejection became a gift, revealing my true purpose beyond the corporate world.

The Lioness Awakens

Looking back, I see the power of stealth; the wisdom of moving in silence, the discipline of waiting, the courage of knowing when to act.

I have been tested by loss, strengthened by faith and sharpened by experience. My journey has taught me that true power does not always roar, sometimes, it moves in quiet conviction, trusting in the unseen forces that guide it forward.

I am a lioness, moving with stealth and living with faith. And this is only the beginning.

ABOUT LERATO

Lerato is the founder and leader of Think and Grow Rich Africa, a coaching and transformational development organization with a vision to ignite a paradigm shift empowering Africans to understand, harness, and utilise the immense power of their minds and thoughts, leading to a new era of success. Her purpose is to catalyse a revolution of self-discovery and empowerment, guiding Africans to unlock the boundless potential within their minds and thoughts, thereby igniting transformation.

The mission is to build, train and develop great people and high performance teams, believing that great people are those that understand the power and capacity of their minds and thoughts, use that power to create their success, achieve their goals and fulfil their purpose in life. This is done by equipping tools with a robust set of tools, techniques, and methodologies that facilitate transformation including design thinking, coaching, education, consulting mentoring and training. She is an ICF certified coach and is also a Napoleon Hill Institute certified coach.

Lerato is a former senior partner and global leader at Deloitte and she is a results driven executive business leader with authentic, inclusive and innovative leadership style. Her career of over thirty-three years spans across public and private sector industry growing her career from being a procurement clerk to head of procurement; senior manager at IDC, director at Alexander Forbes, general manage at Umngeni and Blue IQ and Murray and Roberts, executive mManager at Accenture and senior partner at EY; Africa managing director at ERM.

She has served as an executive board member of Deloitte Africa and a member of Remco; board member and ethics committee member Deloitte Consulting and ERM chairperson of the Africa board and ERM global board member.

Lerato is a keynote speaker, a facilitator and an executive leader, she has driven strategy and delivered consulting services in both private and public sector as well globally which includes the US, Spain, Czech Republic, France and the UK. Lerato is a master in business development and sales as well as revenue driven practice management.

Lerato is also co-founder and executive producer of a film production company called Urithi and she is a movie actress featured in a movie called *Moms Rising*. She also founded a perfume brand called LERADIS.

Lerato is a proud mother of five and a wife to Solly, her husband of thirty-three years.

She is a World Leaders Conclave Business Excellence Award 2025 winner, Finalist for the Woman Changing The World Award for 2025, and she was named one of the Africa's Top 10 Most Empowering Women Leaders of 2024 by the *CIO Views* magazine.

MARIAM ELHOULI
GUIDING LIGHTS

In the symphony of life, there are melodies of belief, pathways of planning, flames of determination and whispers of intuition. These elements, woven together, guide us through the labyrinth of challenges and triumphs, teaching us valuable lessons along the way. Join me on a journey of warmth and wisdom as we explore the transformative power of faith, strategy, determination and stealth.

UNDERSTANDING FAITH

Close your eyes and feel the warmth of faith radiating from within. It's the gentle whisper that assures you of your potential, the gentle hand that steadies you amidst uncertainty. Faith, dear friend, is the compass that points us towards our dreams, urging us to trust in the unseen and embrace the journey ahead.

But let us not mistake faith for blind optimism. No, faith is the quiet confidence that blooms from self-awareness and inner strength. It teaches us to believe in ourselves and our abilities, even when the world doubts our potential. Through faith, we learn the invaluable lesson that belief is the first step towards achievement.

THE POWER OF STRATEGY

Picture yourself standing at the edge of a vast wilderness, armed with a map and a sense of purpose. This, my friend, is the essence of strategy. It's the art of charting a course towards our dreams, guided by clarity of vision and intentionality of action.

As we navigate the terrain of entrepreneurship or any endeavour, strategy becomes our trusted companion. It empowers us to break down our goals into manageable steps, guiding us towards success one strategic move at a time. Through strategy, we learn the importance of planning and preparedness, understanding that foresight is the lantern that illuminates our path in the darkest of nights.

THE ROLE OF DETERMINATION

Feel the fire of determination burning within your chest, urging you to press forward despite the obstacles in your path. Determination, dear friend, is the relentless drive that fuels our journey towards success. It's the unwavering commitment to our dreams, the refusal to be swayed by adversity or setbacks.

In the face of challenges, determination becomes our guiding light, illuminating the path forward with unwavering resolve. It teaches us the invaluable lesson that success is not measured by the absence of obstacles but by our willingness to overcome them. Through determination, we learn the transformative power of resilience and perseverance, understanding that every setback is merely a stepping stone towards our ultimate destination.

My entrepreneurial journey was fraught with challenges and setbacks, each serving as a test of my determination. There were moments of doubt and uncertainty, where the road ahead seemed insurmountable. Yet, it was in those moments that my determination burned brightest, propelling me forward with an unyielding resolve to succeed.

EMBRACING STEALTH

In the cacophony of voices clamouring for our attention, the art of stealth emerges as a guiding principle. It is the ability to block out the noise of doubt and scepticism, to trust our instincts and forge ahead despite the odds. Stealth empowers us to make decisive moves quietly, even when others question our judgment or sanity.

Stealth is not about secrecy or deceit but rather about strategic discernment and calculated risk-taking. It is the art of moving with purpose and intentionality, leveraging the element of surprise to gain a competitive edge. As the saying goes, 'Don't ask about travel to a person who has never left home.' Similarly, don't seek advice from those who have never ventured beyond the confines of conventional thinking

In a world filled with noise and distraction, stealth becomes our trusted ally, enabling us to block out the doubts and fears that threaten to derail our journey. It teaches us the invaluable lesson, that sometimes, the most powerful actions are those taken quietly, with purpose and intentionality. Through stealth, we learn to trust in our inner wisdom and intuition, understanding that true strength lies not in the volume of our actions but in their strategic precision.

My own journey embodies the seamless integration of faith, strategy, determination and stealth. Each element played a distinct yet complementary role in shaping my path to success. Faith provided the foundation upon which I built my dreams, strategy illuminated the path forward, determination fuelled my actions and stealth enabled me to navigate the complexities of entrepreneurship with finesse.

Through trial and tribulation, I learned to trust in the symbiotic relationship between these elements, recognising that success is not the result of blind faith alone but a harmonious blend of conviction, foresight, resilience and subtlety. It is through the integration of these principles that we unlock our fullest potential and chart a course towards fulfillment and prosperity.

As we journey through life's myriad pathways, let us embrace the warmth and wisdom of faith, strategy, determination and stealth. Let us cultivate belief in ourselves and our dreams, guided by strategic vision, unwavering resolve and quiet confidence. In doing so, we unlock the transformative power of these elements, illuminating our path towards fulfilment and success.

ABOUT MARIAM

Mariam Elhouli is an accomplished entrepreneur, mother of five, award-winning author, and film director. As an international keynote speaker, she inspires and empowers audiences worldwide with her expertise and impactful insights.

ADREA L PETERS
STEP BY STEP ALL THE WAY UP! UP! UP!

'You have one person on one side of a pole holding a rope and another person on the other side holding a rope …'

My thought bubble … *Hang me now.*

My interview for THE Microsoft Corporation was tanking right before my eyes and this guy, this hiring manager, is talking about ropes and poles. For the love of …

He goes on, 'What is the degree of the rope if both let go of their ropes?'

My mind filled with mathematical symbols. Sweat tickled the edges of my hairline. It was hot, so very hot. Hands … clammy, gross. I wondered if the stench from my armpits wafted across the table between us.

'No idea,' I said.

He made a check on his tablet and moved on.

Heart sunk. Then fluttered sporadically. I gripped and wiped the seat cushion of the desk chair holding me in place. A few seconds earlier he'd asked me the difference between a Mac and a PC. I'd given him the same stellar answer. To appear smarter, I think I added something like, 'I really have no idea. I've had very little exposure to either.'

'Last one,' he said.

Thank you, baby Jesus.

'You walk into a room and try to turn on a light, but it won't turn on.

What's the first thing you do?'

I replied, 'Am I standing in the dark?'

He smiled. 'Why?'

'I'd find a flashlight or another light nearby first.'

Smiled again. 'It's light enough for you to see.'

'I'd check that it was plugged in.'

'Thank you,' he said.

He returned the excess pages he's flipped over the top of his legal pad and placed it face down on the desk. He stood. 'Thanks for coming in.'

I weaved and bumbled to my infrequently high-heeled feet, pressed my skirt flat and managed, 'Thank you! I hope I did okay.'

To which he said … nothing.

I left thinking, *There is no way on God's green earth that I got that job.* What. A. Disaster.

A month or more later, I got a call.

The same hiring manager that interviewed me was now offering me a co-op internship at THE Microsoft Corporation.

Co-op means you get paid. I think I made around $17,000. It was 1990 into 1991. I was twenty. This was big.

'Are you sure?' I asked.

To which he paused. Faux chuckled. Then said, 'Yes.'

'Did someone else drop out?' I continued in utter disbelief.

'No,' he said. 'So, what do you think?'

'You are sure you want me?'

'Yes.'

'Then WOW! Yes!'

And off I went to Bellevue, Washington, just outside of Seattle, after the school year ended.

Little did I know how powerful my one year at Microsoft would be. Not only is it the highlight of my résumé still, three decades later, that year gave me a foundation from an extraordinary company. I was treated like a professional and expected to be a professional. It was a phenomenal place to learn what *good* looks like. As I reflect on it, it made a colossal impact on who I am today; an award-winning author, executive strategist, award-winning entrepreneur, writing mentor, retreat host and C-suite technology consultant.

How you begin, whenever that is, matters. How open you are to being in over your head and learning to swim quickly, matters. Listening. Thinking. Processing. Digesting. Sharing. These are the five keys to my success as a leader in all that I do.

How did I get there?

Bulldozing. Over-reacting. Failing. Interrupting. Hoarding.

Not all at once … but sometimes all at once! Seemed like every time I got a little more confidence from a little win, I soon fumbled all over myself again.

And that was a GOOD THING! How else would I have learned? It's so important to fail; to do the direct opposite of what we know we should do or even could do. We must understand the light *and* dark sides of ourselves to constantly evolve and expand.

I hope you noticed that it is the direct opposite of my ideals that make up my downfalls. Opposites keep us balanced.

Bulldozing. Over-reacting. Failing. Interrupting. Hoarding.

vs.

Listening. Thinking. Processing. Digesting. Sharing.

We all walk the bridge between our desires, which I like to think of as synonymous with destiny, and our cringies, which I like to think of as those things you wish you could take back almost as quickly as you released them. This is life. This is what we all do. We're in this together, which is a lovely equaliser. We bounce between that joyous ideal state and that cringe-worthy state, until we understand how much better it feels to live in our ideal.

Once we hit that realisation, life gets quite sweet. Many never decide to stop the cringies. They accept it. They adapt to it. That's when we know we're in trouble. This is where I encourage people to be quite black and white, yes or no, holy wow or holy no! May we adore the fringes, the edges, because that is where we *feeeeel* life. Where we LIVE life. If we don't push the limits – on both sides, good and bad – we never discover what we are capable of. To be capable of greatness, you must also be capable of not-greatness.

As a woman leader at a Fortune 35 company in the 1990s and early 2000s, I didn't have a lot of female mentors. I was often one of maybe two or three other women around a table of thirty, forty, fifty male execs. I loved it. In the nineties, my women friends and I played along, noticing all the nepotism and bullshit mansplaining. We didn't report every infraction to HR. We fought back. We called bullshit when bullshit flew. I learned the good and bad ways to do things. I was tougher and rougher than I should have been or needed to be as I rose up the ranks. Maybe that paved the way for women after me? I don't really think so. I wasn't proud of how I felt I had to lead. This is why, as I teetered on the edge of the VP track … I quit.

Yes, you read that right. I quit right as I was about to really rise in corporate America.

Here's why: I was NOT a man. I could not lead as a man and I could not stand the thought of not becoming the woman I wanted to become. I can't say I was this clear that was my reason for leaving at the time. It took years for me to be able to voice the internal battle I faced. When I left the corporate world and started my own consultancy, I told myself and others it was to write books. I needed to control my time. I needed to not be owned. I wanted to be paid for every hour I worked; no longer letting them work me for fifty to sixty hours a week whilst paying me for forty.

Over time, I went deeper, because I finally had the time to! I know now that it was because I wanted to lead like a woman and stop imitating the male leaders surrounding me. I was tired of moulding and shapeshifting to 'fit in'. I wanted all the parts of me to be honoured. I wanted to take everything in without everything being a fight, or only about the bottom line. Don't get me wrong, I love money. And I love integrity, kindness, love, laughter, joy, sharing, talking and enjoying life equally. I wanted to become Adrea. I wanted to see exactly who she was and what she was capable of.

Turns out, I was capable of a helluva lot more than I ever imagined! And that continues to be true … which surprises me daily! I'm learning and expanding more now than ever before because I trust my instinct, which is driven by my gut! I teeter ever closer to the edge on the regular. And each time I take a step off the edge, I'm that twenty-year-old taking a call from THE Microsoft Corporation, where I'm in awe, filled with surprise and wonder that *you're sure you want me?*

'Yes.'

ABOUT ADREA

For nearly two decades, Adrea has dedicated every spare moment she could carve out from her busy consulting career to pursue her true passion – writing. Her stories and articles reflect the heart of her curiosities: love, physics, food, wellness, logic, grace, cleverness, wordplay and the belief in the beauty and potential within herself and others.

A proud valedictorian with a journalism degree from the University of Colorado at Boulder, Adrea continued to pursue her craft with determination, later earning a master's in popular fiction writing from Seton Hill University. Her creative spirit led her to co-author several inspirational alphabet books and an app with Teffanie Thompson through Pictureless Books. Together, they also co-wrote *When I Go Outside, I Go Inside*, published by MMH Press. Their collaboration extended to the award-winning textbook *Many Genres, One Craft*, a valuable textbook for writers.

Adrea's writing has taken many forms, from magazines to screenplays to full-length novels. In 2020, she released the first two books in her *Becoming Truitt Skye* trilogy, with the third installment, *The Equation for Imagination*, released in 2024. She also created the *Quantum*

Collection, including the award-winning bestseller *Quantum Thinking*, a compilation of affirmations designed to evoke new possibilities in perspective and help readers unlock their full potential.

Her latest project, *The Power of the Pause*, co-written with Karen Weaver, will join the *Quantum Collection* in spring 2025. This marks their second collaboration, following the success of *Quantum Love*, released in 2021. Both *Quantum Thinking* and *When I Go Outside, I Go Inside* were chosen for the 2021 Academy Award gift bags, a special honour given to the nominees for best actor, actress, director and best supporting actor and actress.

Adrea is deeply committed to supporting other writers, mentoring them for over two decades. Her passion for helping others find their voice and share their stories shines through in her work, as she guides aspiring authors with both compassion and clarity. In 2021, she released *The Science of Story: Mastering Your Nature*, an award-winning book that has inspired a series of workshops where she empowers individuals to see themselves as the heroes of their own lives.

Her achievements were recognised in 2021 when she was named one of *Brainz Magazine's* Top 500 Entrepreneurs, alongside names like Oprah, Jay Shetty, Mel Robbins and Jessica Alba. This honour celebrated her entrepreneurial success, her commitment to making a difference and her unwavering dedication to helping others achieve their dreams.

Adrea now resides in Vermont, where she continues to write, mentor and inspire. She would love to connect with you, so please feel free to visit her at adreapeters.com.

ADORA CRYSTAL EVANS
FROM VISION TO REALITY:
FAITH IN ACTION

What does stealth and faith mean to you?

Whenever I think of stealth, I think of power and beauty, but it's faith that is, and continues to be, a hugely important part of my life.

Whatever vision we create for ourselves, how we want our family to be, our body to look, our world to be, our business to be, a book, our dream, it's first about having a vision for what we want and then having the faith to believe it can happen.

In my experience, even though I now live in a very *conditioned* state, with years of affirmative statements, years of self-love and years of mastery and success, life is still bumpy; it's messy and imperfect. But having faith means trusting the tough times will pass and it won't be long before you're back on track. When I'm meeting a new edge in my courage or stepping into the unknown, I remember my early years of discovering the possibility of being more, being different and becoming my highest self.

Back then, 99% of my baggage and old ways were driving my actions 99% of the time. I was living an automated way of being. But 1% of the time, I would get a little sliver of *something,* maybe an hour, maybe a day of flying high, when everything is awesome. And then I would collapse back into dealing with all the old stuff: the drama, a breakup, old beliefs.

But that glimmer of hope grows, and then you get a Hallelujah moment when you just know life can be amazing. And that's the beautiful and underestimated thing about faith; you know you've been 'called'. You realise other people have figured it out, so you're going to figure it out too.

Miracles and crazy quantum leaps have happened for me in my life. From dancer to TV producer; from living in a boarded-up home to an $8,000 one-time cheque; from not sure what's going to happen next to walking on red carpets and working with celebrities, wearing $20,000 dresses.

Although a lot of this appears like it happens overnight (and it can), there's also a dichotomy.

It's possible that little moments of faith, a tiny moment in time, can set off into the quantum reality, creating major shifts, major miracles, major immediate changes. But it's also important to consider the really 'small' choices we make every day, again and again. You don't go to the gym and suddenly have six-pack abs and the butt of your dreams. It's the tiny choices that pay off over time, and then suddenly the character emerges, and all the work and the positive choices can be seen with the eyes, or it shows up in your bank account, or in the divine client, or in that new radiant soul.

With a vision and a little bit of faith, the small choices you make daily will enable you to see things differently. Things that used to be a big deal, just aren't as important anymore.

Back then, not now, I would look in the mirror and see all of my faults. Learning about the principles of self-love, it still took a while before I was able to say, *Wait, wait, wait. You're supposed to love yourself. Look at yourself and say it out loud, I love you. I love you.* I was caught in a wild cycle; I'd even beat myself up for not thinking positively; *I should be thinking better. I should be kinder to myself.*

When you notice that you're not being kind to yourself, just give yourself grace. Don't camp out there, but those pockets of awareness are huge and you'll be surprised how they will yield incredible results in your life.

Right here, I want to let you know that some people actually think, *When I've been doing this* right *for twenty years, everything will come together and I'll never have a self-limiting belief ever again!*

But this is just not true – no amount of life mastery will guarantee you *never* have moments of self doubt. No one can ever be perfect, but you can get *better* at it.

The seed for a better life is planted in the visualisation of the dream, then when the reality of it comes into your life, it's just magic. I call it *life-magic.* What I love about those miracle moments is how they raise your vibration when life is pulling you down. Life is going to happen, no matter what, and we can only control what we do and the actions we take. When our vibration is raised, we can see our challenges as roadblocks before the breakthrough. When we are faced with a struggle, we grow into it. We must grow into the person we need to be to take the very next step to receive what it is we want. Once you have that perspective, there is no stopping you. Challenges are there to serve you, shifting your future to embrace them with an open heart.

Through my faith, I have very strong rituals throughout my day to remind me to be in gratitude, to remind me of how great my life is, the vision I'm creating and where I'm going.

For some people, depending on where they are, it can feel hard to think of being in a high vibration when life has gotten you into a momentum where you feel isolated and desperate. But a tiny glimmer of hope and faith can set you back on track. It's not about denying your emotions either though. Don't cover up or push away what you feel, embrace it, acknowledge it and look for the hope that will eventually come.

Being patient with our emotions and our emotional state is imperative. With the advent of social media, we think we can from zero to hero in ten minutes, but this just causes frustration. We must accept our emotions and hang on to the faith that things will work out – even if it does take some time. Those little faith moments all add up and add to our belief in ourselves.

Remember that what you focus on is what you grow. Find one thing to be grateful for and you'll start to notice many things to be grateful for. Smile at the flowers, and everyone is smiling with you. Is it possible to be sad when you are smiling? The opposite is also true; focus on feeling frustrated and you'll find more things to be frustrated about. So, get good at what you're tuning in to, while still embracing all your emotions. Otherwise, they will just be suppressed and anything suppressed is likely to explode at some point! If you deal with what you're feeling and honour it, with a perspective of optimism, progression and learning, you won't hold on to it.

Part of stepping onto trailblazing or unchartered paths, where you take the wheel and you're the boss of your life driving in the direction you want to go, means you're going to have to throw out the rules you've held on to for most of your life; get a good education, a good job, be a good citizen, marriage, kids and retire when you're told to. If you're going to step out in courage you might just need to make up some rules of your own. Faith comes into its own when the reality doesn't quite match the vision. Your vision might be that you're supposed to be a *New York Times* bestselling author and two people have bought your book. Faith is holding on to the vision and continuing to take action and steps towards your dream. One of the highest forms of faith is taking continuous action even when you can't immediately see the outcome you want. It's at times like these you need to be the courageous roaring lioness; brave, stealthy and consistent.

A couple of times in my life I've let my stealthiness take over. I've set some cool intentions and gone on a fun ride – without telling anyone. When you tell people, you have to deal with expectations and goals, controlled by steps. Instead, I set an intention and go on the journey – and the results have been bigger than I could ever have imagined. But it does take discipline to show up, and to build momentum when I just want to roll over and go back to sleep!

Just like for me, the dream may sometimes feel out of reach, but when you have faith, you can count on yourself to keep your word, knowing the universe is buying into you and what you want to achieve.

ABOUT ADORA

Adora Crystal Evans is a highly sought-after elite connector and producer with a passion for creating strategic partnerships and helping others to achieve their goals.

With her talent for collaboration and alliance-building, Adora has earned a reputation as a trusted advisor and strategic partner for entrepreneurs and business owners alike.

As a producer, Adora has a track record of success, having created a number of successful events, both in-person and virtual. She is skilled at bringing people together and facilitating collaborations that drive meaningful impact.

Adora's keen understanding of collaboration and creating environments where people can go faster in collaboration makes her the go-to hired wing gal for some of the best leaders in their field. Adora has co-produced Destination Diva's TV Show on WE Network and soon to be travel channel, The Can You Really Think and Grow Rich Tour with the Napoleon Hill Foundation, and several events with Denis Waitley, Les Brown, Bob Proctor, and other thought leaders.

PHILLIPA VINCENT-CONNOLLY NAVIGATING STRENGTH & FAITH

In the intricate dance of life, we often find ourselves navigating the realms of stealth and faith. Whether it's the quiet resilience we muster in facing adversity or the unwavering belief in ourselves despite the odds, these qualities profoundly shape our journey. For individuals like me, living with cerebral palsy, life takes on added layers of complexity. Having cerebral palsy – or CP – presents a unique set of challenges, shaping all aspects of daily life. From navigating physical limitations to confronting societal perceptions, individuals with CP, like me, often employ a blend of stealth and faith to discover the power to transcend limitations and embrace our fullest potential. In this chapter, we delve into the intricacies of living with cerebral palsy, exploring how the interplay of stealth and faith can guide our journey.

Cerebral palsy is a neurological condition that affects movement, muscle tone and posture, stemming from abnormalities or damage to the developing brain, often occurring due to a lack of oxygen to the brain, and in my case, being born prematurely at twenty-six weeks, weighing 2lbs 2oz, which back in 1970 made me a 'miracle' baby, surviving such odds. Developmental symptoms vary widely, with manifestations ranging from mild motor impairments to severe physical disabilities. My CP manifested in me walking with a bent gait, never being able to run, climbing stairs without a rail, wearing high heels … and not walking along the pavement in public without being stared at. Then, there was the diagnosis, years later, of dyspraxia and dyscalculia. While the challenges posed by CP are diverse and multifaceted, they often extend beyond the purely physical realm, impacting my social interactions, self-perception and personal aspirations.

For some, like me, the challenges are apparent and subtle yet pervasive, demanding adaptability on my part and creating an unwavering resilience of character to navigate the challenges of everyday life.

As a child, until the age of nine, I was institutionalised in a Shaftesbury Society boarding school for disabled children. In some ways, it was an expected experience because being in a school like that did not require me to adapt or try to conceal my disability, though I couldn't hide it even if I wanted to. My gait and lack of balance made me walk as if I were permanently intoxicated, without the alcohol! I was the least disabled of my school peers at that time. Through my strength of character, I was usually the student who would try to stand up for my peers or perhaps walk quickly down the corridor, in my nightdress and bare feet at night, to find one of the nurses or the matron because someone had fallen out of bed, or needed the bathroom, in the middle of the night. I was the pupil who challenged the staff, complaining when we couldn't watch television after tea and were made to go to bed, and be asleep at pm. I was always the outspoken one.

As a child, I was friendly, and my mum said I would speak to anyone when we were on a bus or out and about. Strangely, I had a lot of confidence and was complimented for my pleasing personality. However, that changed when I started mainstream school with all the 'normal' kids because that was when I realised I was different. It was a harsh lesson to learn in more ways than one. At that time, my consultant and doctors advised me to use walking sticks, which I reluctantly did, to help me acclimatise and navigate a much bigger school with the physical challenges that presented me with. The students at that middle school reacted to me very differently. Some with pity in their eyes, others with fear because of a lack of understanding of disability. Very few treated me the same as them.

As a teenager, I got into fashion, art and music with the rise and popularity of the 'new romantic' movement and the new wave music of the early eighties. For me, dressing as a goth, with jet black, sugared and watered hair spiked up toward the ceiling, with half a can of hairspray daily, wearing velvet dinner jackets, mohair jumpers, a crucifix and back-knotted Victorian skirts, allowed me to defy my mum, and stepdad, as well as gravity! I was only 5'2, so the added height of spikey hair made me appear taller. The youth culture of that movement at the time allowed me to hide my disability behind a persona, *a look*. I thought that the more outrageously I dressed at the weekend, the more make-up I wore to school, the more crimped and spiked my hair was, the more 'people' would look at how I was dressed rather than how I *shuffled*. In secondary school, I was insular. Quiet most of the time, I tried to keep myself to myself so I wasn't bullied … but that didn't always work. So, after attending the usual Friday night youth club disco, I spent most of my weekends reading books, drawing, listening to music or watching old black-and-white movies on Saturday afternoon TV.

During this period in my life, I was trying to conceal my disability, the essence of stealth; I felt I'd never have close friends because of my disability, let alone have a boyfriend, get married and have children. My paradigm was invested in what society expected a disabled person to be – unable to contribute anything of any significance to the world, for others to write their story, to be institutionalised, out of sight and out of mind, because of the perception that your presence in anyone's life would not amount to anything worthwhile. Stealth, in the context of cerebral palsy, embodies the art of navigating the world with grace and subtlety. However, it could be argued that dressing like a punk or a goth was neither gracious-looking nor subtle! I was trying to master the delicate balance between concealment and revelation, choosing when to disclose and talk about my disability and when to try and blend into the fabric of society unnoticed. For many individuals with CP, the desire to fit in, be liked, loved even, and be treated as an equal to their 'normal' peers, often drives this stealthy approach. This is where my character, determination, persistence and faith developed.

I vividly recall many instances that encapsulate the essence of stealth in my life. It was during my teenage years, fraught with insecurities and the relentless pursuit of acceptance. Despite my cerebral palsy, I strived to appear 'normal,' masking the physical challenges with long skirts, crazy-colour hairstyles and different looks to distract from my disability and the constant fear of rejection that lurked beneath the surface. Outwardly, apart from my waddle, I may have seemed like any other teenager, but beneath the facade lay a constant battle against self-doubt and the fear of being perceived as different. Stealth, in the context of cerebral palsy, encompasses having a pleasing personality, not speaking up for yourself and navigating the world with a modicum of grace and dignity, often concealing the outward manifestations of a disability. For many individuals with cerebral palsy – me included – the desire to be treated as equals usually drives the instinct to camouflage the physical challenges we face. From adjusting our gait to hiding involuntary movements, stealth becomes second nature, a silent testament to our resilience and adaptability. It's about striking a delicate balance between authenticity and assimilation, choosing when to reveal one's vulnerabilities and when to try and blend as seamlessly as we can into the fabric of society.

In the face of adversity, faith emerges as a guiding light, illuminating the path forward with unwavering conviction. It's not merely about religious belief or faith in God but also a profound trust in oneself, the universe and who God created me to be. Faith takes on a multifaceted significance for individuals with cerebral palsy, serving as a source of strength, resilience and hope amidst life's challenges.

My journey as a disabled person with cerebral palsy has been intertwined with moments of profound faith, where I dared to defy the limitations imposed by my condition and embrace the boundless possibilities that lay ahead. One such moment stands out distinctly in my memory – the day I decided to step into the personal development community. Like so many, I watched the movie *The Secret* (2006) in 2014, presented by Bob Proctor, Joe Vitale, John Assaraf, Michael Beckwith and Jack Canfield. I loved the idea of the law of attraction and wanted to manifest a new flat to rent because the house my two boys and I lived in at the time was plagued by black mould and unsafe, rotting floorboards. I began looking into Bob Proctor, watching his YouTube videos and eventually joined his free live events, which he presented on social media. Despite hearing of the success stories of Bob and the results of his coaches and success advisors, I had doubts and uncertainties about the material Bob taught and that, because I was disabled and imperfect, this material wouldn't work for me. It was the paradigm I had about me and my disability that plagued my mind, not whether the material worked, but whether the material would work for me or not ... because of my disability. Over time, and through the uncertainty of the COVID-19 pandemic and the lockdowns in the UK, I participated in more events with Bob, and my paradigms began to change.

With God (yes, I say, God, instead of the universe, but you can choose whatever higher being you prefer) and faith as my compass, I embarked on a journey of self-discovery, firstly through a year-long mentorship program that I manifested with Bob, to embarking on a training course with a mentee of Bob's, an Irish lady, who now lives in America, called Cliona O'Hara, when she set up The Napoleon Hill Institute. The way Cliona teaches Napoleon Hill's material, which Bob always taught, she shares from her heart and from her intuition. It's a way of teaching this material that resonates with me. I have been trained as a global certified NHI coach to mentor from the heart, with authenticity, love and faith, transcending the physical constraints I have lived through, which previously constantly threatened to hold me back. In the face of adversity, I became a certified coach with NHI in August 2023. Then, in October 2023, I visited the Napoleon Hill Archives in Virginia as a founding member of NHI, meeting Don Green at The Napoleon Hill Foundation and, of course, Cliona and the NHI team, studying with them all in person. The goals and results I desired, which I had written down on goal cards years before, such as becoming a certified coach in this material, had manifested, which increased my faith in the principles I studied and confirmed that God had put me on the right path. Through doing the work, being persistent and getting into action, faith emerges as a steadfast companion, offering solace and strength when working on your 'inner self' and breaking down old paradigms amidst living in the present of life's circumstances. It's not merely about studying and learning the principles, but applying the principles based on intuition AND study, then getting into action to achieve the results in life you desire. Studying and applying personal development material is a lifelong lifestyle encompassing belief and faith. Faith is about believing in a higher being (God) and a profound trust in oneself and the universe to know that you WILL manifest your goals at the right time and that faith acts as an illuminating, guiding light during the darkest days.

For individuals with cerebral palsy, faith serves as a guiding light, empowering us to transcend the limitations imposed by our condition and embrace the boundless possibilities that lie ahead.

My journey with cerebral palsy has been intimately intertwined with moments of profound faith, where I've dared to defy the odds and pursue my dreams with unwavering conviction. Despite the old paradigms sometimes re-emerging, I've rejected them, refocused, and I've learned to trust in the inherent resilience of my intuition, my belief, the Holy Spirit, and most importantly, God or the universe (whatever or whoever we choose to put our faith in) believing wholeheartedly in my ability to overcome whatever possibilities and challenges may come my way.

It is through this definiteness of purpose – to teach and help other disabled people realise their true worth and what they have to offer society - that I have now set up a community interest company or charity called AIMS (Accessibility, Inclusion, Mindset and Service) for Life – coaching for disabled people, to sponsor, without charge, disabled people to be mentored and coached, so they can find out their life's purpose, realise their goals and manifest dreams that they genuinely desire. Disabled people have so much to offer, and more often than not, many disabled people have positive affirmations of themselves, however, we have different experiences of life in comparison to non-disabled people as our lived experiences are not considered 'normal', because our bodies, sometimes our minds, and often the societies in which we live, often restrict us because of our disabilities, (known as the social model of disability). The social model of disability, our identities as disabled people, and our concepts of our 'self-image' disabled us, which create entirely different paradigms from our informative years, creating not only physical challenges to overcome but paradigms to rewrite and inner work to do. It is from this mindset that I have founded AIMS.

I started AIMS as a step of faith to help other disabled people navigate the complexities of life. This is where the interplay of stealth and faith becomes paramount. It's about supporting other disabled people to find the delicate balance between resilience and vulnerability, helping them to courageously forge ahead while embracing the inherent uncertainty of the journey. I believe this dynamic interplay is both a challenge and a source of profound growth, shaping identity, self-image and life perspective in profound ways.

One of the most heartfelt lessons I've learned along this journey is the power of authenticity. While stealth may offer a reprieve from judgment and scrutiny, true liberation lies in embracing one's authentic self, flaws (disability or superpower?) and all. It's a lesson I've had to learn time and again, shedding the ghosts of fear (or paradigms), I so meticulously allowed to take over, and instead, now, making myself vulnerable to be seen, indeed seen, for who I am.

In the tapestry of life, the silk threads of stealth and faith intertwine, weaving a narrative of resilience, courage and unwavering determination. For individuals like me, living with seen or unseen disabilities, these qualities serve as guiding beacons, illuminating the path forward amidst the darkness. Through the art of stealth and the power of faith, we discover the strength to transcend our limitations, embracing our true selves with unwavering conviction. As I continue this journey, I carry with me the lessons learned, forging ahead with courage and faith, knowing that the possibilities and challenges I face only make me stronger, so long as I make decisions about those possibilities and challenges by acting on them.

With my definiteness of purpose, I move forward as a role model. I am a product of Napoleon Hill's principles to help disabled people find their strength and faith, to support them in finding, and becoming, the best version of themselves, or their *other self* – the other self God always intended them to be.

ABOUT PHILLIPA

Phillipa Vincent-Connolly is a historian, writer, and published author specialising in historical fiction and nonfiction. Known for her expertise in disability history, she is a sought-after consultant and broadcaster, particularly after the publication of her ground-breaking book *Disability and the Tudors* (Pen and Sword). This work, the first in a planned series examining disabilities in different historical eras, draws from Phillipa's experience living with cerebral palsy, offering a unique and empathetic perspective.

Phillipa holds a degree in History and Humanities (2011), a PGCE with QTS (2014), and an MA Graduate Diploma in History (2020). She has spoken at prestigious institutions such as the National Archives and the British Library, earning widespread acclaim for her engaging and authoritative presentations. A Fellow of the Royal Historical Society, Phillipa's teaching background further enhances her ability to connect with diverse audiences as a public speaker.

Her writing has been featured in *History Today*, *Blitzed Magazine*, and various BBC radio programs. She has also appeared in mini-documentaries, sharing her passion for history and disability advocacy. Phillipa's research and writing span various topics, including archives, artefacts, architecture, fashion, and royalty, making her a versatile and dynamic historian.

As an activist, Phillipa is dedicated to amplifying the voices of disabled individuals, both from the past and present. She uses her platform to challenge societal inequalities and promote greater representation of disabled people in historical narratives. Her deep empathy, informed by her experiences, drives her commitment to social justice and equality.

In addition to her nonfiction work, Phillipa is an emerging star in historical fiction, with her *A Timeless Falcon Dual Timeline* series garnering attention for its rich historical detail and compelling storytelling. Based in Poole, Dorset, Phillipa's work extends beyond the United Kingdom, reflecting her extensive global research interests. With her unique combination of historical expertise, personal insight, and literary talent, Phillipa is shaping the future of disability history and historical fiction. She has the research and writing abilities to adapt to any project and is the future of the past.

LAURA MUIRHEAD
FAITH BEYOND THE FLAMES

I lay there in the hotel bed, trying to allow myself to drift off to sleep after the longest day of my life. The shocking events of the day played over and over in my mind. How did the life we dreamed and worked for over the past fifteen months lead me here – this hotel, this bed, this moment?

We had dreamed of having a house on the water for years. Finally, we were ready to look for that house. It was only a couple of years after hurricane Sandy hit the New Jersey shore so housing prices hadn't completely recovered from the storm and were still somewhat reasonable.

When I say we were looking for the right house, I mean we looked. We must have looked at every house that was remotely in line with our parameters. It was important for us to get the right house because we planned to live there for a long time. Luckily, we found a real estate agent we really liked and trusted. That was a must for me when we began our search. And, again, luckily, he went along with us looking and looking. When a new listing would pop up I'd text him, *Have you seen this one yet?* He'd respond with something like, *Just saw it, want to have a look?* He was patient too. Houses that had crawl spaces meant he and my husband would go in for a look.

I really liked one of the first houses we saw. We even made an offer on it, but we discovered it needed extensive repairs to the bulkhead, so we pulled out. There were a couple we really liked but weren't quite right. It was a bit of a process, taking more time and effort than my past house buying experiences.

We finally were set on a house and made an offer. There were the typical negotiations and attorney reviews before we were officially moving forward, or so we thought. Remember I said that housing prices hadn't bounced back from the hurricane yet? Well, the appraisal came in low.

Quite a bit low. Good for us as buyers, right? It would seem that way but the seller was a bit in shock I think. It took a full three weeks for him to respond to the low appraisal.

Ultimately, we agreed to a purchase price that was a bit higher than the appraisal, but not what the original agreed price had been. At that point the seller was in a rush to get everything closed within a week or two.

We quickly took action, packing everything up and storing it in a moving container we had delivered to our driveway. We were ready and anxious to get into our new house.

I still don't know what happened but, two months later, after the seller was in a big rush, the deal had not closed. There we were with all our belongings packed up, sitting in our driveway, us in an empty house, and Thanksgiving closing in quickly. Normally we would be baking pies and cooking a big meal. It was easier to buy the new essentials we needed to celebrate the day than it was to go digging to find them in the container. So, we did … and had a simple dinner that year.

Things were dragging on the seller's end. We were frustrated and anxious. Now Christmas was approaching and here we were with our house still packed up in the driveway.

Some might have said these were signs to walk away and look for a different house. For some reason, we didn't feel this way and pressed on. We had been ready to sign on the line for over three months!

During that time, we had ordered some new furniture. There were many calls made to reschedule the deliveries. The same thing went for the container taking up our driveway.

Finally, we had a closing date about a week before Christmas and were able to get into our new house. It was such a relief to have the keys and start getting settled into our dream home.

With any move, it takes a while to get used to new routines. We had two dogs and two cats, and of course, it was an adjustment for them as well.

What didn't take any adjustment at all was the view. Our backyard faced south over the Barnegat Bay. On clear days, we could see all the way to the lighthouse a few miles away. Every day there was a different breathtaking view. A portrait of colours to appreciate. At night, we could see the moon and the stars through the oversized windows in our bedroom.

One thing we hadn't initially realised was that at times, with the right amount of rain and tide, part of our street would flood. We probably should have known, since we lived on Island Drive, that under certain circumstances, it became an island. It soon became apparent that I needed to trade my low-sitting convertible for a higher profile car. It was early October before we actually got around to trading in my car for a new SUV.

About that same time, we fell in love with a puppy. She was a rescue and although we knew it would be another adjustment for our menagerie, after careful consideration, we adopted her.

It had been a fun summer filled with early morning jet ski or boat rides for my husband and me. There was quite a bit of boat traffic in our area of the bay, so we liked to take advantage of the still mornings or more quiet evenings. My son was in college, so the weekends frequently included a house filled with his friends and water activities. We fully enjoyed those summer days.

But now it was fall and chillier weather was settling in.

30 October was a sunny warm day for autumn. We spent the afternoon outside casually visiting with family. In the evening, we turned

to watching a Cubs' playoff game – a miracle in itself for this lifelong fan. As the game moved into the later innings, we moved upstairs to watch from bed and drift off to sleep. Our furry friends were tucked into their normal spots, our new pup safely in her crate by our downstairs back door.

Thank goodness my husband jolted awake about 3:30am. He noticed a light flickering outside our bedroom window. In his sleepy haze, it wasn't registering what that light could be. The blur turned to panic when he realised the back of the house was on fire. He gave me a quick push and yelled to get up and out of the house. Somehow, I heard his words even though I don't remember them now.

I was up and out of bed and grabbing my phone in one quick motion. Noticing the flames dancing just on the other side of our bedroom windows, I dialed emergency as I ran down the stairs. Standing in the kitchen, it didn't make sense how the fire had started. And it didn't matter in those moments, as Dan pulled the puppy's crate open and she ran into my arms.

Just then, the 'hurricane resistant' windows started to burst. Smoke and flames were now flooding the house. It was only then that the smoke alarms went off. Up until that point the fire had remained outside, having started at the back of the house on our screened-in porch. The overstuffed cushions on the furniture out there being the perfect recipe to fuel the fire. We found out later that the fire likely started as an electrical issue in the lights, right above the furniture.

I found a leash by our front door and grabbed a sweatshirt jacket for another makeshift leash for our other dog. As I was getting the three of us out of the house, hearing the smoke alarms triggered our oldest dog to run back upstairs, quickly followed by my husband calling to her, pleading to come to him. Once upstairs, he took a breath to call a second time, only then realising there was no more oxygen in the air. Fortunately, she came to him and they joined me outside. In only our night clothes and no shoes, we temporarily huddled in our car in the driveway for warmth.

The next hours were a flurry of police cars, fire trucks and water. For a short time, I watched our house burn from our neighbour's house across the street. My heart and hope for saving it sank when I saw the flames bursting through the front windows. What we didn't know until later, was that had we stayed in bed, even for a few more minutes, we wouldn't have gotten out of the house at all.

My brother-in-law lived a few minutes away, so I spent the morning there. Dan was back and forth to our house until the fire was completely out.

Dan is an action-taker. He had put in motion steps to secure a long-term hotel room for us. I call it our 'three room mansion'. It was two bedrooms with another room serving as a living room and kitchenette all in one.

Before checking in that evening, we made a stop at the mall. We had been loaned mismatched clothes from our neighbour for me and jeans and a shirt for Dan from his brother. He was lucky to have discovered a pair of his shoes in the trunk of our car. Our neighbour also found a pair of flip flops for me to wear.

That is what we had on when we walked into the mall. We knew we had to get at least a few clothes and essentials before checking into the hotel that evening. Any care of how we appeared to anyone else was out of the question. I imagine there must have been a faint smell of smoke wafting around us. Somehow my driver's license was somewhat intact, the edges melted, but usable. That's what the store clerk used to look up my store account so we could buy new shoes, a couple of shirts and some jeans.

We also made a stop to get a brush and a hair dryer, not realising until the next morning that I had forgotten to buy a comb. Since I work from home as the CFO of our family business, it was a priority to get a new computer.

Earlier in the day, Dan had replaced his cell phone, since he didn't have time to grab his.

At one point walking through the mall I had a moment where I realised that the treasured Finnish Iittala glass collection, part of which was given to me by Mom, was gone. It was then I started to cry, but just as quickly the moment passed, knowing it was gone, along with so many other treasures, and crying would not bring any of it back. The only way was forward.

Sometime in the morning, my son and his fiancé came by offering their help. Phone calls were made, including one to my best friend in California. She immediately offered help and asked if she should fly out. In my daze, I told her I didn't see what she could possibly do to help.

As we laid down to try to sleep that night, my phone buzzed. It was my best friend saying she was on a red eye flight and would be there in the morning. Thank goodness. I can say that now looking back. There were so many calls to make; credit cards to replace, utilities to cancel, our car had to be towed because the keys were lost – new keys had to be made. Even months later, my friend's notes were there to refer to when needed.

When I look back, I'm so grateful for her showing up despite my initial refusal of help. In times like that, having your best friend to support you, to talk with and, yes, even to laugh with, is huge. It's one more experience we have shared together.

And my new car? My car was in the garage. They tried searching the remains of the house but didn't find the keys. But then an idea came to my son to try to start the car. Miraculously it started! That meant the keys were in it. A quick search discovered they had somehow fallen in the back seat. A few days before the fire we had taken our dogs to the park in that car and must have dropped the keys when we returned. We were grateful to have immediate use of that car.

The day after the fire, Dan discovered one of our cats cowering in the wet soot of the house. She was scared, wet and smelled like smoke. She's not a cat that likes to be held, but Dan kept her on his lap for the short ride to the vet's office. It was once they were in the examining room that she tried to bite Dan … and we knew she would be okay. The vet completely checked her out, and she was indeed, 'okay' and is still with us today.

In the days following, we were able to gain back some of our brain space as we tried to move forward one step at a time. Our main focus was to find a place to live. We were grateful for our three-room mansion but with three dogs and a cat, you can imagine it wasn't an ideal situation. Again, we were grateful to accept help. My son and his fiancé often came to take care of our pups. Just walking the dogs was time-consuming and we didn't like leaving them alone at the hotel, knowing they would probably bark at every car door closing or someone talking in the parking lot.

Of course, the insurance company was helping with the search, but it was obviously more of a priority for us. We called our real estate agent (yes, the one that climbed into crawl spaces with my husband) and we searched online for rental houses as well. Because of being our own best advocates, a month later, we were moving into our temporary house.

In that month, we had started to replace some of our belongings. That continued in our rental house as we also had a new search; a search for a new permanent house. We had decided not to rebuild on the bay – for a few reasons.

After one house didn't work out, we did find one that was a good fit for us and moved into it in July of that year. In the meantime, we had also started spending time in a town that I loved from my childhood in Michigan.

The months in the temporary house allowed us to realise that we not only wanted a new home in New Jersey, but also a second home in

Michigan. A month after closing on our New Jersey house, we closed on our new Michigan house.

Months after the fire, we spent days meeting with insurance adjusters trying to recall and list each and every thing we had owned. It was agonising. Because we lived on the water, and I was adamant about avoiding losing our belongings to a flood, we stored many of our cherished possessions in our attic. Well, we didn't anticipate a fire that would wipe out the upper areas of our home, including the attic and its contents. What we learned from that is to take a video of each room of your house with cabinet doors and drawers open. That will save you from trying to scroll back on your phone looking for pictures that might show some of what you had.

A house fire isn't something I would ever want to experience but I am grateful for what has come from that. I believe that every life challenge comes with the opportunity to learn and grow. That's why I say *a funny thing happened on the way to my life* is the overarching theme for me. We have had opportunities to expand our lives into Michigan, opening an art studio there, as well as having an investment property. My core principles of *The Queen Code* also served me well in the days, months and years since the fire. We have learned to be grateful for and focus on what remained after the fire took almost everything we had.

When our house burned, we quietly, cautiously rebuilt our lives with what we had left – the faith that we would be okay, and that our lives would continue. They have and we are thriving.

ABOUT LAURA

Laura Muirhead is an international bestselling author, accomplished artist and the CFO of her family's multimillion-dollar company. She is also the creator of the Queen Code program and the Queen Code Oracle Card Deck, which guide multi-passionate women to find clarity, set boundaries and elevate both life and business, stepping into their full potential. Laura's work bridges creativity and business, demonstrating that success can be achieved on both sides of the spectrum.

Her personal journey is as dynamic as her professional life – she is a licensed pilot, an energy healer and the author of *A Funny Thing Happened on the Way to My Life,* as well as a beloved children's book and three journals. Laura's life story is one of resilience and reinvention. From navigating the unexpected twists of life to rebuilding after a devastating house fire, she draws inspiration from her experiences to empower others.

Laura enjoys photography and exploring the world. She splits her time between homes in New Jersey and Michigan. Laura cherishes time with her husband, grown children, close friends, two Labrador retrievers and a life filled with creativity and adventure. Learn more about Laura by visiting lauramuirhead.com

JOANNA HUNTER
ALBERT EINSTEIN ONCE SAID, 'THE ONLY REAL VALUABLE THING IS INTUITION'

From a super young age, I have been aware that we live in a world of two realms; the seen realm and the unseen realm. Our physical reality is boldly declared as the only tangible truth. Solid matter, facts, statistics – they reign supreme. Then there's the unseen realm; a mysterious universe of soul whispers, intuition and dreams. Often dismissed as 'woo-woo' and fantastical, it's a realm where ideas float like ethereal whispers and reality is shaped by the formless dance of the mind.

To the mainstream, the seen realm basFks in legitimacy, while the unseen realm languishes in the shadows of scepticism. Yet, this dismissal does a disservice, not only to individuals, but to the very planet we call home. I've come to believe that in our modern world dominated by algorithms and unfeeling reason, the intuitive mind of the unseen realm, guided by ancient universal laws, is a beacon of wisdom and a wellspring of untapped potential.

Intuition, in my humble opinion, is *the* tool of the next gen of CEOs who wish to stand head and shoulders above everyone else in the marketplace, rising above the cacophony of the online noise and saturated markets. It's also one of the best tools for navigating life with higher consciousness and with deeper emotional intelligence.

To many, intuition is deemed irrational, almost crazy, relegated to the fringes of acceptability. Even contemplating intuition as a business tool can invite judgements, as if one has succumbed to some form of mental affliction. My soul's mission is to dispel this notion, to usher in an era where intuition is not only accepted but celebrated.

For me, intuition is a legitimate way to connect with results that seem like magic and can unlock a world of infinite possibilities that defy logic or explanation.

Allow me to share my journey as a 'walker between realms'.

I was born with a deep awareness of the unseen realm, living in a world that mostly only acknowledges and appreciates the seen, physical world realm. This gift was character-building as a child. I was called a 'daydreamer', told I had my head in the clouds, that I needed to get into the real world. Indeed, my unseen world experiences were not deemed legitimate nor real.

I began questioning my sanity before I was even nine years old. The 'wispy people' were another set of 'people' I could see as clearly as if you were sitting across from me right now. I was often told these people were a figment of my imagination. However, the evidence didn't stack up that this was all in my head. Just like most of humanity, the wispy people went about their business not bothering anyone, though some would, on occasion, nod or smile in my direction. Some would even speak to me, asking me to deliver messages to their solid loved ones.

All normal until I discovered that most of humanity could not see these wispy people and the solids would often gasp upon discovering the wispy person I was speaking to was, in fact, dead. This was all in my imagination according to some people, but details, messages and accurate descriptions of folk I had apparently never met, were given to me by people who appeared to me as real as you are!

Most people were unable to open their minds to the place where a logical higher consciousness explanation could be found, so I was dismissed as having an overactive imagination and called 'strange' or 'weird'. At best, I was met with curiosity. At worst, I was met with fear. Often, my experiences were invalidated and dismissed, just so the adults around me could explain away the unseen realm and squish me into a neat little box in their seen realm.

Calling me a 'weird little girl' was better suited to their narrative of the world than expanding their consciousness to a new one. Despite what others said to me as a child, these experiences were very real.

My parents, however, thankfully blessed me with open minds. They neither discouraged nor fully encouraged my unique experiences, leaving me in a neutral space – at least within the confines of home. However, other adults were not so tolerant, thus by the time I was nine, I was so gaslit that I'd started to question my sanity. As an antidote to this questioning, I began to develop a love of science to prove I was very much sane, and that my experiences with the unseen world were indeed real and could be scientifically proven.

Now in my adulthood, I can confidently say that my young love of science blossomed into a lifelong love affair with metaphysics.

Like most young lovers, these paths are not always straightforward, but filled with twists and turns. As I grew older, I found society's expectations, coupled with the relentless march of the seen realm as the sole reality, pushed me further away from the unseen world.

I worked diligently to suppress my spiritual gifts that manifested at inconvenient moments, akin to an embarrassing inappropriate relative. In young adulthood, I pretended not to recognise these gifts to avoid the discomfort they brought. I did everything I could to pretend to be '*normal*'.

This facade, this mask of normalcy was something I became proficient in and only those closest to me glimpsed the real me. Even then, I occasionally faced the accusation of being 'freaky'. Like many spiritually gifted individuals, I learned to hide my true self to fit within the boundaries of societal expectations.

Then disaster struck. After years of building and operating multiple six-figure businesses, while hiding behind my mask that had now become one of over-achieving, I collapsed at home with multiple organ failure. This was not some stealthy thief in the night; my body had been signalling distress for years. However, those signals resided in the unseen realm; the realm I had been routinely ignoring in order to fit in.

Hospitalised with a diagnosis of multiple organ failure, I was told I wouldn't leave the hospital alive. Death loomed; the imminent consequence of years spent out of sync with my true nature. In that hospital bed, with only the comfort of the angels I saw so clearly waiting for me, to guide me home to the unseen realms, I vowed that this was not how Joanna Hunter's story would end!

In that darkest hour, as life slowly ebbed away, the light of the unseen realm began to seep back into me. The medical verdict of multiple organ failure was a prognosis that left no room for hope. Yet, in that dire moment, I turned inward to the unseen realm – the realm I had abandoned but had always been there for me.

My decision to sign myself out of the hospital defied the doctors' pleas to stay where I was. The nurses told me it was a bad idea to leave the hospital and sincerely asked me to think of my family and of the distress I would cause them when my body finally succumbed to my prognosis. However, the unseen realm whispered that recovery was possible, and against all odds, I chose to believe. I bet on myself, for the first time in what felt like forever!

Recovery was not swift; it spanned years. Yet, every step was guided by the unseen realm as I stumbled into a new life. This journey wasn't just physical recovery, it was spiritual rehabilitation, a reawakening.

Overnight, everything had changed, yet nothing at all had changed. The bills still required paying, my children still required care and feeding, the sun and moon were still caught in their endless cycles of rising and setting, chasing each other across the sky above, but for me personally, nothing was ever the same again.

My businesses were sold, and the once-abundant flow of money dwindled. The constants in my life vanished and, what I once took for granted, my health and mental wellbeing, was no longer assured.

Days blurred as I navigated a new reality. Confidence hit rock bottom, only to rise from the ashes and be rebuilt. My finances were in disarray, yet this chaos paved the way for the creation of new income streams aligned with the new/old emerging 'me'. Every inward gaze found the unseen realm offering guidance, like a Wi-Fi connection to the metaphysical world. Faith, trust and discernment became my allies in this unseen journey.

In my childhood, the unseen realm was a source of comfort and grace, manifesting as a deep connection with the spirit. Now, as an adult, it became my salvation. Trust and faith, initially perceived as tests, were in reality strengthening my resolve and my connection to this place I had once turned my back on.

Money, a sacred teacher of the unseen realm, became a significant hurdle. Embracing my lack of money, seeing the fear as a spiritual teacher, rather than succumbing to it, allowed me to navigate the seen realm more adeptly.

Understanding that I am the conduit through which my reality flows, I realised that healing my conduit from limiting beliefs was crucial. The unseen realm's tools of intuition and knowing, coupled with the healing of my inner world, became the key to unlocking results that seemed like magic in the physical realm.

Trust, faith and intuition turned inward, becoming tools for navigating the unseen realm and tapping into the universe's limitless potential. This internal relationship, dubbed YOUnity consciousness in my world, forms the foundation for navigating both realms.

Acting with inspired action, avoiding the push. Hustle had now become 'persona non grata' and was for people who don't know how to flow. I committed to the internal flow of the universe within me. Listening to internal nudges that might seem illogical in the seen realm became a guiding principle.

I have healed my health to the point where I no longer have the incurable, lifelong chronic illnesses doctors told me I would have to live with forever.

I healed relationships that were once a cause of major stress and drama to me.

Then I healed my finances and became a self-made millionaire, all with the guidance of unseen helpers. What's more, I help others do the same every single day!

I went on to become the founder of the world's largest metaphysical experiment, called *My Million Dollar Experiment*. An experiment asking the question; 'can mindset and intuition training, along with a million-dollar plan make you a millionaire in just one year?'

In 2021 I proved that it could, with one in every 268 participants becoming a millionaire in just one year! Guiding others to create results that seem like magic, results that defied logic, had become my jam.

I have an invite for your consideration: I want you to contemplate the idea that every human creation originated as an idea – formless, lacking in matter, yet very real to the person envisioning it. Ideas become things. The birthplace of all things is, unequivocally, the unseen realm. This profound truth hints at the vastness of the unseen realm and its limitless potential for expansion, within our seen realm.

Consider that every object in your home, every creation, started as a thought, an idea. Society often dismisses the unseen realm as nothing more than products of imagination. This dismissal is a poignant oversight.

In entrepreneurial circles, there's often an obsession with 'how' something is achieved; a mindset anchored more in the seen realm than the unseen.

The frustration many encounter in their quest for the elusive 'how', even if found with step-by-step instructions, stems from ignoring the unseen realm. It took a lifetime of learning and unlearning for me to navigate the unseen realm as my primary tool for crafting a life by design.

True industry leaders, like Steve Jobs and Elon Musk, have understood the importance of navigating both realms. Jobs drew inspiration from meditation, a tool of the unseen realm, while Musk talks about accessing a stream of consciousness from which all his ideas and inventions come.

Allow me to guide you through the process I employed to manifest bold goals – like making a million dollars in one year – from the unseen realm where it was just an idea to its manifestation in the seen world. These steps form a road map, a blueprint for transforming dreams into solid realities.

Set the Intention: Pure intentions act as footprints in the sands of the future, guiding your energy in the unseen realm.

Make a True Decision: The word 'decision' shares more affinity with words like herbicide and homicide than any other in the English language. A true decision involves cutting off/killing off any alternative avenues, embracing a singular focus, and even eliminating failure as an option.

Declaration of Your Decision and Intention: In the formless world of the unseen, nothing has matter – yet. It falls on us to anchor both intention and decision into the solid world of the seen realm. This step transforms formless ideas into tangible reality, with a simple declaration. Tell others, anchor in the choice.

Own It: This step is about ownership. If you can't own it in the unseen, the chances of owning it in the seen realm are greatly diminished. In my million-dollar experiment, many struggled to own their desire to be a millionaire, succumbing to fears of judgement in declaring it. Fear, the mind's killer, introduces doubt, diluting the focus and creating mixed-bag results.

Embrace Fear as Your Sacred Teacher: Fear, while capable of paralysing the mind, can also be a teacher – an opportunity for expansion in the physical world. Listening to and understanding our fears reveals what needs healing in our inner world. By healing these aspects, the light of creation flows through us, paving the way for creation.

Understand You Are the Conduit: For lasting results in the physical realm, healing your conduit from limiting beliefs that distort your reality is crucial. The more healed your conduit is, the more readily available results that seem like magic will become to you.

Turn Inward to Trust, Faith and Intuition: These are the tools for navigating the unseen realm. They all originate from the self-relationship you cultivate in your inner world, what we call YOUnity consciousness. If you can't trust yourself, how can you trust the internal guidance leading you to extraordinary results?

Act with Inspired Action: Avoid the push, 'making it happen', and other forms of hustle. Instead, listen to internal nudges that may not make sense in the seen realm but will guide you to effortless results. Lean in and act when you feel excited and inspired.

Receive As most would think, the challenge of receiving something desired doesn't usually lie in the unseen realm. More often than not, the final step of receiving becomes the hardest. Not because the unseen realm fails to deliver, but because we aren't always open to receiving.

This is because the journey of receiving from the unseen realm is not just a series of steps; it's a profound exploration of self, of limitless potential waiting to be harnessed. It offers a different perspective on creating the reality we desire – a reality crafted not just in the seen realm but intricately woven with the threads of the unseen, with ourselves as the conduit!

ABOUT JOANNA

Joanna Hunter, an international metaphysical teacher, author, speaker and channel for the transcendent collective consciousness known as Skylar, is on a soulful mission. She's here to weave the teachings of Skylar into the fabric of Earth, reviving magic, abundance and a profound connection to source. Joanna brings a refreshing, no-nonsense approach, often hailed as the most down-to-earth 'woo' coach you'll ever encounter.

Website: joannahunter.com
Find her on all socials: @joannahuntercom

ELLE LIKOPOULOS
GET YOUR F****** ASS UP & WORK

'Never lose sight of the fierce lioness within you. For it is she who will guide you to victory, against all odds.'

In the realm of self-help and personal empowerment, a guiding principle emerges; the fusion of stealth and faith. 'I have the best advice for women in business,' Kardashian told *Variety*. 'Get your f------ ass up and work.' A quote that went viral for all the wrong reasons and was met with a lot of criticism, but within it lies a deeper truth.

In the pursuit of success, women often find themselves entangled by the craving for approval and acceptance. However, those who are able to reach the peak of achievement possess a unique quality – they move with stealth, undeterred by external validation, channelling their energy into relentless pursuit rather than idle chatter and overplanning. They embody the essence of a lioness, a symbol of unwavering self-faith, requiring no external affirmation to forge ahead towards their aspirations.

Reflecting on my own journey, I recall a steadfast sense of identity and purpose that guided me from my earliest memories. While the specifics remained undefined, I had a deep understanding of the principles that defined me within my spiritual core and sense of self, that would lead me to my path of success, which ultimately is fulfilment; this is what we truly strive for. The oversight in our society often lies in neglecting to nurture this inner compass within our children, focusing instead on societal constructs of success. But life's tapestry is woven with unpredictable threads, and without a firm foundation in our intrinsic values, we easily veer off course when faced with adversity.

Inevitably, there come moments when you will feel lost, seeking solace and direction from external sources. Yet, amidst the uncertainty, there must exist an unwavering faith in oneself – a beacon guiding us through the darkest of moments in our lives. I have always navigated the terrain of my life without soliciting directions, my faith serving as both compass and map. Through trials and tribulations, I persisted, trusting in the trajectory laid out by my unwavering belief in self.

Thus, the path to fulfilment and success is not defined with accolades or societal validation but with the quiet resolve to heed the call of one's inner voice. With stealth and faith as our allies, we navigate life in our pursuit of happiness.

One of my earliest recollections of discovering my core spiritual principles was when I was around the age of five or six. It was a cherished ritual with my mother, delving into the nostalgic world of *Nick At Nite*, an American night time programming block featuring classic sitcoms from the sixties and seventies. These moments before bedtime held a magical allure for me. I was captivated by the retro fashion, enchanted by the melodies and enthralled by the sensation of time travel into a bygone era. It was our sacred time, free of distractions, just my mother and me, nestled together on the couch.

One night, as the opening credits of *The Mary Tyler Moore Show* graced the screen, it felt as though the universe had aligned to deliver a message directly to my soul. The narrative unfolded, depicting a young woman named Mary navigating the bustling streets of a metropolis, seemingly alone in the crowd. Yet, amidst the bustling cityscape, the spotlight remained squarely on her, underscoring her individuality and resilience. The melodic strains of *'Love Is All Around'* by Sunny Curtis reverberated through the room, echoing a poignant sentiment.

In that electrifying moment, as Mary tossed her hat skyward, a surge of exhilaration coursed through me. It was as if her bold act of defiance against the backdrop of the urban jungle mirrored a yearning deep within my own soul. In that instant, it dawned on me like a beacon illuminating the path ahead, that I yearned for nothing more than *freedom and independence* above all else.

From that pivotal moment onward, my aspirations crystallised into a vivid kaleidoscope of visions; a kaleidoscope of financial independence and worldly exploration. I yearned to travel the globe, to immerse myself in the vibrant tapestry of cultures and experiences that awaited beyond the horizon. I dreamed of a life in Paris, with its allure of new sounds, fragrances and fashion, beckoning to me as a beacon of possibility. While the specifics of my career path remained trivial, the overarching vision of a big and bright future self-propelled me forward with unwavering determination.

However, fate had other plans in store for me, unveiling its first major curveball during my final year of university at the tender age of twenty-one. What began as a suspected ruptured appendix swiftly spiralled into a life-altering revelation – cancerous tumours lurked within my ovaries, casting a shadow of uncertainty over my future. As I emerged from the haze of surgery, grappling with the stark prognosis of a potentially limited lifespan, my inner lioness roared into life.

Enduring a night of harrowing tests and scans, I found myself thrust into the realm of oncology, confronting the prospect of major abdominal surgery that would determine the trajectory of my fate. In the cold sterility of the operating theatre, the surgeon outlined the gravity of the situation.

I was to undergo major abdominal surgery, cut open like a gutted fish, from the top of my stomach down to the bottom, to see what fate lurked for me beneath the layers of my skin. I remember the surgeon explaining to me that, depending on what he found, he may have to remove more than he wanted, leaving me unable to have my own children. I responded that it was okay because children were not in my vision and he smirked and said, 'They weren't in mine either at your age, but I am going to do what I can to give you that choice.' They put the oxygen mask over my face and the song rolled into my mind, as my eyes rolled to the back of my head.

I clung to the flicker of hope ignited by his promise to preserve my choices, even amidst the looming spectre of infertility.

Upon awakening, I embarked on a month-long journey to reclaim my strength. My surgeon, in a bid to grant me the choice he had promised, removed one and a half of my ovaries while preserving the rest. Determined not to let my academic pursuits falter, I devoted my time in hospital to studying, steadfast in my resolve to sit for my exams and graduate without delay. Despite the uncertainty shrouding my future, I clung to the faith that I would persevere along the path toward my envisioned future.

Throughout this tumultuous period, my high school sweetheart and boyfriend, now my husband, remained a steadfast presence by my side. I vividly recall a poignant moment when, as I sat propped up in my hospital bed immersed in my studies, he tended to the mundane tasks of daily life, washing his clothes in the bathroom sink and hanging them over the shower rail to dry, refusing to leave me alone, even for a moment. It was during this intimate moment that our love was put to the test by the probing question of the oncologist: 'Do you think you are each other's *one?*' Without hesitation, we both responded with resolute affirmation, cementing our commitment to each other amidst the trials that lay ahead of us.

With the cloud of infertility looming over us, the oncologist presented us with a stark reality; the best course of action would be to undergo IVF and freeze embryos, given the precarious nature of the remaining partial ovary. Thus, within a whirlwind six-week period following my release from the hospital, we found ourselves exchanging vows, propelled by the urgency to fulfil legal requirements for embryo freezing. And within three short months, I found myself pregnant with our first child. There I was, twenty-one, married and having a baby, with no idea how I would ever fulfil my vision of financial independence, freedom to travel and success.

Within the early years of our marriage, life seemed to unfold according to plan. I graduated with honours, revelling in the joy of academic achievement. Our marriage flourished, and we embarked on the journey of homeownership, building a nest for our growing family. Welcoming our firstborn into the world filled us with indescribable joy, and the prospect of another addition only added to our happiness. Despite the demands of parenthood, I remained focused in my belief that my career aspirations were within reach.

However, life had a way of testing my resolve. The shadow of cancer returned, casting a heavy dark cloud over my dreams yet again. Enduring further surgeries and health challenges, I confronted each obstacle with unwavering determination. The pregnancy of our second son brought its own set of uncertainties, with the looming possibility of significant abnormalities. Yet, I clung to the belief that this child was meant to thrive, steadfast in my conviction that our journey was guided by a higher purpose. Though a very difficult period in my life, my second son was born healthy, further encouraging me to continue to follow my instinct, with faith, that I was on the right journey.

As the years passed, I found fulfilment in my role as a devoted wife and mother. Due to my health issues and complications with my second pregnancy, I never pursued a career within my studies. Instead, I spent my time working within my family's business, allowing me flexibility to care for my boys, as well as helping to earn money for our household. While I excelled in our family business, the realm of business brokering, dominated by men, presented its own set of challenges. Despite my capabilities, I was relegated to the sidelines, deemed unfit for succession due to societal expectations and the demands of motherhood – I was completely overlooked.

Yet, despite the boundaries around me, I remained undeterred. I continued to pour my heart and soul into our family business, all the while nurturing the flicker of ambition that burned within me. Though I may not have been the chosen successor, I refused to allow my aspirations to be stifled. I was determined to carve out a path of my own, one fuelled by passion and the unwavering belief that my journey held the promise of greatness, regardless of societal constraints and what was expected of me as a mother to young children.

Fast-forward to the present, some fifteen years later, and I find myself immersed in a life beyond my wildest dreams. Still happily married to the man who stood by my side through every trial and triumph, I am now a mother of four children and hold the esteemed title of CEO at one of Australia's most successful business broker agencies, my family's business. Alongside this, I have become a bestselling author and an advocate for gender equality, travelling the world to spread the message of holding faith in one's value.

But let me assure you, this journey was far from easy. It took nearly eight years of relentless perseverance to expand my family, overcoming countless hurdles and facing moments where defeat seemed inevitable. Despite the well-meaning advice of others urging me to 'accept my lot', I held onto my belief that my family was destined to grow. Through the trials of infertility treatments, the loss, the grief and the many failed tests, I simultaneously built my reputation as one of the country's top business brokers.

Yet, even as I achieved success in my professional life, I encountered resistance at every turn. The patriarchal landscape of the industry offered little support, and I found myself met with scepticism and sarcasm when I became pregnant with my twins. But I refused to let motherhood dampen my ambition or diminish my capabilities. With unwavering determination, I continued to climb the ranks, challenging societal norms and striving to prove that women, especially mothers, belong in positions of leadership.

When my youngest son was diagnosed with autism, I faced yet another obstacle. Balancing the demands of his therapy with the demands of my career, at times, seemed insurmountable, but I refused to back down. I doubled down on my advocacy efforts, determined to carve out a path that defied expectations and championed inclusivity.

Today, I stand at the pinnacle of my career, travelling the globe to inspire change and challenge perceptions. Yet, despite my achievements, I still encounter discrimination and exclusion in the corporate world, yet I refuse to be deterred. I continue to fight for recognition and equality, knowing that every step forward paves the way for future generations of women.

I embody the vision of the determined young girl who sat beside her mother, dreaming of a future filled with purpose and possibility. Through the years, I've harnessed the power of stealth and faith, unwavering in my commitment, to chart my own course.

Success, to me, isn't just about achievements or accolades, it's about the fulfilment that comes from staying true to my core values and principles. It's about honouring my instinct and navigating life's challenges with unwavering determination.

My journey has been marked by moments of uncertainty and doubt, but through it all, I've remained steadfast in my belief that my path is guided by a higher purpose. With faith as my compass, I've forged ahead, trusting that each step taken brings me closer to my ultimate destination.

As you embark on your own journey, remember this – success isn't about waiting for the perfect moment or seeking validation from others, it's about trusting in yourself, embracing the power of stealth and faith, and forging ahead with unwavering determination. Believe in your abilities, stay true to your values and never lose sight of the vision that fuels your soul. For it is through quiet perseverance and unshakeable faith that you will achieve greatness beyond your wildest dreams.

So, I challenge you to 'get your f------ ass up and work' – and never lose sight of the fierce lioness within you. For it is she who will guide you to victory, against all odds.

ABOUT ELLE

Elle Likopoulos, renowned as one of the highest achieving business brokers in the Southern Hemisphere and CEO of Absolute Business Brokers. Elle has carved a reputation for representing more females than any other agency within her industry. Her unwavering commitment to fostering inclusivity and support for women has set her apart as a beacon of change. 'In order for change to occur, change must be seen.'

Driven by her vision of creating a nurturing work environment, Elle's leadership has propelled Absolute Business Brokers to unprecedented success nationwide. Despite being a mother of four, including a child with special needs, Elle tirelessly advocates for the balance between career aspirations and motherhood. Her personal journey fuels her passion for championing the cause of women in business, inspiring others to pursue their goals fearlessly.

Beyond her achievements in the business world, Elle is a prolific author and public speaker, using her platform to ignite inspiration and education for future generations of female leaders worldwide. Her bestselling books and captivating speeches resonate with audiences, offering invaluable insights into navigating the challenges of entrepreneurship as a woman.

Through her continued success and exposure from public speaking roles and accolades, Elle remains steadfast in her mission to forge a path where every woman can thrive in business and beyond. She is a true advocate for gender diversity and empowerment, shaping a brighter future for women in the business brokerage sector and beyond.

VIKKI SPELLER
FAITH TO FACT

I'*d like a quick, easy, close park please,* this is my inner dialogue with the universe whenever I need a carpark in a busy area. There are moments when I hear people complaining about how hard it was to get a park, especially in the holiday season; however, hand on heart, when I take a moment to check in and ask, this is something I never need to concern myself with, for once I ask, I have total faith that I am looked after. When opportunities arise, I like to offer a different perspective by asking, 'Have you thought of simply asking for a park?' to which some reply, 'Ask who?' and I answer, 'Who or whatever you have faith in.'

You see, my life has been filled with countless moments where my faith has turned into fact. An easily found carpark is only one small example of how, when holding onto such trust, reality has no choice but to follow.

Faith. A simple five-letter word, yet it's meaning holds immense power, having the ability to shape our reality. At its core, faith is a belief; having confidence in or a deep trust in something unseen or unknown. For me, it's holding the conviction that there is meaning and purpose behind life and that we are part of something greater than ourselves. Holding a belief in something greater than what you can physically see, or having a deep trust in whatever it is you believe to be true for you, can literally be life-changing. And while the concept of faith may seem abstract or intangible, in my view, its impact on our lives is anything but.

Faith has directed my path throughout my journey on Earth in a multitude of ways, whether that be through holding faith in myself, having faith in spirit or having faith that I am supported by the universe. In my experience, this feeling of faith holds such powerful energy, yet it can also be fragile and easily broken, through fear or a lack of trust. I have personally experienced both sides of the spectrum.

There have been times in my life where I have faithfully followed my heart completely, even when outward circumstances would suggest otherwise. These moments have turned out to be some of the best decisions I've made. Yet there have been moments in the past where I allowed doubt and fear to creep in, not holding enough faith in myself or my abilities, therefore, at the time, sabotaging some wonderful opportunities that had come my way.

For those of you who've had times in your life where your faith in yourself may have also been limited, some may look back with remorse. However, I'd like to offer you the perspective of viewing life through the lens of faith. I firmly believe and deeply trust that everything unfolds exactly as it is meant to. Each circumstance that has played out in my life, regardless of the experience, has led me to be in this precise moment for a reason, and I am exactly where I am meant to be. In this instance, I am currently sitting in my writing studio, sharing my innermost thoughts with you.

As the years have unfolded, my faith in the universe continues to strengthen, as well as my faith in spirit and myself. I feel proud to say that, for the most part, as I have journeyed through life, I have held a deep trust in following my heart and allowing my inner wisdom to lead the way. I've held a faith, a silent knowing that I'm always supported and have total trust that all is working out in my favour, even in those moments where, externally in the physical world, it may not look like it is.

As I reflect upon my journey and feel into the energy of faith, I am reminded of a time in my life when I had almost given up, when the young teenage version of myself felt so deeply broken. As a teenage girl who once felt like life wasn't worth living, I remember how tough it was. It felt I was stuck in a dark hole with no way out. It's a hard place to be in when you think your life is falling apart and you don't belong. The depths of heartache are so real, that they cause physical pain in your chest and an all-consuming heaviness that doesn't want to leave you.

But you know what? Throughout this period of my young life, I held onto hope. I held faith that it wouldn't always be like this and that these feelings of turmoil would pass. There seemed to be a quiet voice inside me saying, *Everything is going to be okay.* I felt supported by something bigger than myself, even though at the time, I didn't understand what that was. As each day passed, I felt my faith strengthen, trusting in the universe to support me, knowing that the feeling would lift and everything would work out. And it did.

I now know this time in my life was such an important part of my journey, giving me an understanding of the depths of turmoil that can be felt, and how the act of faith has the ability to lift you up and out of the trenches. It helped me to strengthen my belief in my inner wisdom, my self-worth and my faith in the universe, knowing I was fully supported, even in those moments when life felt like it was falling apart.

It wasn't an easy journey, and I hold immense love and pride for that young, teenage version of myself. She taught me just how strong I am and how holding onto faith can move you forward in life, shift perspectives, and allow for positive opportunities to appear. And now, I'm grateful for every single day I get to spend living my life to the fullest, with the essence of faith filling my heart and propelling me along my path with immense love and trust in my journey on Earth.

We don't always know where life is leading us, but sometimes we simply need faith to take the next step. For me, holding faith became an innate part of who I am, a knowing that, when aligned with the universe, my faith will show itself as fact. That the faith I feel will lead me throughout my life and bring forth the learnings and teachings that the universe is offering me, within the physical plane of my existence. I journey through my days trusting in this unseen world and nurturing my dreams as I harness the power of belief and co-create with the universe. I believe we each have the ability to draw to us what we hold dear. Have you ever felt like there is something bigger than yourself at play in the world? I hold the belief that there undeniably is.

Having faith in the universe and its ability to support me is like having a silent partner who is willing to guide me along my path and offer assistance. I honestly believe the universe conspires in our favour, and our greatest job is to hold trust in the process. Even during those times when we don't have all the answers or know which way to turn, there is true comfort in holding a quiet and consistent faith that *all is well.*

In my journey through life, I've experienced countless moments where my faith has led to fact, where the universe has offered me tangible outcomes and instances where my trust in the universe has manifested in ways that almost seem magical. As each circumstance unfolds throughout life, it has given me the opportunity to build upon my faith in the universe, the spirit world and myself.

Small acts experienced throughout my daily life have strengthened my faith in my belief and given me evidence of knowing I am looked after. Take, for example, the times when I've needed the perfect outfit for an occasion, asking the universe to guide me towards something that is affordable, comfortable and suitable. Then simply letting go of the outcome and trusting. I find the outfit effortlessly, as if it were waiting there, just for me to discover. It's like the universe guiding me and, sure enough, every time I've followed that inner voice, I've been rewarded with a sense of confidence and joy that only comes from knowing you're exactly where you're meant to be.

Then there are those moments when the right person enters your life at exactly the right time, as if they were sent to you by some higher power. I'd asked the universe to guide me along my path of development and trusted I would be shown in time. I remember vividly the night I met my dear friend and mentor, Brenda Arber, author of *Hear My Words,* who has been instrumental in the development of my spiritual growth. I have always held faith that the right person is sent to us to help us with the next step in our journey, and for me, Brenda was one of these people. It was a chance conversation through a friend, or so it seemed, that led me to attend her class back in 2012, but I firmly believe it was anything but random. It was divine intervention, the universe conspiring to bring us together in that exact moment when I needed her most, and once again, my faith led to fact.

Of course, faith isn't just about trusting in the synchronicities of life to unfold but also about believing in yourself and having faith in you and your abilities. Back in 2008, I was required to have trust in my skills and intuition, when I took a leap of faith and started my business, Intuition Plus. In those times, things like mindfulness, coaching and spirituality weren't as easily accepted as they are now, but I trusted that my business would succeed. And you know what? My faith paid off. Over the years, my business has touched the lives of hundreds of people and brought me immense joy and fulfilment every single day.

But perhaps the most profound example of faith leading to fact, as a family, was almost twenty years ago, when my husband and I decided to purchase our home at auction, even though our property hadn't yet sold. It was a giant leap of faith, to say the least, a decision based on deep trust rather than certainty. And yet, through faith that we would be looked after and visualisation as a family, everything fell into place. After signing the contract at the auction, our own property sold, and we were able to move into our new home with ease and grace. Faith in the universe had paid off once again, and it was as if the universe had orchestrated the whole experience from the very beginning.

And then, of course, there are those moments in life when having faith in the universe saves us from unseen dangers, like the time I missed a turn while driving to my appointment, only later to hear that I had avoided a serious multiple-car accident by doing so. In moments like these, I am reminded of the power of faith, trusting that we are always being guided and protected, even when we don't realise it.

But here's the thing about having faith, it's not always easy. Life can test us, especially in those moments of uncertainty. However, I have found over the years that by practising faith on a daily basis, it can be extremely beneficial when life throws you a curveball. Since you are in the habit of holding faith, it makes it easier to fall back on when challenges arise or when going through times of struggle, since faith becomes an innate part of who you are and your belief system.

This building of faith can then be drawn upon through major life experiences, where you may be at a crossroads in life, a relationship breakdown, a health crisis or experiencing grief. Faith is giving you the strength to navigate this time with greater ease. By trusting in the universe, we open ourselves up to infinite possibilities as we let go of the need to control every aspect of our lives and instead surrender to the flow, knowing that we are being guided to exactly where we are meant to be. And in doing so, our faith creates space for miracles to happen.

As a woman navigating her early fifties, I am finding that my faith in myself, spirit, and the universe is growing stronger every day. It hasn't just been the big events throughout my life that shaped this belief, but the little things too – the everyday moments that continually showed me that faith turns into fact and the everyday experiences that reaffirmed my trust in the unseen world.

My faith has also been shown to me over the years through those moments that touched my heart and reminded me of the magic of life. Like the butterfly that landed on my hand and stayed there for twenty minutes as I walked on the sixth anniversary of my mother's passing. Or the simple act of connecting with my best friend over the phone as we listen, support and lift each other up. Or sharing in laughter with our three grown-up children, a testament to the love and connection we hold as a family.

Even small acts of kindness from strangers, a genuine smile or the offer of holding open a door – all of these moments serve as gentle reminders that we are all interconnected and that there is goodness to be found in the world. These everyday moments may seem insignificant on their own, but to me, they give me faith in humanity, in spirit and in the universe. They serve as building blocks, filling my life with meaning and purpose, grounded in the belief that we are all supported as we journey through life.

Looking back on my life, I hold so much gratitude for the power of faith – that quiet knowing that has shaped my journey. Faith is a guiding force, offering a source of strength that can carry you forwards. And as I continue along my path, I do so with a heart full of faith, knowing I'm always guided and supported by the universe, trusting that the best is yet to come.

May the essence of faith envelope you as you walk your path, and may you be reminded of the power you hold within to create your destiny. And if you're feeling lost or uncertain, or wondering whether you'll ever achieve your dreams, I invite you to have faith, to trust, to take inspired action and to be open to receiving support. You are worthy of all the good things that life has to offer. Have faith in yourself and your abilities, and in doing so, watch as your reality begins to shift in ways you never thought possible. For when we have faith, anything is possible.

ABOUT VIKKI

Vikki Speller is a highly respected intuitive women's coach, meditation and mindfulness teacher, international speaker and bestselling author, who embraces her calling to support others. Through her business, Intuition Plus, founded in 2008, and as an internationally certified women's circle and retreat facilitator, she provides nurturing spaces for women to come together.

Through one-on-one coaching, events, writing and speaking, Vikki has empowered, inspired, and provided support to hundreds of women and children, guiding them to overcome challenges, nurture self-love, and cultivate their intuition.

With a compassionate heart and drawing upon her own life experiences, she has a deep understanding of the challenges women face. Approaching her coaching practice with a genuine desire to uplift and support individuals on their unique paths. Drawing on her intuitive abilities, energy healing and holistic counselling background, Vikki empowers people to tap into their inner strength, make aligned decisions and manifest their dreams.

Vikki's insights resonate in books, anthologies, magazines, online platforms, docufilms and podcasts.

As a published children's book author of *Finding the Magic of Love* and *The Magical Friendship Spell,* Vikki weaves tales that inspire self-love, instil a positive mindset and encourage the practice of mindfulness and affirmations. These stories not only entertain but also educates, including bonus mindfulness tools, making them valuable resources for parents, carers and teachers.

Vikki anticipates the release of her upcoming children's card packs; each designed to uplift and guide young souls on their path to self-acceptance and compassion for others. It is Vikki's aim to inspire and educate the importance of the spoken word and the ripple effect it creates within lives.

She is deeply passionate about nurturing children and adults alike in holding a strong sense of self and has an array of creative projects underway including a range of women's oracle cards and affirmation card sets, an inspiring spiritual self-help book series and online courses. Her latest release, *Mandalas of Reflection: Colouring and Journaling,* is an adult colouring book that combines intricate designs with empowering affirmations and guided journaling to support self-reflections and personal growth.

Vikki is a regular columnist for *Holistic Bliss* magazine where she shares empowering messages. As an author, you'll find more of Vikki's writing in powerful anthologies such as: *Ubuntu On Whose Shoulders We Stand* compiled by Dr Tererai Trent, Oprah's all-time favourite guest, forward by Duchess Sarah Ferguson. International bestseller, *Voices of Impact Volume 4,* empowering stories from female visionaries and entrepreneurs. And bestseller *Hear Us Roar Lion Edition,* stories of courage and perseverance. Vikki will be a regular co-author within the pages of each of the *Hear Us Roar* book series and docufilms.

Vikki lives in Queensland, Australia, and treasures spending quality time with her much-loved family and creating memories together. As Vikki's journey continues to unfold, she invites us to embrace our own, knowing that within each of us lies an infinite capacity for growth, wisdom and the power to create a life filled with purpose and joy.

Website: vikkispeller.com

Instagram: instagram.com/vikki_speller_intuition_plus

Facebook: facebook.com/intuitionplus.vikkispeller

LinkedIn: linkedin.com/in/vikki-speller-author-coaching-intuition-plus

TikTok: @vikki_speller

LISA BENSON
CHALLENGING
STEREOTYPES

'How many kids do you have?'

I close my eyes, it feels like I'm in slow motion. I've been asked this question more times than I can put a figure on.

'Um, I actually don't have any,' I reply through clenched teeth.

'Oh.' There is always silence following the drawn out 'oh'.

I often try to guess their thoughts. *Oh, you poor thing. What on earth is wrong with her?* or *How unusual.*

I can't read minds though. I can only go by verbalised responses, and more often than not, people offer an unsolicited solution to my 'problem'. 'It's not too late, there's still time.' Everyone has a story of someone they know who had a baby in their forties, or even fifties. Others say, 'Don't you like kids?' or 'Oh, what a shame.'

'I didn't meet the right man until it was too late, and he has three grown up children of his own.'

I used to find myself filling in the blanks, to justify or ease their discomfort. I would go on, seemingly unable to stop myself: 'The most important thing for me has always been to be happy within myself, and finding a compatible partner is secondary. Only then are children considered based on our unique circumstances. I never thought to seek out a partner for the purpose of being a father to my children. That seems back-to-front to me.'

Did I just press play on a recording?

Why do I feel the need to explain myself? I know I've been trained to ease situations with politeness, ensuring I don't make anyone else feel uncomfortable but could it also be because I'm in a minority?

According to the Australian Bureau of Statistics, the percentage of women who have no children is on the rise. In 1986, 9% of women never had a child compared to around 16% in 2016. Nowadays, it's approaching 20% of the population – still a considerable minority. Why do I feel as though I am *out* of the inner circle when I haven't performed exactly as society expects women to? Why don't mothers have to justify their choice to *have* children on a weekly basis? Without trying, by living my life, I have become a challenge to the stereotype of what a woman of my age should be, simply because I have chosen not to have children.

In one of my favourite books, *The Four Agreements*, Don Miguel Ruiz explains how humans are domesticated similarly to the way pets are. Often without knowing, our parents indoctrinate us with learned behaviour, just as they were conditioned by their own parents. As children, we were rewarded for doing what our caretakers considered 'well-behaved'. We were given attention and accolades for keeping within mediocre guidelines and doing what other people wanted us to do, instead of being allowed to express our originality – the gift intended for us to share.

Once in the school yard, my conformity was tested. One of my primary school friends tried to coerce me by saying, 'If you sit with me at recess and tell Sally she smells, I'll be your best friend.'

Was this part of my training to be a people-pleaser? Was it where I first heard cruelty?

In school it was common for cliques to form and gang up on people who were in any way different. We all know the kids who, for some unknown reason, seem to be in charge of the playground; those who bully and wreak havoc. I can still recall the gaping void in my stomach, my dry throat and the intense pressure in my head from the tug of war between my desperate need to be accepted and my inner compass. I never considered beyond the superficial, how Sally's parents were struggling financially and couldn't afford basic hygiene products or soap. In my group, we simply judged her because she was not like us. I never did tell Sally she smelled. I was too scared, and it didn't feel right. Perhaps it was the first moment where I challenged, by stealth, my own willingness to conform to pressure.

I knew, even then, that excluding someone was an unfair punishment. Something inside me understood that it was heartless to label people as outcasts for not being part of the majority, even though I played along. It seemed as if some kids took pleasure in making others feel left out. Here then, is where I learned I was different. I knew it was wrong, and despite how desperately I wanted to be part of the cool gang, I simply couldn't follow through with the behaviours that would win me that validation. Perhaps this is where my faith in my authentic self began; but I wouldn't learn that til much later in life.

As adults, we hopefully learn through experience and maturity how to behave respectfully, but some of us continue to play childish games into adulthood.

We discriminate based on disability, race, sex, gender choices, religion and cultural rituals, just to name a few. When there are no differences, we manufacture them – you have ginger hair, you wear glasses, you're too tall, short, large, skinny. We all have our time being the new person at school or in the workplace. None of us escapes discrimination and judgement, we are simply scrutinised and assessed at different levels of intensity, for diverse reasons.

We can have empathy for others, but we have the most impact when we speak from our lived experiences.

I've defied the norm by being a forty-nine-year-old woman who has never had my own children. But it isn't the only example. I was married at forty-three and realised my goal to publish a book – my memoir – at forty-eight, which by conventional timelines is considered 'late'. It makes me shudder when I hear young women voice their concerns about being 'left on the shelf' or passing their 'use-by date'. I have faith that women today are more aware that they have more choice than ever before. It is part of what the women's movement has fought for all these decades – to empower us to forge our own paths and not to conform to societal beliefs about the timing of life's big milestones, or even the necessity to tick them off at all.

I am also a 'second wife' to my husband. This has provided enough material for me to write another entire book. In the early years while we were dating, I was judged and scrutinised as the shiny, new, younger wife by some of my husband's inner circle. It was like being an intruder on a reality TV show. Intruders are rarely accepted – everyone just wants them voted off. A second wife, I discovered, has to pass tests the first one typically does not.

All I wanted was for people to see me as a whole person, not to imagine me as a stereotype. I had recently left a toxic relationship, after losing my dad and all four grandparents within three years. I was ready to live a fulfilled life and be free from the suffering of my past. I had fallen in love with a man who allowed me to be myself; I had no doubts I'd found my soulmate. In those early years of our relationship, I was unsettled by outside influences and judgements, which left me feeling like Sally in the playground.

But all of this life experience has, by stealth, given me empathy for anyone struggling in a blended family or starting a relationship later in life. I know how toxic judgements can be, and how 'harmless comments' can bruise us.

'Oh to be retired at forty like Lisa,' was one such remark that often came back to hurt me.

Perhaps that's what people saw. What they didn't know is that I'd left my job, after much agonising, to support my husband with a new career which involved travel between two homes. I struggled to process losing my financial independence I'd worked so hard at since I was fourteen years of age. Comments like this upset me. But looking back, I see the damage was mostly to my ego. I'd been the main source of income in previous relationships, so when anyone insinuated I was mooching off my husband, I felt undermined. But then, my husband encouraged me to pursue my dream to write a book, which softened the pain of our huge life change. He had faith in me, at a time when I lacked faith in myself.

I was far from 'retired'. I worked harder than I ever had to become a writer. I didn't try to explain myself. I knew that eventually, the time I was investing in writing workshops, being mentored and writing hundreds of thousands of words, would pay off and the results would speak louder than any empty justifications.

We all have an innate need to belong to our families and communities. When we're excluded, it brings up feelings of not being good enough or rejection from the past. So ironically, some of our feelings of being judged are sometimes partially self-inflicted – amplified by our exposure to stereotypes and concern with other peoples' opinions. Our insecurities play into the judgements, and we live out the nightmarish consequences of this clash.

After time and healing, I have surrendered to the faith of being unique. When we experience discrimination, we have the chance to become more connected to our own stories and to that of others. It has certainly made me more compassionate to others and I now appreciate each person's differences as something to be cherished, not judged, criticised or rejected.

I have always admired people who exude confidence and don't care what other people think. As teenagers, we are hardwired to try to be like everyone else. It's a developmental milestone to want to look the same, act the same, eat the same and dress the same. At that tender age, now exacerbated by social media, we are brainwashed by the media and emotional marketing to believe we have to replicate ourselves or face being an outcast. Many of us get stuck in this place, wanting to be like everyone else, instead of growing into an understanding that each person's quirky traits are what makes them beautiful and attractive. 'Why would you want to fit in when you were born to stand out?' as Dr Suess so aptly puts it.

I was in the kitchen, cutting the skin off an orange with our granddaughter (from my husband's previous marriage), when I noticed her wide eyes as I sliced the top and bottom off to make a flat surface. Then I guided the knife around the rounded sides of the fruit, allowing the long, curved pieces of peel to drop onto the chopping board, until I'd gone all the way around.

'Mummy doesn't cut them like that,' she said.

'There are lots of different ways to cut an orange,' I smiled.

Maybe I should have said, 'Mummy does it one way, I do it another, but you will find an even better way that is right for you.'

When we teach the next generations how to do things 'our way', we limit their imagination. If we suggest that everything isn't locked in, we can encourage limitless possibilities and kids might adopt a growth mindset.

'You should,' is an outdated model, in my opinion. The fact that young couples feel pressure to marry on a predetermined schedule, surely contributes to the high divorce rates. Of course, if people are wanting kids, biological constraints are a factor, but if being single or choosing to have no children were equally valid options, perhaps more women would end unhealthy relationships without fearing time was running out. As we age, we may panic that we've run out of time to get to know a new partner, so we end up settling in a mediocre pairing.

If I had gone through life looking for answers outside myself, I would never have achieved personal fulfilment. Life began to flow more easily for me when I tuned in to what was right for me, instead of following the rules society imposed on me. Marriage and children might be perfect for you. As might being a single parent. Or adopting a child. Or any other variation that makes sense to you.

Sometimes we struggle to tell the difference between conforming to a stereotype and our inner desires. We've all lived so long immersed in a culture, that we can barely distinguish what we want from what we're *taught* to want. But beneath the static, our true emotions can guide us on the path we were destined for. While writing my memoir, I was plagued with self-doubt and anxiety about what others would think of me. So, I meditated on this question that had me paralysed: *Should I still proceed with publishing my book if my loved ones don't approve of, or support the book I have written?* I played angelic music and burnt some Palo Santo and did some breathing exercises to centre myself. The answer was instant and overwhelming. *Yes. Of course. Yes.*

Tears rolled freely down my cheeks. My conviction to finish what I'd started was stronger than any negativity or backlash I might face. Those were all beyond my control. I was determined to not be limited by outside forces in that intimate, personal moment. When I opened my eyes, I was calm and had complete faith.

I often think I could have chosen a more traditional career; one where I was less vulnerable and exposed to the judgements of others. But I have become clear that staying within my comfort zone is not what I'm here for. Since that day in the playground, I have always known I was being called to expand myself, not appease the masses. How can I inspire others to push through the hard times and be authentic, if I don't show the way by being vulnerable myself?

As a chronic overthinker, I get consumed and paralysed by my thoughts. Whenever I've gone through times of struggle in my life, I've always secretly known things would get better. I had faith in the tiny voice deep inside me that always whispered to me, *You are here for a higher purpose. There is no rush. This is your pathway and you can't bypass the hard parts.* Having faith means not expecting anything at a specific time. It's about trusting in the universe's divine timing.

I still struggle sometimes to not get caught up in others' expectations. The world is full of 'too' assumptions. Too old, too late, too long, too much, too little, too early, too this, too that. The sooner we learn no-one cares about what we are doing, the sooner we are free to live the life we were destined to. Sometimes all we have to do is challenge a stereotype thrust upon us and tune into our inbuilt guidance.

I have done life a little differently. Even though I've people-pleased my way through much of my life and put up with behaviour I shouldn't have, when it came to the 'big' decisions, like getting married and having children, I've found the inner strength to stand up for myself and not succumb to external pressures. It was as if I tapped into a higher power. In these moments, I listened to the messages from the universe. My intuition knew when to say *no.*

Many people – including my late Nanna – warned me about my decision not to have children, that, 'You'll regret it one day.' Of course, I've wondered *what if,* and perhaps I will do so more as I age. Every choice is a fork in the road. It's natural to question how our lives would have turned out if we'd made a different decision. I'm sure those with children often fantasise about life without them sometimes too. I've made peace with my choices, which doesn't mean they come free of regret.

Stereotypes help us fit in to an 'accepted' category. We feel part of the collective when we belong to a mainstream group. But seldom do we find fulfilment by following the crowd. The most common regret people have on their death bed is that they lived a life governed by other people's expectations rather than their own. It doesn't matter what path you follow, as long as it's your own.

In the age we live in, women are challenging stereotypes in all kinds of ways. We are only just starting to be taken more seriously, even though we have been tirelessly working towards equality in the background for decades and beyond. If we each challenge the patterns indoctrinated by the patriarchy in our own lives, we add to and continue the momentum. It seems though, that we often lose faith and give up right before our breakthrough moments. We can learn from the lioness, to move shrewdly through our days with faith that we will achieve our deepest desires if we stay focused and don't give up.

When we lack conviction in our decisions or haven't yet learned true acceptance of self, we search for ways to fit in and fulfilling a stereotype sometimes offers us a way in. No matter how far away I am from widely held beliefs about what is okay or not okay, I feel I belong when I am calm and accepted for being the most authentic version of myself. Only after much self-development, research and experience, am I more comfortable within myself. Feeling the freedom that often arrives in midlife has helped. I am grateful for the positive side-effects of aging.

When I least expected it, life sprung a wonderful surprise on me. I am blessed to have the opportunity to look after our two-year-old grandson once a week. It feels as though my natural motherly instincts now have a place, and at the same time, I am helping my husband's daughter live a fulfilled and balanced life.

I have complete faith that I am on the path meant for me and I am embracing my blessings with open arms.

Now when people ask me how many children I have, I answer more confidently, with just a few words. I don't feel the need for an elaborate explanation. I know who I am.

Sometimes, by stealth, we become a role model without intending it, simply by being someone who hasn't followed a conventional path.

ABOUT LISA

Lisa Benson is a self-diagnosed recovering perfectionist who spent five years writing her multi-award winning memoir, *Where Have I Been All My Life?* During this time, she lived part time on a boat on Sydney Harbour which she found to be a peaceful and inspirational space for her writing. Lisa and her husband continue to lead a 'double life' travelling between Newcastle and Sydney each week.

Lisa has a Bachelor of Business Degree with a major in tourism and marketing. She previously held various sales and marketing positions in hotels and resorts, and also worked in a real estate office. It wasn't until Lisa was in her forties that she decided to pursue her lifelong dream of becoming an author, and she now writes full-time.

Lisa has received multiple awards for *Where Have I Been All My Life?* from Literary Titan, Global Book Award, NYC Big Book Award and The Bookfest (x2). Lisa's memoir has also been translated to Czech and has been praised by women from the Czech Republic and Slovakia.

Lisa's motto is *Stop Trying – Start Being* although she spent most of her life doing the exact opposite. Her writing is honest and relatable, and she hopes her vulnerability helps others feel less alone. Lisa would love to inspire women to stop wasting time living up to other people's expectations, to discover the magic of living an authentic life and to be free of self-imposed limitations.

If you would like to hear more from Lisa, you can follow her on Instagram (lisabensonauthor), Facebook (Lisa Benson Author) or LinkedIn (Lisa Benson). Lisa's website is www.lisabensonauthor.com

LAURA GOLDBERG
FROM LION CUB
TO LIONESS

It has taken me many years and many roads to get to this place in my life where I am totally content in my own skin. A place where I feel comfortable in sharing my life, and my story, in a way that I hope will inspire and lead others to believe in themselves. It took me forty plus years to realise I have a voice … and I want to use it for good. I refuse to be a silent warrior, like so many women before me. I have learnt a million lessons along the way, but I've come to recognise that each lesson is a blessing. Have you ever stopped and reflected on how far you've come? I absolutely recommend you do, because you'll be sure to find someone stronger, more resilient and more powerful than you ever thought possible.

I was born in Johannesburg, South Africa, daughter to a migrant father and first generation South African mother. All my grandparents came from Madeira, a small island in Portugal. They were farmers, mostly, but also driven to provide their family with a better life, so when the opportunity arose to move to a country that would provide them with what they thought was a better life, they took it. My maternal grandparents set up shop as fruit and veg merchants, while my paternal grandfather worked as an electrician for the South African government and my paternal grandmother stayed home to look after her three children. A strong work ethic has always been a dominant characteristic within my family and I'm sure every single one of my aunties, uncles, brothers and cousins has this built into their DNA.

Being white in South Africa afforded us certain privileges, but my parents also worked hard to provide a solid education for my brothers and me, plus all the mod-cons available at the time. We wanted for nothing and I'm grateful for my wonderful, loving childhood. All four of my grandparents were a solid fixture in my life. I have many amazing memories of the times my brothers and I spent with them, along with my myriad of cousins. I realise now how fortunate I was to be loved and cared for by these amazing people. We come from a long line of strong, fearless women, and I hope I can pass that trait down to my own daughter.

My school life was as normal as the next guy and I was a high achiever, especially when it came to sport, where I excelled. Tennis was my passion, and I spent many hours on courts all over Johannesburg honing my skills with various coaches and playing whatever tournaments I could. And I was no different to girls all over the world, where friends, boys, make-up and the like took up most of my spare time. I was a talented tennis player and once I had completed high school, I went to the US on a tennis scholarship, I thought the transition from Johannesburg to Mississippi would be easy, but I was sadly mistaken. The weather was not what I was used to; freezing and snowing! (I had never seen snow before in my life!) The homesickness was intense. In truth, I was ill-prepared for life outside my tight family unit and, in hindsight, should have done more research into moving abroad as a naive eighteen-year-old. I did not last long and returned to South Africa a bit bruised – but not broken. I knew what I wanted, I was just unsure on how to get it.

I enrolled in a local university and around the same time took a more permanent role in the family business. My degree in psychology meant I was exposed to several important causes, such as becoming a volunteer for Lifeline and an amazing organisation called Kids Court Support, which allowed us as psychology students to help kids navigate the court system before they were called in to testify. Tennis continued to be my priority, and training and playing was always at the top of my mind. At twenty, I was afforded another opportunity to study in the US and took it with both hands. I was older and wiser! Life, however, had other plans for me and after just one semester, I returned home as my father had been diagnosed with Ménière's disease. I continued studying via correspondence and took over the family business full-time. Two degrees and a few years of hard graft later, I decided to emigrate to Australia to be with my older brother and start a new chapter. My life in South Africa was becoming unfulfilling and I was sick of working seven days. Crime was at an all-time high and I felt the time was right to move.

Emigrating to a new country is not for the faint-hearted, but I was fortunate enough to be embraced and cared for by my brother and his wife. Despite all my working experience and university degrees, getting a good job in Australia was not as easy as I had predicted. After many interviews where my past experience was brushed aside, I took a job I was overqualified for and was treated in a way that dented my self-worth and confidence. I stayed for two years; two years too long. I was lured to another job with the promise of promotion and what I thought would be better working conditions, only to be thrust into another mindless and unsatisfying job. I am certain, however, that I learnt how I did NOT want to be treated, and vowed to find a job I would be proud of. My partner encouraged me to pursue my passion, and with that, I enrolled in a personal trainer's course. My life as a PT was the most fulfilling thing I had ever done. I was using both my psychology degree and my love of physical exercise, all day every day! Running my own business was exactly what I needed and the new skills I learnt were invaluable in my evolution. Many of my clients held important corporate jobs and I learnt so much from each of them. In fact, I am still friends with some of them today, including one particular lady who has inspired me along my journey of self-fulfilment.

I was a PT for seven unbelievable years, until it was time to move to the next chapter of my life as a mum. My son was born prematurely at nearly thirty-five weeks. He was so tiny and fragile, and I was very afraid, as I had no idea what to expect. I remember feeling empty as my baby was whisked away from me after a forty-eight-hour labour. My little fighter stayed in the special care nursery for a week before coming home. To say the next thirteen months were a blur really is an understatement. I fell pregnant easily for the second time, with my daughter, but having *two under two* was challenging. Although my daughter was a relatively easy baby, I was losing my sense of self and I struggled with the loss of identity. An opportunity presented itself within my husband's restaurant business and I almost begged him to allow me to start working with him. He was so supportive and welcomed me into the fold with an open heart and mind. What started as a two-days-a-week affair gradually turned into a full immersion into the business, which I was happy to be a part of. To have a partner as supportive, enthusiastic and unwavering as him, I believe, is rare, and I thank the universe for sending him my way. We are a team; a unified force. Our value system is the same. We are aligned in our vision of the future and, while working with your spouse is not for everyone, I am grateful to work with someone who has so much knowledge and understanding of a very diverse and ever-changing industry. He's calm and considerate. I'm fiery and spontaneous. We are a perfect match.

I do what I do every day so, like my parents, I am able to provide my kids with a stable, well-rounded life. My kids are my biggest inspiration to do more, be more and, most importantly, to serve others more. I like to think that despite my imperfections, my kids are learning about what it takes to be a truly worthwhile human. They are my biggest cheerleaders, and I'm so proud to be their mum. As a parent, there are many challenges but so many more rewards. Hopefully, even through adversity, I am teaching my kids about mental toughness and resilience, while remaining kind and fair at the same time.

So, while I was navigating this new life as co-owner, partner, mother, friend, sister and daughter, I still felt a nagging emptiness in my heart, yet I had no idea what I needed to fill the gap. A few major hiccups, a couple of 'failed' business pursuits, a GFC and some interesting times passed. We managed to open and close a few businesses in that time, including internationally, and things seemed to be settling into a period of calm. In December 2019, we kept hearing about this disease in China, and because we had a business in Beijing, the rumblings got louder sooner for us. What happened next needs no further mentioning, however, I do feel a sense of gratitude for the lockdown, as my husband and I were becoming more and more stressed about business and life. Being in the hospitality industry during a global pandemic is no joke, but we relished in the family time, and walked many miles in self-reflection, vowing to do whatever it took to keep our family afloat; most importantly, to keep the family home. After the first lockdown ended, there was a moment in my life that potentially changed everything. People speak of the sliding door moment and this was mine. I was invited to a women-led conference in Brisbane and decided to take a chance and go. I had nothing to lose and everything to gain. Little did I know it would lead me on a path that has led to immeasurable growth and understanding, as well as the acceptance that I was destined for greater things. Talk about opening your heart and mind! I am so grateful to the amazing people who believed in me before I believed in myself. Sometimes you just need to put yourself out there.

With this new-found confidence and zest for life, I started to become the leader I had always aspired to be. However, in June 2021, I got two calls that would upend my world. The first was from my daughter's school, telling me she had fallen off the play equipment and had a possible broken arm; the other was from my mum in South Africa – she did not sound good. We were hearing about the potential of another lockdown in Sydney and my mind was reeling. Throughout the pandemic, we kept reminding my parents the importance of keeping safe and healthy, but somehow, they still managed to get infected. Dad was admitted first, and Mum followed shortly after. My brothers and I were in total shock. It was our worst nightmare coming true before our eyes. The tyranny of distance exacerbated by the fact that the borders were closed, meant that every day we were talking to doctors and nurses in South Africa. A few days later while my dad was recovering well, my mum had taken a turn for the worse. Agonisingly, she was intubated around the same time as my dad was released. So, between my daughter recovering from a broken elbow, my parents in a dire situation, my uncle dying of COVID and our business closing again … I was in a world of strife. My anxiety was through the roof, and I felt I had no choice but to apply for an exemption to go be close to my parents. Somehow, I managed to get back to South Africa and what followed was an intense period of grief, despair, hope and pain, coupled with many highs and lows. I managed to find a strength and courage within myself I did not think was possible. And through the depths of my despair, I was able to find my faith again. To say that I prayed hard would be an understatement. There were prayer groups and prayer circles across the world for my mum, and even though we thought we might lose her numerous times, she managed to defy the odds and pulled through. I am grateful every day for the miracle that is my mum, and I made the conscious decision that once she was released from hospital, I would strive to become the best version of myself. Two sets of hotel quarantines also meant I had time to reflect and spend a lot of time by myself. While it truly was the hardest time of my life, I am conscious that it gave me a chance to be still within myself, opening my heart to experiences that would ultimately change everything.

My whole perspective on life has changed and I'm proud to say that through the roughest and most challenging time of my life, I was able to come out on the other side, stronger, more resilient and more open to learning from other inspirational people.

So back to where we started. Whilst I am totally conscious that I am one of the lucky ones, I have been able to use my life experience and my business to make a small difference to the people around me. I am determined to use my knowledge, experience and faith to influence others and teach them that while you may not think what you are doing is important, there may be many people in the background who are watching, listening and learning from you. I have also learnt about the power of friendship and camaraderie. I never knew how important this would be until I met a group of women who have become my mentors, sounding boards and my forever friends. Everyone needs these people in their life, and sometimes it takes a leap of faith to find out who they are.

So back to my original question, what's stopping you from becoming the person you want to be? Is it the fear of failure, the fear of not being understood? I'm here to tell you that you are your own worst critic and if you try to look beyond your own self reservations, you might surprise yourself. Your life is just as important as the next person's, and I have decided to make it my life's mission to make all people, but especially young girls, realise that their dreams and aspirations are just as important as anyone else's. This shortened version of my life has not even touched the edges into the woman I am, however, I feel it's important to note we are the sum of our parts. Every experience, every emotion and every opportunity can and will lead you down a certain path, but it's what you do with these that really makes the difference.

How loud can you roar? How LOUD can you roar?

ABOUT LAURA

Laura Goldberg, BA Psych (Hons) & BComm in Marketing. I'm a proud mother of two wonderful children, Ethan and Gia. Originally from Johannesburg, South Africa, I was raised by Portuguese parents. After a brief stint on a tennis scholarship in the US, I returned home to pursue two degrees at the University of South Africa. During this time, I took over my parents' leather and luggage business, witnessing significant growth while studying through correspondence. In 2002, I immigrated to Australia, initially working for international clothing brands before following my passion for personal training,

Today, I am the co-owner of Hurricane's Grill Restaurants alongside my husband Craig, who founded the brand in 1994. Our South African/Australian styled steakhouse has expanded to three restaurants in Sydney (Brighton Le Sands, Circular Quay, and Castle Hill) and a couple of franchises. We've also ventured into Dubai, Indonesia, and China, with exciting plans for more growth. Additionally, we are partners in our hospitality group, C and L Hospitality group. Recently, I launched my new co-brand, 'The Sausage Sizzle Company,' providing catering services for schools, charities and BBQ events. I am also the director of a South African Leather brand called Jekyll and Hide.

Our restaurants have won multiple awards, including the Australian Small Business Champion award and City of Sydney local business award. Personally, I have been honoured as a finalist for Business Person of the Year in Bayside, Sydney City, and St George councils and well as being in the running for Entrepreneur of the year for the Australian Small business Champion Awards. I've also been a finalist in the Australian Women's Small Business Champion Awards for two years running and finalist for five categories of Ausmumpreneur Awards. One of my proudest moments, however, was being named Volunteer of the Year for Easts Rugby Club.

Beyond business, I am passionate about empowering girls and women to become their best selves. I try to lead with compassion and authenticity. I mentor a variety of women and girls across a broad variety of industries and I believe that I have found the main purpose in my life here. In March 2023, I had the opportunity to join a female founders' tour to London and Paris, where I was featured on two international panels discussing my entrepreneurial journey. As a co-author of the Amazon bestselling and multiple-award-winning book, *Curiosity Killed the 9-5*, as well as being a co-author in an upcoming book called *Women Making a Difference.*

Beyond being a mum, daughter, wife, friend, mentor and now author I am involved in various charitable organisations and where I can, I volunteer myself and time. I will continue to dedicate my life to be of service to others and to inspire as many women to recognise their self-worth.

JAMES HENDERSON
CLARITY

I began my career as a hairdresser seventeen years ago, at just eighteen years old. I was eager to learn, driven to succeed and extremely motivated to create something magical in my life. I grew up in a large family of eight children, my parents divorcing when I was fourteen. Of course, like all families, we had an array of challenges over the years. These challenges led me to wanting to be the best version of myself and inspired me to bring my own spark of magic to the world. No challenge was ever going to dull my shine. In fact, every moment that, at first, appeared to be a challenge, has turned out to be a pivotal moment of growth and realisation, helping me to see my own strength as a person.

I've always been passionate about creating a successful career, so when I began hairdressing, I found it to be a great outlet of creativity and a source of connection between myself, clients and other staff members. I discovered an industry where I had the freedom to be myself, something that had been a struggle in my life. I always felt I had to hide parts of myself or dim my light so I wasn't too bright. Not as a hairdresser though. I was free to be me, and I met so many beautiful people who accepted me just as I was.

I always had a deep faith that I could create something special through my career, not only for myself but for every person I met along the way. I was very much a silent achiever until people began to see my brilliance; there was something special about me that not everyone was offering. It was a sincere heart, care for my clients and extraordinary skill that set me apart, as well as my desire to give every client their dream hair. I just loved seeing people happy. Through every connection I made with my clients, I was able to not only make them look beautiful but feel beautiful too. I was able to inspire them in so many areas of their life. Growing up in a large family with diverse personalities and a lot of adversity, I found I was able to relate to many different people, with an open heart and a deep level of understanding, as they shared their hardships. They knew they weren't going to be judged, just heard and accepted for who they are. Not only was I inspired by their stories, I was also able to learn so much about people from all walks of life.

The first four years of my career was a lot of fun and hard work, building skills, connections and confidence in my work. I had moments of realisation that *I am brilliant at what I do.* In fact, I created a process I would apply when I started working with new clients. I would say to myself before I started their hair: *This person is going to have the best hairdressing experience they have ever had. They will love their hair and always rebook. They will enjoy their experience with me so much that they will keep coming back.*

I loved making people feel joyous. Without even knowing it, I was creating this as my reality. I built a phenomenal and loyal clientele in a short period of time and became a very reputable hairdresser in Adelaide. It was at this point I knew I wanted my own salon one day. I would say, *When I'm forty I'll do that.* It felt so out of reach as a twenty-three-year-old, but my heart knew it was something I desired. I held the faith that it would happen at the right time, and I always knew that when I did it, it was going to be my dream salon. Whenever I'm creating my vision, I am very clear on how I want it to be. This doesn't mean I'm not open to flexibility or change, but I have a clear vison of my dreams and then trust it will unfold … just as it is meant to.

I worked at the same salon for the first eleven years of my career. I had drive and was always edging for the next move. I and two other people were managing a team of thirty; it was a great learning experience working with a variety of personalities. Back then, I wasn't as receptive to change, hence my eleven years in the one place, however, I knew my time was coming to an end when it didn't bring me the same joy it once did. As I left and began another phase at a different salon, it felt like a true catapult for change in all areas of my life. I grieved for the previous salon while finding my feet in a new establishment that had only two other hairstylists, but also several other amazing small beauty businesses that truly inspired me.

It was during this phase that I began to connect with myself on a spiritual level, understanding there is more to life than what we can physically see. I've always had a deep feeling that we're here for a reason and have a purpose. Through my own life experiences and meeting so many people throughout my career, I also had an understanding of how we are strongly governed by our past. We can choose whether we allow it to be a negative thing and become stuck on our stories and trauma, or we can choose to grow through them, to shine our light even brighter. I've always chosen the latter option and faced challenges head on. During this time, I felt I was awakening to a more spiritual aspect of life, helping me to heal from my past, to be better able to handle my emotions, to process them, letting go of past pains and to truly see the magic I had held within for so long.

During this uprooting period of life, I decided to end the relationship I was in as it didn't feel right for me to be with him anymore. It was extremely challenging to end the relationship, as I was fearful of breaking his heart, and I stumbled for several months before making the decision. I was confused as I felt love for him, but I couldn't decipher my exact feelings. My mind and heart were in chaos. I just had to trust my deep inner feeling. My body was screaming to end it, as I was experiencing extreme moments of anxiety and panic attacks. I had a pivotal moment when I knew I had to make the choice …

I was at the dinner table with him, his mother and sister. His sister and mum were sharing a story of a friend falling in love with another friend. His mother in an instant said, 'She loved him – but as a friend.' I felt a huge pulse of energy rush from my feet to my head, and back down again. It was as if a moment of relief passed over me, to say, *This is you, you love him as a friend.* I knew from that moment I had to end the relationship. And I did it the next day. I was heartbroken as I wanted the relationship so badly, but I also knew I had to honour my deepest feelings and let him go. It wasn't right to hold him back from meeting the love of his life, and it wasn't right for me to hold myself back either. I wanted him to meet someone who would love him as much as he loved me, and I wanted to release myself from the pain of not feeling I could give him that same love.

One of the most beautiful things I've ever had said to me came from this time, when he said to me, 'Thank you for teaching me how to love again.' My heart melted in that moment, and I thought, *Why couldn't you always be this open and expressive?* (Hahaha.) I now see the gifts in it all. I saw the gift that I am, and that for everything that doesn't work out the way we wish it to be, there is a greater lesson to be learned. This whole experience was teaching me to have faith in what I feel … and to trust it. With the pain of the heartbreak, I slumped into a deep depression which I found hard to shift. I knew there was no turning back, only moving forwards and finding ways to overcome this deep sadness. They were some of the darkest days of my life, but also the days that have taught me so much.

With this ending, I had brilliant new beginnings. I started my business on a small scale: *James Henderson Hairdressing.* I had drawn and written out my vision for my dream salon and knew what I wanted, but as I was learning everything happens in divine timing. I started by renting a chair from the salon where I worked.

A few months in, a dear friend opened up a cosmetic clinic and set up a small studio salon space there for me. It was literally a 3x3m room with a mirror, a chair and a basin. It was super cute though as she has an amazing eye for detail. I transitioned over to the new space, and it was an amazing opportunity to learn about business and operate on a small scale, so I could learn what I needed to know. As I held the faith in my heart that my big salon vision would come to reality, I was embarking on an incredible healing journey where I met the most amazing and trusted healers: Nicole Whitty, Darren and Ryan from the Elysian Sanctuary in the Adelaide Hills. They have helped and supported me every step of the way. They have been there for me with everything from family relationships, my relationship with myself, past pains, trauma and emotions; everything that has ever held me back. They have taught me incredible tools, energy healing, breath work and meditation, to be able to help myself on a daily basis. It was through my own healing that I began to notice my hairdressing clients were also going through their own personal pain. I started to feel an inner calling to help on a deeper level.

During this time, I could feel I was getting closer to opening my dream salon. I'd been thinking about it a lot and saving money to support it. All I had to do was to have faith it was going to happen and that I would be guided to exactly where I needed to be. Two years prior to this, I'd already asked the universe what the name of my salon was going to be and I was shown the word *Clarity*. As the time came closer, I asked again, *Is this was still the name for the salon?* And, of course, was shown it again and again!

I finally accepted this was to be the name of my salon. I knew where I wanted it to be, so I started putting it out there that I wanted to be shown the building where it was meant to be. I would occasionally jump online and look at commercial real estate, and one particular day, I found myself looking at the most perfect building. It was exactly what I had envisioned – two storeys, open, with lots of natural light, several rooms and different spaces for a waiting area, salon floor and basin area. It was beautiful, white, clear and beaming with love. I knew it was the one as soon as I saw it. I contacted the agent and organised a time to view the building. I have to say, all this time, I never felt ready; I was purely acting on faith, as well as holding the faith in my heart that everything was going to work out for me. I had faith that this space was *Clarity*. In fact, it was a deep inner knowing and it was everything I dreamt it to be and more. Even though I didn't feel I was ready for this big move, I had faith in myself that I could do it. I was still navigating my own personal healing journey, but I was never going to let that stop me from creating my dream.

Three months on and *Clarity* was here. I put my heart and soul into creating the space; every detail was created with love. I held a vision in mind and then saw it taking place in the physical reality. I created *Clarity* to be a place where people leave, not only looking beautiful, but with a heart full of love. I want everyone who enters to feel their brilliance to know they are incredible; to look in the mirror and see they are more than their physical beauty, that their inner beauty also shines bright.

It was from the people I've met over the past seventeen years, as well as my own desire to heal, that I then chose to become a coach. My inner calling was to help people on a deeper level, and it was something I had to act upon. Having faith that I can heal from the past, knowing and experiencing that is possible, has shown me that if I can do it, anyone can. I am here to help those who are ready. If I can create my dreams and hold the faith that anything is possible, then anyone else in this world can too. It is my calling to help others achieve this. All you need is to have a vision in your mind, have the faith that everything will work out for you ... and have faith in yourself. It doesn't matter where you come from or what you've endured in the past, you can overcome anything life throws your way.

We didn't come here to live a small life; we came to live our life to our fullest potential, to shine brighter than the brightest star in the night sky, to beam brighter than the sun and to bless the world with our God-given gifts and talents. From the bottom of my heart, I have faith that everyone walking this Earth has the ability to do just that.

Believe in yourself, have faith and the rest will unfold, just as it is meant to for your own divine path.

ABOUT JAMES

My names is James Henderson, my passion in life has been to make this world a better place for everyone I cross paths with and even those I've never met. I have always inspired to uplift others and bring love, joy and laughter into people's lives. I have worked as a hairdresser for the past seventeen years and have been a successful business owner for just over five years.

Six years ago, I began my own healing journey which I reached a point in my life that I needed help emotionally. I sought out a holistic approach in processing my own emotions, healing trauma, learning a deep forgiveness from the past and accepting myself and others on a deeper level. Throughout this time, I met Nicole, Darren and Ryan from the Elysian Sanctuary who helped me to heal and taught me incredible tools to move through any adversity in life. While on this journey and working as a hairdresser I had the blessing of connecting with thousands of clients who shared their life with me. I realised even more so that there were many people out there that also needed help. This inspired me and created the desire to help people on a deeper level as I knew it was possible to overcome the things that people would share with me. This all let me to the decision to become a mindset coach so I could help people achieve the life of their dreams. I have always found it easy to be kind and loving to others, knowing that I can inspire and have an impact on someone else's life is what sets my heart on fire and is apart of my life's purpose.

ELISE BONATO
INNER ALCHEMY

The instinct often arose during the mutable twilight of evenings, curled into myself and gazing upon the fading sun cast through weighted lace; shapes of wavering light, painting along veneered wood and coloured glass in my room at the end of the hall. The left cheek perpetually warmed by the sunken pillow and echoes of night filtering into my right ear, given the bed pressed into this corner of my seclusion. Framed into stillness, amidst this liminal space, I would welcome the invitation of my imagination and ritualistically submerge myself into the oceanic expanse that became internalised wonder.

Many nights of my childhood through to my youth were spent this way, exploring the craft of imagination to evoke various states of creative expression and sensory awareness. There were very few times that I did not believe the elements I envisioned were untrue either, with the amount of attention I bestowed in creating them to great detail. This internal cinema became a canvas upon which I would often draw upon for comfort and sanctuary, reconciliation and analysis, prospection and creation. Each pursuit of imagining led to an exploration of myself and consciousness from an early age, that only recently I have begun to recognise and even appreciate for the simple principles that this practice entails. I did not realise I was continually immersing myself in a state of faith of what I imagined to be true or possible. The ways in which I envisaged my life, the way I yearned for it to unfold, idealising potential outcomes and prospective situations in a manner that I believed foretold of all that I dreamed to experience and encounter. Precious fragments of dream-like splendour that I saw within, as solidly as everything I experienced without in the world.

This practice of devotional ideation – an inner alchemy – also served as a means of processing my lived experiences. The emotional landscape within my family home as a child was regularly changeable and, to a further extent, challenging. My own disposition became withdrawn, as I matured in age and the volatile nature of these dynamics affected my ability to understand or relate to my developing sense of self, as well as to others in relationships. The humming threat of mental and emotional instability in the home ultimately resulted in depression and onwards, an accelerated self-inquiry of my grasp of living reality. While this did come to shadow my experience in my youth through to early adulthood, employing imaginative visualisation and expressing this through other forms of impassioned creative engagement, was a vehicle of salvation for me that I never wavered to employ. For this reason, it became an avenue of healing as well, a precursor to my body of work to this day as an intuitive healer and multidisciplinary artist.

Fortified by beloved film soundtracks, orchestral masterworks of classical origin, vivacious pop albums and eclectic dance anthems – all lovingly labeled and ensconced in a CD folder – would be selected by that same intuitive inclination to explore within. Slotted gently into my purple-lidded Walkman, these plentiful scores were surrendered to a ready ear, primed to explore all that would arise within. As if in meditation, I would unfurl my body and cast my awareness faithfully into the night, as one would a pilgrim seeking a coveted inner sanctum. Closing my eyes to see vividly what was as true as anything I would witness by day. With each practiced expedition of my imagination, I entrained myself to filter visions of what was, into what could be, and eventually surpassed this to invite what was yet beyond the capacity of my experience in the faith it would result when I awoke each day.

This meditative practice developed over time to inform my creative ambitions for years; from my formative training as a classical dancer, performer and traditional martial artist, through to my professional practice as a multidisciplinary artist later on. I ultimately employed a stealth of envisioning what I deemed fit to be the results and unfoldment of my life. I cast myself into consistent imagining of the experiences I strove for, virtues I longed to embody, and conclusions of my efforts that would yield into lived existence. I consciously invested my attention on these already being so, with the same wondrous curiosity that compelled me to in my childhood. This activity of employing my imagination to condition my awareness into the lived reality, has become so entwined into my nature that only now, as I settle into the rhythms of my life path, I am registering how impactful this has been on what I have ultimately experienced. The universal effectivity of employing faith and creative resolution in harmonious conference, while also pursuing the intended result with a stealth of character that devotes itself, without concern of the opinions, notions and presumptions of others.

Underestimation, criticism, misperception and manipulation have often operated at the periphery of these endeavours from the purview of other people. I was keenly aware when these counteractive intentions were present in those around me and, as a result, have since made an effort to lead myself into each forthcoming moment with covert devotion in my ambitions. My dedication to the creative arts was, at times, met with ridicule from peers and even teachers, which only inspired me further to nurture myself with the imaginative wonderings of my own making – of triumph and bliss in the form of dance, art and music. This also translated later on when people sought to influence my creative direction, when I was developing the visual arts language of my professional practice. There were multiple instances when I was confronted for my choices in presenting my work conceptually for a contemporary context. Yet, in exhibition, my originating foundation of ideas consistently transcended that of others' preconceived or misplaced conclusions. I learned swiftly to apply stealth in all my pursuits of enterprise, whether in learning or success. Enriching my applications to create and serve with a faith that emerged in the evocative spectrum of my personal journey and professional undertakings.

Twelve years ago, I was coming to terms with being in an emotionally manipulative relationship, completely isolated from any support of family and friends, and progressively ill from the effects of that situation. Seeking a safe resolution to free myself from the entrapment that was escalating, I visualised – day and night – being physically, emotionally and mentally capable to leave, and eventually pursue my goal of continuing my art practice internationally. An opportunity to apply for an international art residency in New York City emerged and I subsequently dedicated myself to configuring my application for this possibility. Even while bedridden, my physical health having declined to the extent I was in constant pain and unable to walk or care for myself, I was determined to welcome this opportunity and apply myself to the notion of it already confirmed. I recall vividly, while contorted in pain but resolutely focused on breathing softly into the tunnel of my imagination, burying myself in visions of walking the streets of New York, taking the subway, seeing masterworks in galleries, through to painting in an open, high-ceilinged studio with white walls. I never questioned or entertained that this was not already a truth of my forthcoming experience. I was seeing it vividly and had bestowed quiet faith to myself, amidst painful uncertainty and withering safety, that it was what I was meant to do. Just over a year later, I was walking, pain free, in Brooklyn's downtown, on the way to my studio, enveloped freely in the art residency program.

When someone made mention or passing comment about the fortuitousness of a previously doubted positive outcome regarding my vocations, the constancy of my achievements or my intuiting a conclusion despite opposing judgement preceding the event, I met this with the grace of curiosity. This authorised me to develop an unyielding response to these situations and engagements with people in which I would then refocus on my original intentions and craft an even more vivid internal cinematic of what I was devoting myself to create. The embodiment of this has been stealth and faith in due practice, sustained into an ability to carve out my own trajectory of success to formulate and magnetise the idealised result, according to my unique preferences, while remaining in balance with life itself, and permitting all in choosing to live, perceive and do as they will.

'Elise has presence,' people closest to me would say. Hearing this uttered over my head when I was younger, I eventually came to question what this referred to, especially as it was spoken in reference to any supposed achievements. My invigoration towards that which was abstract, transcendental, obscure and esoteric in nature was duly founded upon a perception I developed as a child. This 'presence' of embodied imagination may have also been the state of awareness that I remember diffusing into – like a meditation – of complete faithful concentration when invested in any form of creative expression. Meditation, an integral part of my daily practice now, has been framed by these levels of perception of self that complement where my attention ventures, towards projects of professional and personal relevance.

How could anyone be perceived in comparison to anything or anyone else, other than themselves? Especially as each's existence is justly informed by their own internal imaginings. I always observed myself as thus; a product of a heightened, envisioned inner world. Would it not be impossible to evaluate one's affective presence to another, given their imagination would touch upon a completely different spectrum and quality of being? Could it simply be that determining and deciding what you intend to create or achieve with complete faith and reverence – this state of awareness to know the self and its capacity for imaginative willpower – not require any affectation of difference or uniqueness to any other? We all have this innate capacity to imagine and make known what we intend, especially if it is in confluence with our true nature and life purpose. Apply yourself to this possibility, regardless of the narratives and dialogues operating around you, with an unreserved stealth of devotion and glorious curiosity of imagining beyond the immediate known.

Approximately six months preceding an invested path of spiritual enquiry and holistic healing I was yet to embark on, while I sat stationary in my car one afternoon, a piercing thought materialised within my inner vision, as I reflected; *were that I could heal instantly at the touch of my hands.* At the time, I had been encountering intermittent wave-like sensations of drowning, fatigue, uncomfortable itching and skin rashes, anxiousness, depression and remnants of nerve pain. Encountering these symptoms whilst in the midst of furthering my professional art practice, I deliberated whether there even existed reachable, forgiving solutions, as I progressively oscillated at the edge of folding into the suffering. A spark of some otherworldly notion, of healing myself with the touch of my own hands, as they rested gently upon my thighs, cast itself across my awareness. It came forth like a lightning bolt during the attempt to mentally reconcile the discomfort I was experiencing in that moment. Breathing deeply into the emerging impression of this existing as true in *any* reality, not questioning the supposed impossibility, that old quiet wonder awoke, and I entertained it. It played on the edges of my imagination through to the day I enrolled in my first course of hands-on energy healing, to learn how to apply this modality to heal myself of all that I was navigating. A decade since, I am now offering my services in this field, facilitating professionally as an intuitive healer and energy alchemist for people worldwide.

Uphold being resolute upon the internal visage of one's creation, not swayed by wayward illusions of fate, but lead by what one actively lives according to envisioned determinations and earnest faith that it will be so – because it is you who has made it. As one would, exerting a purposeful movement in their surrounding space, dancing to a rhythm that resounds in the body. Or as a stroke of golden ink on paper, mapping gilded communion by that very shape formed by the hand. Or as words spoken or sung with deliberate precision of the sound uttered in the time required for them to form via the mouth. Of this, I have always treasured the aspect of myself that maintained loyalty to the creative agency we all inherently have access to, which is to magnify our lived experience with the imagination. The stealth of devoting oneself to cultivating a world within and therefore beyond into the surrounding landscape of your reality that reflects the natural beauty of a soul's essence into everything one is capable of doing and applying. I observe this as faith catalysing into actioned reality. To act into the world with a quiet reverence, fuelled with whatever colour and creed you may have evoked in inner deliberation. Mesmerising the self into a state of being where, regardless of any surroundings and events that exist about you, there remains a luminous flame of potential that you choose to reinvigorate with fervent devotion and intention for that which is 'other'.

Employ this with a quiet stealth of knowing your power – the creative radiance that spills into the centre of your awareness each moment. This activity has directed me into a ritualistic constancy of visualising the optimal, even transcendental, outcome of what I yearned to witness, experience and embody in my lived reality. The rhythmic practice that inscribed itself upon my psyche, now the architecture framing my life, as I now apply this reverence for creation and cultivating beauty to share with others. Being invigorated by a will to support others into this immersion of faith that they can pursue life with their own innate capacity to imagine beyond the immediate circumstance. And to do so with furtive care, knowing they need not be subject to or dissuaded by external influences, if it is their will. Each is capable of creating and contributing to the world with their unique rapture of self. What you imagine your life to unfold as need not be confined to the armature of your mind. The elements of imagining only begin there, but like a seed in soil, you nurture it with all the necessary variables of heartfelt ambition, gracing the world with your inner illumination.

We are all transient echoes of one's imagination made manifest into form. To bestow faith upon yourself and the universe's majesty that meets you there in that very envisioning, when charged with a stealth of your devotion, will beckon marvels to you as innately as the sun rises to meet the horizon.

Only, you are both that sun and horizon, with no separation or distinction – formed of the same quality of your imagination to believe it so.

ABOUT ELISE

Elise Bonato is a multidisciplinary artist and intuitive energy healer based in Adelaide, Australia.

Elise's predominantly experimental arts practice investigates contemporary notions and versions of the sublime and mysticism that she identifies as 'a visual-aural arcane', through a synthesis of moving image, performance, installation, drawing and painting. Since 2012, she has exhibited and performed at galleries, arts institutions, festivals, and site-specific spaces locally in Australia as well as internationally in the USA and Singapore. Elise has also completed a diversity of arts residencies and facilitated public art projects across Australia (VIC, SA, TAS) and the United States (NY). She has been the recipient of numerous grants and awards, including the Australia Council for the Arts ArtStart Grant, the American Australian Association's Dame Joan Sutherland Fund and the Helpmann Academy Grant. Elise's artwork currently resides in collections within Australia and beyond in New Zealand, Canada and the USA. Her contributions to the arts ecology in Australia has further extended to her industry experience as an independent curator, arts writer, public programs facilitator and gallery director for a multitude of local South Australian and wider national projects.

For the past nine years, Elise has also been offering her services as a fully trained and qualified intuitive energy healer in-person across Adelaide, Australia, and by distance for clients worldwide. She is a reiki master-teacher, SKHM seichim master-teacher, karuna master-teacher, and Shiloh Rae advanced alchemy energy healer and master. In all that Elise creates and offers by means of these services, she is wholly dedicated to being a pure vessel for universal intelligence to emanate through and as a truthful embodiment of divine source energy – in illumined service to others, for the highest good of all.

Beyond, Elise is also an established independent graphic designer and photographer, experimental filmmaker, a dance teacher of eighteen years experience specialising in an array of classical methods and contemporary styles, and adept mixed martial artist. In recent time, Elise treasures practising archery, being immersed in the beatific evocations of natural landscape, writing poetry and crafting ambient soundscapes from field site material recorded at her property on Peramangk Land in the Adelaide Hills.

NICOLE WHITTY
DIVINELY INSPIRED

It started with coughing uncontrollably, constantly, to the point where my insides were contracting. I couldn't breathe; the anxiety, fear was overwhelming as tears flowed. I felt alone and didn't have anyone to call for help – those I could weren't answering. I had to pull myself together, focus and get a cab to the hospital, knowing there was no other way.

As I lay on the hospital bed, unable to move, my body spontaneously coughed more and more, the muscles between my ribs spasming from the inflammation. While they did tests, I started to send healing to the causes, for myself, using energy healing, asking my lioness guide to help me.

I knew from my years of doing energy healing on clients that there was a deeper cause attached to my symptoms. Everything we go through, that we don't transform back into creation energy, is stored within us as energy with information on it. If the data, information stored is not life energy, if it's based in trauma and negative emotions, energy and beliefs that are not true, they tend to surface as physical symptoms and negative emotions, thoughts and beliefs that cause suffering in our minds, bodies and lives.

For most of us, we don't know what is there, stored within us, at different levels of consciousness in our organs, our energy centres, our heart, the subconscious and our soul – until a catalyst triggers them to be revealed. I knew what I had to do. It was my turn to heal something big, but I didn't know what it was until I went within myself.

I also wasn't conscious at the time that this was my upgrade for what I was going to create later.

Previously, I'd had a huge amount of family drama; lots of nastiness and unnecessary behaviour towards myself and my son that I was forgiving and healing from.

I offered healing, help, assistance, love and support to them over the years, but we find with people who want to create problems and that aren't mentally stable, they tend to find a problem in anything they can, even if you are being kind and offering to make peace and make things right.

It ended up being an ongoing thing for so many years, I was just tired of it. In fact, after over a decade of toxic drama and attacks, I had to choose myself and my own family, out of self-preservation, if I wanted to be okay and healthy in my mind, body and for my own state of being.

I learnt that I don't have to show love by putting up with extreme worlds created from inner wars that wound. That sometimes, I have to love myself enough to say no.

It does take a toll, when you have mentally imbalanced family members who are convinced that punishing cruelty over the smallest thing (that is often imagined), is okay to do to others.

When I distanced myself completely, I would hear about the latest saga, but chose to not respond to them, as I knew they had already made up their minds that it was okay to try to harm and destroy based on their justifications, grudges and agendas. Anyone who gets involved just becomes another target.

I accepted I wasn't qualified to know how to help them and trusted that, if they chose to, they would get the help they needed. I forgave them for not knowing any better and applied understanding to what I didn't understand, instead of judgement, as their beliefs and programs in their subconscious were creating and influencing their current life experiences, just as mine were. Who was I to judge? Who was I to decide what they should be based on what I wanted for them or what I wanted them to be, when they didn't want it for themselves? Why keep on trying to save people who don't want to be saved?

I realised through their punishment of everyone around them that they were addicted to punishing themselves and would attack anyone who didn't let them continue their own self destruction. You can't create peaceful relationships with people who aren't at peace with themselves.

These were big lessons.

Every time something happened, I looked at myself instead and asked, *What is within me that is attracting this?* I was aware that everyone who impacts us intensely is an inspiration to uproot what is underlying, to transform it into something that becomes a benefit for others.

The trick is not staying in the emotions of what happened and to go beyond it when we can find a way, to free consciousness, as we are born to do, otherwise, we can get stuck living in the past and recreating it with different people over and over again for years. I wasn't up for that.

I am here to free myself, not to relive suffering, experiencing each thing, positive, neutral, negative, creation or destruction, and meeting it with universal life force energy, finding the gold within it that stimulates more growth.

Deep down, I was afraid of how this had taken its toll on me, but I knew when I was in the hospital not to just look at the obvious events or things I knew had happened; there's always something deeper that I didn't want to miss, as I didn't want to go through it again.

As I used my energy healing skills to go into the subconscious information in my lungs, I could see visions of my mother and father, as children in the hospitals they were put in, and knew these deep-seated memories of abandonment, feeling like no-one cared, feeling alone, them both having pneumonia, were in my body as inherited generational subconscious memories that were physically now being expressed in my body as a severe lung infection.

I was exhausted but continued to heal myself as they gave me medication to calm my body down. They decided I had to be sent to Flinders, a larger hospital, so put me in the ambulance, and I was cared for by a lovely paramedic who made me feel safe, reassuring me I would be looked after. More tests were done. I was awake all night from the coughing, feeling delirious. Throughout this experience, I thought to myself, *If I am going to die right now, am I living the way I want to live and where I want to live?* The answer was no.

So, when my partner came to see me, I told him I wasn't going back to where we were living – I would find somewhere else. Anywhere but there. The area was nice, however, we had screaming neighbours. There was never any peace, there was always some sort of commotion going on and I was living near my family. I felt I was living in hell, not able to relax or feel at ease from all the random outbursts, reflecting the noise of the memories I had stored in my subconscious, from being so used to this environment from my dysfunctional family.

I had to take responsibility for creating all of it and change what I had to inside myself, to change my outer world. So, the next voyage of healing and letting go began. I decided, *That's it, no more of thinking I must just accept what I don't want to accept.* I went even deeper to find the sadness, the pain inside me and I was going to heal it, to not manifest it into my outer world … ever again!

I decided I wanted to live at a retreat style place away from everyone to do this; no neighbours, away from loud imposing noise and chaos. At the time, I knew I wasn't in the position to buy such a place, but there was no other option if I was going to get better physically and start repairing some of these deep-seated generational memories. As I was recovering, I stepped back from my business of helping others, as I was literally stopped from distracting myself, so I could heal and help myself.

I realised, *this is what people do*, they distract themselves with being so busy, because it's easier than facing what's within that's so painful and we don't even know we are doing it, until we hit the floor and have no other choice but to face *everything*. Another big lesson to make sure I take care of me is to give time for my self-care and wellbeing, while I help others. Instead of the other program of sacrificing myself for others, out of people-pleasing; there needed to be a balance.

I went within. I called on my lioness guide, my soul family, my ancestors and my father who is in spirit, to help me find the perfect place to live, heal myself and heal others. I was now running purely on faith, in a higher power, and I realised this higher power was within me, even in my most vulnerable state! I knew intuitively this was it. I had to do it and my burning desire for change gave me the inner fortitude to accept nothing less.

A week later, I was woken up at 2am, hearing my guide saying, *The place is online now, get up!*

Half asleep, I got up and got online and I was led straight to the place; it was the first one I saw.

I asked her, *Is this the place?*

She answered, *Yes.*

I applied straight away, putting my faith into action and was relieved, I would be leaving where I was and starting anew.

A few weeks passed; they were taking a while getting back to me. I ended up in hospital again from the pain from the internal inflammation and spasming from my ribs' muscles being torn, sending excruciating pain up through my back. I was over everything, but I had complete faith in my guide, who had been with me for so many years, and started thinking, *Why are they taking so long?*

Just as my faith was waning, I got the call while at the hospital that we had secured the house; the application was successful. We were moving. Relief flooded over me, to get away from that environment and be able to go to a place of peace, open spaces, nature. It was happening.

It was all divinely inspired, all of it.

If I hadn't gotten sick, I wouldn't have found the cause of what was there subconsciously in my body, and I wouldn't have left the place we were living to create the business we have now, that helps hundreds of people every year. I wouldn't have had the level of understanding and training from helping myself, that led me to help so many people through what I was going to create.

I thank my family for everything, because as I didn't trust them, I decided to seek connection and guidance from my true self, my guides and ancestors, that blessed me with accurate, authentic advice, wisdom and truth every time. The experience gave me more faith than ever before, that something higher was guiding my life when I decided to tap into it and ask.

I discovered that responding with gratitude to the things that challenge us the most, and hurt on every level and to everyone who inspired my metamorphosis, opened me to grace and that's where suffering not only ends, but truly turns into a gift that can be used to the benefit of all.

As I devoted myself to this level of faith, it ended up helping so many people who discovered my skills as a conduit, that served for their highest good and aligned with the laws of nature. I never advertised, people were referred through word of mouth from their authentic experiences we shared from working with spirit, source, universal intelligence guiding the way – this is how my business was born ... helping people.

I learnt to surrender my business to universal intelligence, so those I work with are guided by a higher power and I trusted we would connect when divinely inspired to do so. I never would have developed and practised these skills, learning to free my subconscious memories, assisting me in my own transformation of my own quality of energy, if I hadn't had all of these experiences that gave me a different perspective, compassion and awareness of life; an insight into why other people do things, how these things are stored within us and how we can use divine inspiration, insight and healing to transcend what seems insurmountable at the time.

My faith in my guide, dad in spirit and my decision, desire to leave and create a life I wanted to live, a life I didn't need a holiday from, was my motivation for me to create my next chapter. The way I wanted it to be, instead of just accepting what I thought I had to accept out of self-limitation and being used to it. Breaking free from thinking I had to stay in that way of life, because that is what I was used to from the conditioning of my family. I moved out of the belief that I couldn't have what I wanted.

From having enough, hitting rock bottom, being in despair and not knowing how I was going to change it; being in my most vulnerable state, from using my faith in spirit, I did find a way to change it.

My soul's truth was rebirthed and many blessings were born from releasing all that I never was and remembering what I really am. Not just for myself, but for others. Our own transformation truly does end up being the greatest blessing for all.

Although it doesn't feel like it at the time, years later, we see how powerful one decision can be when it is backed with faith and decided to be the only accepted reality.

The space I moved to was beautiful, in the hills, serene, tranquil, perfect for anyone to receive healing and peace of mind.

I again, knew, as clear knowing, this place I moved to needed its own name.

I called in universal intelligence, my true self, my guide and asked her, *What is the name of this place?*

I heard, *Elysian.*

This is why my holistic centre for peace and wellbeing is called Elysian Sanctuary.

Elysian means divinely inspired.

As everything I do and create comes from divine inspiration, if it doesn't come through from this, I don't do it. It has to be divinely inspired, intuitively guided for me to feel the universal intelligence that is the fuel for consciousness to create through my vessel.

As divinely inspired with the intention of love, truth, integrity, authenticity to give the magic that can change lives for the better, respecting all soul paths. Honouring and respecting universal laws, the laws of nature in all I do and create. This is the most important thing to me. My soul knows it; my soul knows it's the most important thing to be my true self and inspire others. Not just think it but be it, vibrationally, as an embodiment of pure creation that is always giving.

ABOUT NICOLE

Nicole is the founder and CEO of the Elysian Sanctuary – Holistic Centre for Peace & Wellbeing in the Adelaide Hills of South Australia.

Nicole is a fully qualified SKHM Seichim master, Karuna master, reiki master teacher, quantum wnergy healer, intuitive medium and has been in service for the past fifteen years helping thousands of people from all over Australia and overseas with these abilities and is a meditation teacher, sound medicine healer and event, retreat facilitator for clients at the Elysian Sanctuary.

She is also a NHI global master coach offering online events to expand consciousness and assists people with creating their best lives through her Mindset for Wellbeing program – YOUR VISION FOR YOUR LIFE!

Always using her skills she offers in alignment with the laws of nature, to help others for the benefit of all, on all levels of consciousness. Everything she does is altered to the specific needs of each person or group she works with for optimum results.

As Nicole's reputation grew over the years from getting fabulous results with her clients, she always operated by word of mouth and letting universal intelligence guide what she does.

Recently being guided to serve globally, she has embarked on now being an author and sharing her stories with the world.

She can be contacted through email: whittyart@hotmail.com or +61403055825

You can find her on FB: facebook.com/Holistic.Intuitive.Healing

JESSICA TELLIS
FACING A HARD LIFE

Seeptember 2017.

Denial. Denial. Denial.

This how I faced my diagnosis. It made it so much easier to accept. There was so much going on and now a cancer diagnosis? I do not have time for this. By denying, I coped with hearing the words you never want to hear, 'It's cancer.'

I remember sitting opposite my surgeon. He was blunt; he didn't sugarcoat anything but even if he had, I figured I would not have liked it anyway. Tears welled in my eyes as I sat in the hospital where I had worked for twenty-seven years as a registered nurse. Now, with those words being uttered, I went from nurse to patient in a matter of seconds. A patient? Nope. Never signed up for that. Anyway, back to tears. As I sat there facing my surgeon, I felt alone. No-one was with me. As a single mum, I didn't want to ask my family to come with me because I didn't want to bother them. Looking back, this was a good reason to bother them and ask for help, but I didn't. I couldn't. I did not want to bother anyone.

Three days before, when I had my routine mammogram (which turned out not to be so routine), they found a lump in my right breast. I was forty-eight years old. A biopsy was performed and I was told to return after the weekend for the results.

I really don't know how I managed to do this, but that afternoon I was asked to speak at a women's retreat at the local community centre

… and I did. I had my son's year twelve music concert to attend that night … and I did. On the weekend, I had a shift at the hospital which I should have called in sick for … but I didn't. I didn't want to let work down as I knew how hard it would be to replace me. So, instead I let myself down. I did not love or care for myself enough to say NO.

After my results from my surgeon, everything seemed to blur. I had to pick my son up from school. The only news I could tell him was, 'Don't worry, I will be okay. We'll get through this.' Without knowing it, these were the most important words I could have said. Five years later, my son told me that was what he hung onto – it gave him hope and comfort. For me it cemented a decision. I was not going to leave my child.

More doctor's appointments, scans, bloodwork and X-rays all told the same story. I had breast cancer.

Telling family and friends was hard. Really hard. Most of them cried or went very quiet. The strange thing was I felt I had to put on a brave face for them. I felt I had to be strong when they cried. It wasn't until I was at home, alone that I realised I just wanted someone to comfort me. I felt I had to be strong. So, I was. My parents were so shocked they could not even talk to me about any of it. It was hard for our family because my uncle was in the hospice dying of cancer, my son was going through his final year twelve assessments and Mum was elderly and unwell. Suffice to say – there was a lot going on.

When the day of my surgery arrived, I felt it would all be simple. The lump would be removed, I would recover and that would be all.

'I'll ring you with the results of your surgery next week.' My surgeon had done a good job. My scar was small and I felt comfortable as I awaited my results. I only had a bit of stiffness but was otherwise recovering well. I spent the week quietly, pottering around at home and doing my best to support my son.

The next week, after I had spoken to my surgeon, I wanted to scream. It was not ok. My results were not ok. Nothing in my world was ok.

The surgery revealed another lump in my right breast that had grown after I had my mammogram, and the cancerous cells had travelled into my lymph nodes. This was a lump that had grown in two weeks whilst I was awaiting surgery! So, I now had two lumps in my right breast. My surgeon was puzzled and I was shocked. Being a registered nurse at this time was not helpful. This now scared me. I knew that a mastectomy, chemotherapy and radiation therapy would follow. That night, I cried and cried, until I had no tears left. That was the first of only two times that I cried. I did not want to appear upset in front of my son or anyone else. Denial let me do that for most of the time, just not that night.

The surgery for my mastectomy and auxiliary clearance was scheduled shortly after. When that day arrived, I dreaded it. I just wanted it over.

The days after my mastectomy were difficult. I was stiff and sore but strangely never had any strong pain. I kept asking my surgeon when I could go home, and he kept telling me that I had to wait for my wound drain to stop draining, so they could remove it. Being a patient was so strange. I couldn't concentrate. I didn't sleep well. I worried about my son who was in the middle of assessments, plus daytime TV was so boring. I just wanted to go home. Finally, that day came. My drain was out, my surgeon wanted me to stay another day, but I refused.

My friend came to pick me up and as I wobbled down the hospital corridor towards the exit, something very strange happened. I felt the biggest surge of energy within me. I went from wobbling to almost sprinting down the corridor, as my friend struggled to keep up. I remember wondering what that feeling was, as it dissipated when I got to the hospital lifts to go the main entrance. It has never returned since.

That night was the second time I cried. My son had his big, final end of year twelve music concert. He was performing in his most important concert of the year and I couldn't attend. It broke my heart, as I sat quietly on the couch, crying and crying. I had attended every one of his concerts since he started school. Now, all I could do was let my tears flow, knowing I wasn't there with him on this special night.

I was given several weeks to recover from surgery before starting chemotherapy. I made sure I ate as healthily as I could, walked every day … and I did a good job of not facing any feelings that were coming up. Powering on was my pathway through.

During that time, I was having regular energy healing sessions with Nicole Whitty, at her beautiful sanctuary. I would flop on the table for an hour and tune out as Nicole would work on me, helping to soothe and heal my body. I continued these treatments after each chemo and to this day I still have regular healings.

Chemo was not fun. I was lucky to have family and friends offer to sit with me during these sessions. Sitting in the comfy recliner chair, I felt awful. I knew what the next steps involved. I had to have an intravenous cannula inserted into a vein in my arm, then the chemo was administered through that. This was a procedure I used to perform for patients and now it was being performed on me! Chemo commenced and ran for several hours. Finally, it was over – it had been a long day. I left the day unit feeling okay. The next day, however, was slightly different. My stomach felt a bit bloated. The next day, a bit more bloated and then after that I felt as if I was twenty months pregnant. It was day 4 post chemo that everything started to crumble. day 4 at 2pm to be precise.

My friends were coming over to check on me, as my uncle was in the final hours of his life and all my family were with him. At 2pm, my cousin texted to tell me the news that he had gone onto the next stage of his journey and, at that exact time, the effects of my chemo kicked in. That combined with the grief of losing my uncle was a moment I will never forget. My friends could see I was not ok as soon as they arrived. That afternoon they kindly stayed with me, looked after me and made sure I knew I was supported. I have never felt so ill. Strangely enough, not sick, but simply horrible. I spent the rest of the afternoon on my couch sipping what was to become my recovery cocktail during my treatments. For some reason a mix of water and lemonade seemed to help my stomach. I continued to drink this cocktail for many months after!

My friends were so kind and supportive that afternoon and that continued throughout the entirety of my breast cancer journey. Their efforts touched me, and I will never forget how they were there for me, whenever I needed them – and even at times when I didn't.

Surprisingly, I managed to sleep through the night and awoke the next morning to a bloated stomach; the most awful feeling I had ever had. I really didn't know what to do with myself. My twenty months pregnant stomach looked flat but felt so big. The day was warm and muggy which added to my discomfort. All I wanted to do was to go outside for a walk, but I couldn't. My strength was not with me, and I was afraid I would fall over. Having exercised for most days of my life, I felt I had to do something. My solution was to devise a walking circuit from my kitchen through the lounge, up the hallway and back to the kitchen. I managed to do this circuit nonstop for twenty minutes and then flopped on the couch. My bloated stomach did not magically deflate but I felt as if I had accomplished something for the day. Rest should have been high on my list but my body kept telling me to walk. From that day on, I walked every day during chemo. Out of the sixteen weeks of my treatment, I only missed fourteen days because it was either too hot, or I was simply too unwell to get off my couch. My neighbour and son would often come with me, as I would walk a short distance then stagger back home. Despite it being hard, I always felt better after. My body kept telling me to move and I found out afterwards that exercise is definitely recommended during chemo, as it aids a quicker recovery.

What surprised me was my weight fluctuations after each chemo. When I fronted up for treatment, my weight was around 51kg. Within four days after chemo, my weight dropped to 46kg. So, with every treatment, my weight dropped by 5kg in four days. The following weeks before my next treatment saw me trying to eat chocolate, ice cream and dessert to try and regain my weight. Whilst I love my sweet treats, I knew this was not the best thing for my body, but I found no other way to regain the weight. Unfortunately, everything began to taste horrible … except my afternoon cup of tea and cake!

Some mornings I would feel so bad I didn't want to get out of bed. My cat, who demanded her breakfast, ensured I did eventually arise but not before I gave myself a motivational speech. I remember telling myself, 'Get up, get up, get up and put your foot to the ground, do it now, get up, now, now, now.' This would go on for ten minutes and eventually my leg would move to the edge of the bed and my foot to the floor. My cat purred in appreciation of my efforts!

With every treatment I had different sets of symptoms.

My hair fell out. I wore one of those soft chemo caps to cover my head. The upsetting thing was the strange looks I got from so many people, especially the older generation. The younger generation didn't seem to look twice.

My food tasted awful. My mouth became so sore I could only eat soft mashed food. In the end, I would often eat baby rice cereal because it was soft. Spicy foods were not an option. Even three shakes of pepper on my dinner were enough to burn my stomach lining so it was sore for a several days.

My fingernails turned a blue/black colour and became loose.

My skin could not tolerate any soap and in the end, I had to use a camel's milk soap as it did not cause any discomfort to me.

I began to itch over different parts of my body … and it drove me mad!!

Chemo sores broke out on my skin.

Heat intolerance. On a hot day I would feel dizzy if I spent even a short time outdoors.

My hands became so stiff I could not hold cutlery properly.

I probably had more symptoms but thankfully have forgotten them now.

Despite having all these symptoms, all the medical staff could not believe how well I coped with my treatment. They may have thought I coped well, but there were many times when I did not cope at all and felt so alone. I guess, sometimes, I did acknowledge my feelings after all.

To this day I believe that I did so well because of the non-stop energy healing and support from Nicole. During that time Nicole gave me powerful healing Sanskrit mantras to repeat and offered many opportunities for me to attend in person events at her Sanctuary. As I lay on the healing table, enjoying the healing energies which flooded my body, Nicole helped me to see that I can save myself.

When I reflect, I see our choices can be to save and help ourselves or hurt and harm ourselves. We make those choices. We have the power to do so.

It is five years on and I am discharged from my oncologist! As I write and relive this journey, many emotions have surfaced which I didn't face five years ago. Looking back now, I finally realise what that powerful surge in my body was when I left the hospital after my mastectomy.

It was my inner lioness … and she was roaring.

ABOUT JESSICA

Hi, I am Jess, an empowering health care worker with over thirty years of experience in helping to support patients and clients through different phases of their health-related journeys. I have a background in nursing, care support work and life coaching.

I love being able to encourage people to be as independent as they can and grow where possible so they can live a more fulfilling life. It is so rewarding!

When I am not working, you can find me on a Pilates mat, walking in nature or baking sweet treats in my kitchen.

MEL JAMES
INVESTING IN OUR CHILDREN IS AN INVESTMENT FOR THE FUTURE

I have the pleasure and the privilege of working in the child protection system as a social worker, and have done so now for over twenty years. I've had the pleasure to work with some of the strongest, most resilient children and young people who have survived and thrived, within, and often in spite of, this system. I have walked alongside children and their families, as well as a great many staff, who have experienced the serious gaps, challenges and downright failings of this system. I built my own child protection consultancy company because of my desire to work alongside, rather than 'in', the system, influencing, impacting and disrupting a system that is, quite literally, in many ways, broken.

This system is filled with children who have been harmed, not only by their parents or supposed loved ones, but by the very system that is meant to keep them safe. They have been (and even continue to be) harmed by some carers who have been inadequately assessed, inadequately funded or who are inadequately supported or trained in the first place. They have been (and continue to be) harmed by case workers too overwhelmed, too under-resourced or too distressed by the abuse and neglect they see every day, resulting in vicarious trauma and compassion fatigue. They have been (and continue to be) harmed by constant changes to policies, processes, legislation and frameworks - a lot of paperwork and not a lot of actual change. It is not that we don't have a solution to the broken system in which we work; we do. But do we have a society which will stand up for the children and young people of the system and say, 'Enough is enough!' Do we have a society that will demand change?

According to recent research, in Australia, one in thirty-two children are abused every year. That's about half a million notifications of harm reported each year. Of the 120,000 children and young people receiving support services, about half of those are children in out-of-home care. They live in some of the sixteen thousand foster and kinship carer homes we have in Australia. The maths here is simple; there are not enough quality carers to support children in need of care and protection. We have thousands of substantiated allegations of abuse in care each year. There are thousands *more* allegations that are not substantiated, and likely many more simply not reported. It should not go without saying - the majority of carers provide high-quality, loving, nurturing homes. It is not their stories that make the front page of the newspaper. It is not their beautiful, warm and healing homes, provided quietly, without reward, badge or trophy, that you hear about in the news. However, we cannot say, 'most carers are great' and ignore the voices of the most vulnerable members of our community - the children and young people within the child protection system who are telling us they don't always feel safe, despite being removed from their families of origin. The decision to approve carers *sometimes* comes down to not having enough options. In some cases, the assessors do not have quality training or are simply not digging deep enough when assessing carers to ensure those we approve are going to provide a beautiful, warm and healing home. Simply having a bed and a car seat does not make a good carer! It may make a 'good enough' carer, but surely the bar should be set higher than that for the children and young people of our society?

So, because we lower our standards and we under-resource the child protection frontline, we have children being harmed, in care, by some state-approved carers. We also have another increasing, distressingly large cohort of children living in residential care services, looked after by a rotating roster of youth support workers, as we just don't have enough kin or general carers for them.

Then we see stories on television of children and young people committing acts that range from silly and mischievous, all the way to sickening, horrifying crimes against members of the general public. The research is less entertaining, yet equally dramatic; more than 50% of children in the justice system are known to the child protection system. When you see the news headlines and watch the presenters talking in dramatic, heightened, almost excitable tones about some 'gang of youths' stealing cars, going on joy rides and, in some cases, causing serious injury or death, there is a public outcry for more serious consequences; more juvenile jails, better 'deterrents' like 'naming and shaming', 'boot camps' and longer jail sentences. The issue is that many of these children have already seen and experienced more harm, abuse and trauma than most others will in their lifetime. If you go by the commentary on any media outlet's social media platform, readers are encouraged to believe that harder, harsher penalties and punishments are what is needed for this growing cohort of children.

Is it any wonder that children and young people within the juvenile justice system become the adults of the homeless, mental health, criminal justice and child protection systems? This isn't rocket science ... but it is science. The research on the impact of adverse childhood experiences (ACEs) is wide-spread and well-known. We know that when you have childhood trauma, you are more likely to experience poor outcomes in relation to your physical, social and emotional outcomes as an adult. However, this isn't nearly dramatic or enticing enough to make the front page of the media. Yet it should! If a critical and proven key to addressing poor mental health, domestic violence, drug and alcohol abuse, homelessness and criminal justice, is in fact greater funding, attention and support for the child protection system (i.e. greater funding, attention and support for CHILDREN) then surely this is a simple, yet dynamic systems change? If it's so simple, why hasn't this change occurred?

When talking about the ACEs and the impact of trauma and abuse on the wellbeing of children well into adulthood, having a basic understanding of some proven 'rules' about the brain and how it develops, perhaps, is critical. The brain does not fully develop until mid-to-late twenties, on average. The last part of the brain to develop is the prefrontal cortex, which is involved in all our executive processing, our impulse control, organisation and decision-making. It really shouldn't be a surprise when children who have experienced significant trauma are removed from their families and communities of origin, then have limited healthy connections and go on to make the occasional unhealthy, illogical, impulsive decision. Why is car insurance more expensive if you are younger than thirty? Because even the insurance companies agree with the research about the brain, recognising that before thirty, young people can make less-than-intelligent choices. Another 'rule' is that *the brain grows from back to front.* That simply means, we're born with a developed brain stem (the part of the brain responsible for automated systems like circulatory and regulatory systems of the body), and we slowly build, grow and strengthen the parts of the brain at the back all the way to the front, the frontal cortex being last. Interesting, isn't it, to consider that if we damage one part of the brain (through trauma, abuse, or injury), it can then affect how the rest of the brain grows, influencing the pattern of development in those later evolving regions. That's why, in child protection, if we see a teen who has emotional dysregulation challenges, we might encourage the young person to jump on a trampoline, play drums or do running, for the rhythmic, repetitive nature of the activity to help retrain the brain's emotional regulatory systems to stabilise. I recall a young person I worked with who would try to take over the care of her siblings in their new foster home, making bottles for the baby, bossing around the toddler, even attempting to discipline them, by yelling or smacking when they did something wrong, despite the carer being in the parental role. This young person was quick to anger, would almost rage when upset, could not handle changes in routine and liked to be in complete control. This naturally and understandably was challenging for the carer, but she was a brilliant, skilled, trauma-informed carer who could look beyond the behaviours for what lay beneath; a young person who had spent much of her childhood protecting herself and her siblings from their father's violent, drunken incidents and horrific abuse of their mother. The young person, from the age of five, would take her siblings into their room, hide them in her cupboard and play babies with them, feeding the babies bottles, singing and rocking the babies to sleep, while their father raged in another room. She ultimately kept her siblings safe during those moments; a burden no child should ever have to shoulder. But all these incredible survival instincts didn't leave her the moment she and her siblings were removed and taken into a safe foster care placement. They had served her well for so long. She had built and honed those skills, so much so that her language was delayed. She read at the level of a year three student when entering high school and struggled in most social settings, resulting in limited friendships. Because her time spent at home was focused on building survival skills, she did not develop her language, social or emotional skills. With a lesser trained carer, she may well not have sustained a stable placement. There are many similar stories, resulting in teens being rendered 'too difficult' and being relinquished, separated yet again from their family and their siblings this time, to end up in a residential care home with four, five, six or more other young people with equally distressing backgrounds and trauma-based behaviours, deemed 'too hard' to manage in family-based care.

When the brain is developing, it is much more susceptible to trauma and stress. This is why adverse childhood experiences are detrimental to children (and young people and young adults) who are aged under thirty. Studies have linked exposure to ACEs to cause problems physiologically, psychologically, behaviorally and, as a consequence, interpersonally. The first ACEs study of critical size was the Center for Disease Control (CDC)-Kaiser Permanente Adverse Childhood Experiences (ACE) Study. It was the first of the large-scale investigations into how childhood abuse, neglect and household challenges affect later-life health and wellbeing.

Ultimately, the original ACEs study found that the more ACEs you experience as a child (your 'ACE' score out of ten), the higher the likelihood of poor social, emotional AND physical outcomes in later life. Higher ACEs was found to be associated with higher likelihood to suffer from alcoholism, experience poor mental health, attempt or complete suicide, or experiment with drugs. Now, you could be thinking, *Well, that's fairly logical.* True! But what was new information was the effect trauma had on physical wellbeing. Those with an ACE score of four were 3.9 times more likely to have chronic obstructive pulmonary disease than those with score of zero. Those with an ACE score of four were 2.2 times more likely to have heart disease than those with score of zero. Those with a score of four are twice as likely to have cancer than someone without any ACEs. People with an ACE score of six or more were found to die twenty years earlier, on average, than those with score of zero.

The incredible thing about this study is the data set and findings has been replicated and confirmed many times over since this study thirty years ago. Like the 2020 study by the University of Copenhagen of one million people, which found children who have experienced repeated serious adversity, such as losing a parent, mental illness in the family, poverty or being placed in foster care, have a 4.5 times higher risk of dying in early adulthood than children who have not experienced adversity during childhood.

What's really important to take from this research, is that adverse childhood experiences are common across all populations. Almost two-thirds of study participants reported at least one ACE, and more than one in five reported three or more ACEs. Australia completed a similar study, released in 2023; the Australian Childhood Maltreatment Study. The ACMS found Australians who experience maltreatment are substantially more likely to have poor mental health, engage in health-risk behaviours and require higher health care services and intervention, more so than people without childhood trauma or abuse. Like the original ACEs study in the late nineties, the data was, or should have been, paradigm shifting for us as a society. It, like many of the studies before it, highlights that ACEs are common, they have lifelong impact and cost us as a community dearly – in poor mental health outcomes, reduced educational and employment outcomes, higher engagement in criminal justice and policing, and require significant financial input at the tertiary health care stage.

Why are we so hellbent, as a community, on locking up children experiencing significant trauma and abuse, vowing that our harsh punishments and cruel consequencing will 'fix' the growing problem, when the evidence is right in front of us. If we want to change the 'system', if we want to impact real, sustainable change for our entire society, and, if you want to be purely emotionless about it, if you want to be economically and fiscally responsible for society, why are we not putting in more supports in early childhood services, delivery and care? Some countries are proving massive systemic change can have significant long-term positive effects on their communities. As an example, Portugal's policy of decriminalising drug use has resulted in a wide-spread reduction in drug-related deaths and has seen reduced crime statistics and reduced pressure on health care systems, due to drug-related injuries and illnesses. Iceland's focus on children's rights, Denmark's paid parental leave policies and even Australia's new domestic and family violence leave are all good examples of steps in the right direction. Yet the rate of children entering the care system continues to increase. And at the other end of the spectrum, the cost on the health, education, policing and criminal justice systems keeps expanding.

Reflect on the major changes in our communities over the past three-to-four decades. Now, where we have two-parent households, we have both parents working; where we have single parent households, those single parents must work to survive. So, there is a growing demand for early education and child care services. Yet, child care workers are some of the most undervalued, underresourced, underpaid and under-educated in our sector. They are quite literally raising our humans for us; they are our lionesses, caring for our cubs. Yet this protective, nurturing and powerful role is undervalued and therefore under-invested. If we invested in child care workers being highly trained, trauma-informed and paid accordingly, then the care they receive when not with their parents would be exceptional, and the role-modelling of best parenting practices by them would be invaluable and immeasurable to parents.

We have commissions of inquiry, policy papers and investigations into all of these matters and regularly come up with 'innovative' ideas; changing the name of the child protection department, changing the ministers responsible for those government departments, spending on logos and updating the email addresses of the child safety workers … as if these are key ways to 'fix' the issues. But when are we going to do something major? Something so disruptive that we might actually fix this broken system. When we do, we will need the entire community to raise up, find their inner lioness - their strong maternal instinct to protect, guide and truly raise our young – and see the value, the asset, that they are. Unless society recognises their inherent value and insists governments better fund early intervention, early childhood and social services, we will not see change.

Maybe we need more emphasis on what works well. Even those with high adverse childhood experiences can go on to be incredibly skilled, successful, positive people who go on to raise skilled, successful, positive children. Resiliency factors can help to decrease the impact of your ACEs! For example, I worked with a young person whose mum had experienced domestic violence, and regardless of her attempts to shield him from it, he too was impacted. Subsequently, she suffered significant and poor mental health. However, she left her abusive partner, the young person's dad. His mother's resiliency and strength to move away from that relationship, seek support, build a strong support network and provide a nurturing, caring environment post those earlier experiences, actually helped to counteract his early childhood traumas. His counselling, his trauma-informed teachers, his supportive network, his stable routine and structure post the move, were all resiliency factors, which may in the long-run help to buffer the negative effects of the earlier DV and poor mental health, as well as the grief and loss he experienced.

Maybe a perfect system cannot be created, but we cannot keep patching this one; doing the same things in slightly different ways and expecting entirely different results. The entire child protection system requires greater funding, greater emphasis and greater support from the general public. How can the system prioritise the needs and rights of children and young people in care, if the perception of the general public is that it does not value young people at all. Until we recognise children are an asset; with inherent value, deserving of great respect and care, then we will never prioritise their wellbeing over money, media sensationalism, and other more exciting, news-worthy matters. When we have more faith in children, and more faith in ourselves, when we as a community become protective Lionesses protecting our vulnerable cubs, only then will we stop investing in prisons for children and start investing in children. Period!

ABOUT MEL

Mel James is the owner, founder and CEO of Social Care Solutions, a progressive and independent social enterprise specialising in child protection assessment, training and consultancy services across Australia and Aotearoa.

Working with children, young people and families for over twenty years, Mel studied at the University of Qld, achieving her degrees in social work and criminology, later completing her masters of social work. After dedicating several years supporting children, young people and families engaged in the child protection system, both here and abroad, Mel soon realised there was a significant gap in the market for high-quality foster care assessment and training services in Australia. And with that realisation, Social Care Solutions was born.

With over seventy dedicated social workers, practitioners, consultants and trainers delivering the highest quality consultancy, training and assessment services, Social Care Solutions has developed a reputation as an industry disrupter, a thought leader and driver of practice innovation to ensure better outcomes for children and young people. A multi-award winner, including recipient of the prestigious 'Professional Non-Government' award at the 2021 Queensland

Child Protection Week, Telstra Best of Business State Finalist, multiple AusMumpreneur Awards and two in the Women Changing the World awards in 2023, Mel has co-written two books and spends her 'free' time teaching at University of Sunshine Coast!

She's a proud mum of three and feels as passionately about their care and safety as she does the children and young people with whom she works!

BIANCA F STAWIARSKI
NGANANGU BUNDARA[1]

Every now and then, I take the time to reflect on a quality I quite often take for granted. People call it by many names: faith, the universe, Ancestors, path, hope, optimism … or countless others. I too alternate between universe, Ancestors or path, but more recently have come to think of this as nganangu bundara, or my morning star. What does this mean specifically to me and the way I see the world? To me, bundara symbolises hope, purpose, passion and opportunity; it is a bright shining beacon of focus in a new day. This is the brightest point in the darkness, when all the other beings are either settling down from their nocturnal lives or starting to wake up. It is when opportunities are limitless and unfettered, and I feel expansive and eternal. When I think of bundara, I don't think about others' interpretation of what this might mean, only what I feel with every part of me. I write this chapter through a process of being Ancestor-led, suspending my logical brain and staying within that timeless flow of conscious being. I encourage you to breathe deeply through ngardi guwanda[2] and travel along the meandering river with me on this journey.

I've always been what people might call 'lucky', or what some of my friends jokingly refer to as 'arsey'[3]. I've had my fair share of childhood

---

1 Nganangu bundara means my morning star in Badimia, also spelt Badimaya – an Aboriginal language from mid-west Western Australia.
2 Ngardi guwanda means thinking, feeling, listening strongly in Badimia. I also describe this as listening with my heart.
3 Arsey is an Australian term meaning very lucky.

and adult trauma, but somehow, I always seem to land on my feet. I used to explain it away, but consciously, I know now that my path is full of opportunities that only I can see. I often share this story when I speak to people but now realise I've never written it down like this before.

Possibly, it's time to share this with you now as it is relevant to the focus of this chapter and also because we all learn and heal through stories. It was around the year 2000. I had just gotten married and was wanting a new adventure (as if being married wasn't an adventure in itself!). My government job felt restrictive and ill-fitting, probably *my first sign* or *nudge* that I was being called to do something else. Maybe because of this, or for some other reason, my husband and I decided we would take up an opportunity to teach English in Japan. Completely different, and seemingly random, to any focus that either of us had previously had. We packed up our home, I took twelve months leave without pay, and we relocated to Adelaide in preparation for the trip. To this day, I'm not sure why we thought it would be a good idea, but I'll let the wind take that thought away, as it's unimportant to this yarn4. Surprisingly, or maybe unsurprisingly if you look at my manifestation skills, we were accepted. But as we were preparing, there was a hiccup – one of us couldn't go. As a result, we both decided not to go. That was a slightly *stronger second nudge*. You'd think I'd start to listen, but unfortunately, I was a bit ignorant of some things at that time in my life. Looking back, it was one of those face-palm moments. Why, oh why, did I not listen? Rather than dwell on that, I'll also send that one to the wind.

Given we both now didn't have work and weren't at home, I contacted my employer, and we returned to the regional town we lived in, settling in to have a family, my husband entering into a farming business. Meanwhile, I was still unsettled with work. I loved having my babies, but it was as if the universe was nudging me … *I think you should move*, I heard over and over. I would have this debate with myself, you know

4 Yarn or yarning is a First Nations term for storytelling with purpose. There are many definitions of yarning.

the sorts of things … *But I like living here, we've got a business, I have my government job, we have a house …*

One by one, the universe reminded me I wasn't living congruently with my purpose; each time the nudges getting stronger and stronger. Firstly, three years of drought and then the locusts descended – *nudge three, You know you should move,* the universe insisted. But I continued to debate, listing all the reasons why I shouldn't move. This time the result was needing to close the farming business – it was literally haemorrhaging money. Yep, that was *nudge four.* Then, as we tried to trade or sell our way out of it, one company sent us to the wall, creating a cascade of events. As a result, we needed to declare bankruptcy; our home and car was taken by the bank and sold. It was like the universe had decided it was done being subtle, picked up a brick and smacked me over the head, saying, *Well, now all those reasons have been removed … MOVE!* After this *more than a nudge – number five,* I finally listened, though I could have saved myself quite a bit of pain and anguish if I only I had listened earlier. As a result, you guessed it, I transferred my work location and moved with my husband and young family to the city.

You'd think that would be the end of it, but no. The universe had got me to the city, but I still wasn't settled. I knew with every part of me that I wasn't walking my path *(nudge six),* that I was still ignoring ng2nangu bundara. This time, however, I wasn't going to ignore the messages. To shorten this yarn, it took three times of applying for a voluntary redundancy from my employer, a divorce and finding myself in a precarious position with two children, single, no job and no savings, before I could finally say that I listened, even though it took another brick smacked into my head *(another more than a nudge seven)* to finally step along the path properly! Thank you, universe, for being so persistent with me. I'm chuckling, because taking seven times to actually follow or even become fully aware of nganangu bundara doesn't seem very smart on my behalf. Oh well, I'm here now.

So, where is here, and what path was so important to warrant the upheaval? I know it sounds a bit cliché, but it was like the clouds parted and I could finally see, appreciate, and understand nganangu bundara. There the path stretched out beyond what I could see, this vast open space, brimming and vibrating with opportunity. This was beyond glorious to witness, and I was energised with the potentiality. Of course, it wasn't all candles and tranquillity. What I didn't tell you was that no-one, besides me, could actually SEE nganangu bundara! I'm sure they all thought I'd gone crazy, drifting off with the fairies. I lost count the number of times my family and friends told me I didn't need to struggle and could just go back to my job. GO BACK? Hell no, there was no way I was going BACK! I knew within myself, that if I went back, I would have failed. Never stepping on my life's path, my life would have withered, all potential lost. I realise that sounds more than a little dramatic, and I can at times have a tendency for the dramatic – cue, some people's eyes roll – but I had gone through so much to be here and I couldn't quit just because it got a little difficult. I was at the precipice of living a life I only ever dreamed of or maybe couldn't even have imagined. I needed to stand in my belief, some might say sheer stubbornness, that I had the strength to venture to this place and succeed. It reminds me of a great quote that has been unfortunately attributed to a few different people;

'Fate whispers to the warrior, "You cannot withstand the storm." The warrior whispers back, "I am the storm".' – author unknown

Wrapping myself up in a cocoon of light, shutting off parts of myself for a while to manage grief and fear, I stepped onto my path, nganangu bundara shining bright for me to navigate my direction. To use the previous metaphor, I became the storm, and much like that weather pattern, I raged through the next few years of the establishment phase, never losing sight of that guiding star. What did this look like? I started an equine assisted coaching business while also diving deeply into higher education, moving through study at double the speed. Firstly, diploma in life coaching (which really helped me too), then half a diploma in counselling, dropping that to start a bachelor in cognitive neuroscience, only to transfer to a master's in counselling practice. That journey firmly placed me on, what I believe, is the right path – well at least it is for now. I stopped studying for a few years to focus on generating more financial resources through my business, while discovering a deep love of writing. At the time of writing this, I have co-authored seven internationally published books and authored three books. I am currently in the process of writing another four co-authored books, including this chapter, as well as undertaking a practiced-based PhD, straddling between Indigenous allied health (mental health) and entrepreneurship! I've also created, some would say 'dreamed into being', a unique and in-demand international social enterprise, creating change at the individual, community and corporate level. I've written online courses accessed internationally, presented at national and international conferences, trained community and corporates, supported a number of people through their unique healing journey, and helped people to start their own businesses. All of this, because I finally listened to my innate Ancestral wisdom, opened my eyes and heart, and saw nganangu bundara. None of this would have happened if I had stubbornly continued to ignore the 'nudges' from the universe and ultimately, my inner wisdom. Neither would this have transpired if I'd listened to others and turned back, choosing a safe and known life for the unknown opportunities of soaring high on thermals.

I can honestly say that I wake up every morning and LOVE what I do. I wake up and check my calendar with excitement, thinking, *Wow, what opportunity do I get to access today, or who do I have the honour of travelling with on their healing or entrepreneurial journey?* Imagine that? Living a life you don't feel you need to take a holiday from? I never wait for Friday night to finally 'live' for two days. Since I started on my path, I have never said, 'Phew … so glad that week is over!' How many others can say that? Although, I do admit my least favourite day is Saturday because in the morning is when I do 'conditioning training' with my personal trainer, Josh. Saturdays, though, are balanced by how fantastic I feel after training, and also that I get to yarn with my PhD primary supervisor, Lorraine, who is incredibly inspiring, insightful and encouraging. I guess you could say I am seeing the light and opportunities of nganangu bundara in a holistic sense; physically, mentally, professionally, financially and spiritually. I am regularly reminded that I avoided this life for so long. It's easy at times to play it safe and float. In the long run, however, it isn't really easy because it requires you to live a lie, to dim your light and never truly fly.

My hope is that through my storytelling, you can see all the places where I could have detoured from my path, the virtual forks in the road that may have derailed me. It was times like this where I needed to stand firm and keep sight of my light, my belief in myself, my skills and higher purpose. This draws me to focus on you, the person reading this book. I'm curious. Why were you drawn to pick up this book? Are you searching for something, or through reading this, does it help you avoid or leave the path from finding your own morning star? There is no judgement in my questions, only curiosity and kindness. Are you navigating through the fog of others' expectations? Tiptoeing around what you innately know is true and congruent for you, but what you know others are unable to see or appreciate. It can be exceptionally hard to stand up to the judgement veiled in suggestions or support. What is it about this chapter that has kept you reading so far? Is there something nudging you, pricking your skin to WAKE UP? Whose permission are you seeking before you finally live?

I implore you … don't wait another day, week, year or decade before you remove your shoes and feel the path beneath your feet. I'm not saying that finding and travelling your path is all light and rosy, it's far from that in my experience. Well, maybe it's getting on the path which isn't so rosy. There is a reason I chose the *I am the storm* quote. Through my experience, once you see, really see the opportunities to step into your potential, your purpose, there is something of a shift. It's not that the path gets easier; I've found it can ebb and flow depending on whether I'm getting distracted or diluted with other interests. What I've found is that there is something in you that changes, kind of like vibrating at a different level, and while you may still experience difficulties or less than positive things, it sort of slides off, repelled by your self-belief or faith in yourself. It's Ancestor-led intuitive knowing. I don't really have one word for this experience. It resonates more like a deep knowing, that while this is occurring, I'm gathering skills for my next expansion – and wow, I'm eagerly looking forward to that discovery!

I'm going to leave you with a quote by Thomas Edison as I think it nicely sums up and finishes off this chapter:

'When you have exhausted all possibilities, remember this: you haven't.'
– *Thomas Edison*

I encourage you to look up, discover your bundara, your morning star. You owe it to yourself, your ancestors and your descendants. As a beautiful friend, who I consider a sister, says:

'Stop thinking yourself as being a dutiful descendant and start seeing yourself as a good ancestor.'
– *Dionne Connolly*

ABOUT BIANCA

Bianca Stawiarski, a proud Badimia and Ukrainian woman, is a centred and purpose-driven healer, mental health and Indigenous healing practitioner, facilitator, coach, international co-author, author, change maker and speaker.

Bianca is the founder of international Indigenous social enterprise, Warida Wholistic Wellness. She's dedicated to healing through a First Nations lens, improving mental health, Indigenous healing practices and economic empowerment through entrepreneurship.

Her approach integrates her innate Indigenous knowledge, knowledge of healing combined with entrepreneurship to empower women and communities. Bianca is recognised for her work in shifting away from Western medical models of dysfunction, instead focusing on healing outside of four walls. Part of this approach embraces the ethos of: gudu-guduwa[1] through ngardi guwanda[2], relationship and connection.

Bianca is an emerging voice in Indigenous literature and a PhD researcher. Her work showcases her rich experiences and deep

---

1 Gudu-guduwa means coming together in Badimia
2 Ngardi guwanda means thinking, feeling, listening strongly in Badimia.

knowledge. A published author and international multiple-award-winning entrepreneur, she's committed to creating community change. Bianca uniquely blends her roles as an author and academic, connecting diverse readers to the wisdom and resilience of Indigenous cultures through her insightful writings. Her PhD research explores integrating ngardi guwanda practices in community-led women's empowerment for entrepreneurship. Bianca hopes that the outcomes from her 'We hold our own Answers' research will empower First Nations communities to choose their own paths.

Want to know more about Bianca and her work in Warida Wholistic Wellness? Check out her website by searching the link here: warida.com. au

BREDA McCAGUE
STEALTH. GRIT. UNSTOPPABLE.
UNSHAKEABLE.

She glanced down at the heavy army boots on her feet. At seventeen, she was in an army barracks for the first time in her life, having just signed up to serve.

Curiosity had brought her to this place, with an interest in understanding why on earth women would not have been allowed into this world, until now.

It was 1993, and I was one of the three teenage girls standing in the army barracks trying to take in my surroundings and the nature of the military culture.

The troops in the barracks struggled with the introduction of women into a world that only men had existed in, till then.

Once, while we stood 'at ease' on the square in the early days before an inspection, one man told me that whilst he was enjoying getting to know us and that we were fun to have around, women would be no good at carrying mortars or heavy weapons.

He said I was unlikely to be able to handle the difficult terrain on a route march, and that my rifle would likely end up being carried by a man, along with his own. He really didn't think the army was any place for a woman, especially a petite, 'five-foot-one', kind of woman.

However, soon after that experience, I noticed some men amongst the senior leadership ranks who appeared to be seeing potential in me and began trying to push me out of my comfort zone. They seemed to be taking an interest in helping me grow. I had never experienced that outside of my home. No external communities had ever told me THEY BELIEVED in me before. No teachers, no coaches. No-one had ever demonstrated true SERVANT leadership to me in my life ... until now.

When I looked back, after many years serving, I realised the men who had taken an interest in my military career were open-minded thinkers, constantly scouting for talent, and had somehow managed to spot some talent in me, that I had not seen. These men did not see women in the army as a threat in any way, and in fact, seemed to be delighted to have fresh minds and perspectives joining their very routine world.

I decided I would stick at it. The curiosity in me had not found its answers in full, so I thought I would persist until I could fully understand it. I certainly never planned to stay in the defence forces for twenty years, but that was what ended up happening, and more!

During those years, and back in my civilian life away from the army barracks, I had also begun to build myself a full-time career in finance, that I ran parallel to my army career. My army career was part-time; I would throw on the combats and boots one evening a week and every weekend. The daytime civilian career saw me in a smart suit every day in the banking world, which I also loved. I found the contrast of the two very different worlds quite fascinating. It felt like I had a unique lens on two extremely different worlds, and this allowed me to compare them both, finding benefits and downsides to each, but combined, bringing me an eclectic mix of pure Inspiration.

My banking career began to take off. I ended up winning awards and quickly learned about the banking world. It fascinated me too, just in different ways to the army world.

My eye was drawn to the leadership ranks in the bank, and I constantly found myself comparing the leadership styles I saw in the army, to the leadership styles I was working under in the finance world.

I found unique leaders everywhere and learned that no-one leads the same; leaders all have their own quirky ways of inspiring people. I learned techniques to motivate people from leaders who told me that other leaders had taught them that particular technique. I began to realise that people hand leadership techniques down through generations.

I became fascinated at the power of leadership, how we can have a massive impact on the world if we become healthy leaders, secure in ourselves and lead by serving others.

I had just found myself a LEGACY worth working for!

Meanwhile, back at the army camp, I had been promoted many times. I'd been trained and promoted to the rank of an NCO (non-commissioned officer) which meant I was now known as Corporal McCague. A year after that, I was sent on a 'standards' course which resulted in my promotion to Sargent.

The role of Sargent was one of my favourite roles, responsible for Corporals and their sections, though not totally responsible for the whole unit. I completed the Sargents course with a Drill Dublin Sargent, called Mal, who really pushed us to our limits. We got roared at, woken up with screaming at 5am, thrown out and tested on the square, half-asleep. They tried all sorts of things to see if we would break and give up, but I realised I liked this kind of challenge. I seemed to be good at reframing my situations like, *Yeah, he won't break me, I'm enjoying this,* as they roared at us. *This will make me more resilient, and I will benefit from this.* It was like I was able to have some fun with my internal narrative while the environment around me tried to test me.

The next course I went on was the officer's course; a two-year course with lots of different parts to it. This was what helped me uncover my ambition.

The first year I was going through the motions and even coasting through it a bit. When I finished the first year, I remember reflecting on the long drive home and thinking, *Did I bring my best?* I realised I absolutely had not. Between year one and two of the course, I reflected and explored what this opportunity could actually do for me if I really put all my effort into it. I came to a number of realisations.

The army needed phenomenal female officers to inspire its culture change. Until then in my life, I had never led one hundred men, or more, in any environment. I'd had the opportunity to do that handed to me on a plate, yet what had I been doing? I'd been coasting. I knew I had great people around me on the course, and I also knew they'd not seen the best of me. I felt bad that I'd been holding back. I guess a lot of my holding myself back was down to the fact that I didn't have the belief that women should be leading troops of men. It was my own inner gender bias actively sabotaging me! The patriarchal society I had grown up in was now leading me to self-sabotage my own success and future.

The second year of the course arrived. I wheeled into the army barracks in County Kerry in my new sports car … and with a whole new mindset! I pulled out all the stops. I untethered my limited thinking and replaced it with healthier thinking. I reframed all of the old unhealthy thoughts and built new ones.

Guess who absolutely smashed it on that course and ended up coming third out of thirty-five amazing leaders! The five-foot-one girl who had finally learned to believe in herself! She had found her inner lioness … and boy did she now know how to ROAR!

As a kid I was the second child in my family, and as many of us know, the second child has to get good at dealing with challenge. As a young teen, I already knew I liked a challenge. I'd been playing music, competitively, on stages since I was twelve years old, and that was a challenge I loved.

As a younger kid, I was very timid and shy in school, yet at home, I was a tomboy. My dad had me doing everything on our farm, from driving Jeeps and tractors to helping him fix things and engineer things. I then went on to progress to doing the bookkeeping and business accounts for the farm. I knew how to calculate VAT when I was thirteen. I barely know it now!

When I was sixteen, he bought me a banger of a computer at an auction, and I began to do his accounts digitally.

My dad had the most exceptional mind. He analysed everything in a way I've never seen in my army or finance life. He looked at things very differently to everyone else in the world. When I was twelve, I would watch him, as he watched nighttime TV. His narratives as he watched the news programs fascinated me. I effectively became his apprentice. He also taught me how to play music; another thing we had in common. He and I were a tight team!

We both drove my mother crazy, as we were usually late going to everything, particularly mass on a Sunday in Monaghan, Ireland. I reckoned the less time I had to sit there, the better; internally disagreeing with the readings and pulling them apart in my logical brain. I still have a bit of that in me and I still really enjoy it! I analyse everything I find in life. I find its purpose, ascertain if it is actually meeting its purpose, and decide if I think it is helping the world, or causing unhealthy beliefs and divide in the world.

My dad's teachings came into their own later on in my life and will continue as part of my thought process forever.

Quite a few years later, things had changed dramatically. The young woman found herself in unexpected life conditions she did not recognise. Sadly, her bright spark began to dim.

After following the guidance and example from her society and the usual path women were taught to want, she found herself existing through a very different type of life experience.

Trauma had entered her life and was frequently present.

She struggled with the trauma, continuously running out of energy, trying to ensure that those relying on her felt protected, safe and emotionally secure. Illness and worry became her new constant.

When trying to establish escape routes from this life, she found nothing was clear or straightforward. One day, she read something that began to shed some light on what she had been struggling to understand; a glimmer of hope began to shine.

She engaged with this information, and became more educated, and finally, things began to make more sense.

Meanwhile back at base, the army boys who had been then reduced to a distant contact were keeping an eye on her wellbeing. A few of them had raised an eyebrow over articles she had shared online. They were worried. One of the mentors who had pushed her to grow earlier in her life got in touch and asked if everything was okay.

She was shocked, as she'd been unable to have very little contact with these people for a full decade at this point. She was, however, extremely relieved at their offer of help.

She packed her things and waited till she could hear the roar of the engines of the vans and lorries that made their way up her drive. Her own army had come back for her.

In army culture, they teach you to leave no-one behind and here she was seeing this actually happen during the worst time of her life. They were not going to leave her to solider alone in such a situation.

The sheer integrity and care from these men and their wives flooded her with emotion. It was at that moment she realised the human divide had never been about 'women versus men' but all about 'toxic versus empath'. The givers and the kind-hearted never stop caring about those they love. They are the precious souls in the human race, the kind of people that make everyone's lives safer, brighter and better.

Humans are complicated. It's a race that needs to be studied in detail for us to gain a true understanding of how it really operates. Most people never get to study human behaviour as she did, but she realised that if everyone had been taught what she had now learned, human suffering could be lesser in volume and impact around the world. If only she could teach others what she'd learned the hard way; to survive and even to thrive, amongst the darkest of days.

A few months later, after she began to share her learnings from the safety of her new environment, she accepted a random request to do a talk for an IT business. She wrote her speech from the heart, teaching the audience about their conditioned subconscious mind, their emotional intelligence and providing them with tools to help them better understand themselves. Her talk was a sell-out, and ended with a queue of men forming, wanting to talk to her in more detail.

She realised that education is how we can change the world. Knowledge is power, and when we humans understand ourselves better, not to mention understanding others better, everything in the world becomes clearer and less chaotic.

She is now a global motivational speaker, and has co-founded an organisation called *Lean In Ireland*, empowering women across the world. She speaks to corporate organisations and at conferences, taking fulfilment from teaching her audiences about conditioned thinking and the impact our childhood environments have had on our thinking programs. It's about how we view ourselves and how those beliefs have been formed.

Her mission is to spread knowledge nuggets across every fold of the globe, driving us all to healthier cultures across the world.

In her view, it is a sizeable legacy, but one she will spend her life delivering on. So far, she has delivered talks in the UK, Scotland, France, Sweden, Germany, USA, Canada ... and she is only getting started!

From here on in, her *word of focus* is ONWARDS and her MISSION is truly mobilised.

Her life quality has improved immensely, her army family still keep an eye on her, her music is back in her life and her spark has now evolved into a full flame.

She is unstoppable, unshakeable and unbreakable. She is ME!

ABOUT BREDA

At the age of seventeen, Breda McCague became one of the first girls in Irish history to join the Irish Reserve Infantry Defence Forces. She subsequently served as her unit's first female lieutenant for twenty years. She has continued in positions of leadership ever since.

Breda also worked across global financial institutions running transformation programs since 2000 and continues into hold a part-time director role with an international financial consultancy as a director of emotional excellence.

In 2016 Breda decided to co-found Lean In Ireland, a global foundation that helps women achieve ambitious goals.

In 2017, Breda's interest began to concentrate more in emotional intelligent leadership. She became an accredited coach. She began to deliver talks across corporates on leadership, decision-making, unconscious bias, emotional intelligence, vision, strategy and growth. She has since been flown to many countries to deliver her lively keynotes.

Out of curiosity, she studied some of the drivers behind why, across industries, we do not have enough women involved in decision-making senior boards and why gender pay gaps continue to prove so troublesome to close. The pipeline leakage is something she works with companies a lot on.

In 2022, Breda did a TEDx talk on hacking mindsets which was promoted to the Global Professional TED.com channel. Breda's material can be found on most of the popular social media channels.

As company director of AIMING4AWESOME Ltd., she builds and delivers unique senior leadership programs laced with a mix of emotional intelligence, mindset mastery and ambitious visualisation techniques. She often runs innovative learning hackathons, bootcamps and workshops for all levels across large European and US institutions.

Breda McCague is a very driven, energetic individual who enjoys educating, inspiring and entertaining others so that they can become the best emotionally regulated and inspiring leaders possible across their societies, communities and work environments.

Breda was awarded the Women of the Year title in the Women in Finance Ireland Awards for 2021 and has chaired and hosted panels at many global finance and inclusion events. She was a finalist in the STEM Mentor of the Year Awards in Ireland 2023 also.

Breda's website & TED talk:
bredamccague.com
youtube.com/watch?v=rcROZ8bdRMA

MICHELLE LANGE
FIND YOUR FAITH & LIVE

Wendy Watson Nelson, the author of *Change Your Questions, Change Your Life* said, 'The power of questions comes from their ability to invite us to reflect.' To me, reflection is those moments in life when we become keenly, even deeply aware of ourselves.

An internal mirror that solicits questions can cause an instantaneous chain reaction of thoughts to navigate a situation. The significance here is to understand that questions guide us to our internal compass, in a hidden place, if you will, that is separate from our day-to-day musings. A lens to see above the noise.

My question is: *What is faith?* Our answers are not based on right or wrong, but rather on deeply personal understandings. For me, faith is a silent strength – a devoted and firm belief where scientific evidence falls short of explanation. It can enhance our confidence and trust in ourselves, serving as a source of a higher power. Faith begins as a small seed that transforms into a belief, helping us navigate how we perceive ourselves. A visual representation of this could be described as an inner power that grows from a tiny seedling into a majestic spiritual tree.

A great question is, *How do you perceive your connection to faith within yourself?* It is important to understand that faith is not solely about seeking a higher power. Rather, it is an opportunity to enhance our awareness of how we trust in our ability to have faith in ourselves. As we navigate life's changes, we can find answers by expanding our horizons of faith.

I believe in the importance of lifelong learning, which has taught me that words hold significant power. The origins of my internal conversations have shaped the external dialogues I choose to hear and embrace. Some time ago, as I prepared for this chapter, New Zealand singer and songwriter Stan Walker released a single for the movie *Origins* titled 'I AM.' The lyrics convey mindful wisdom that resonated with me.

Words, once spoken, can create thoughts that penetrate the depths of our souls, especially when they are rooted in negativity. In my fifty-plus years on this Earth, I realised the most significant harm to my development came from hurtful words. You know the type: 'No-one will ever want you.' Bullies shouting a violent array of insults, 'You are fat,' 'You are ugly and stupid,' or the incessant teasing of 'four eyes' when I wore glasses for the first time. These negative comments echoed in my mind constantly, often without realising it. There is no truth in the childhood phrase, *Sticks and stones will break your bones, but names will never hurt me.* The truth is … they do hurt.

Throughout my life, I have allowed spoken language to create a momentum that led to an overwhelming noise. I have experienced moments where my light was overshadowed by darkness, often due to circumstances beyond my control. One significant event confronted me with the harsh reality of how innocence can be disrespected. While you do not need to know the specifics of these experiences, it is important to recognise that they profoundly impacted me. They shaped my thoughts and, most importantly, affected my ability to connect with my true self.

In this phase of life, I found myself on the brink of an emotional collapse due to someone else's choices. I was experiencing what I now recognise as depression – a coping mechanism for the challenges I was facing head on … in secret. My faith was shaken beyond recognition and my soul struggled to piece itself back together. I suffered in silence, unsure of who would believe me or listen without judgement or blame. The result of this left me flat, unhappy and not the vibrant young woman I once was. I felt utterly alone, afraid and unable to trust or accept my journey – who could at seventeen?

I remember walking to class and looking up at the varying shades of blue in the sky, noticing the fluffy, billowing clouds of pure white. As my gaze followed the clouds, I spotted a spider's web in the nearby shrubs, beside the birds of paradise. I could not help but think that these are all God's creations. At that moment, I asked myself: *Does God know what I am going through right now? Does He see me above those clouds?*

The smidge of faith drew me in, wrapped me up with a warm sense of love that there was someone aware of my yearning and my sorrow. A thought emerged: *Think of something you love.* As the sun shone on my face, I felt its warmth, cherished the blessing and stopped walking. I stood captivated by the beauty of nature, as bubbles flooded my thoughts. They are remarkable creations, some of my favourite memories involve them. My mum would spend afternoons with dish soap and water, bending wire into circular shapes, to make the most incredible giant bubbles that enveloped our little hands before popping. We would giggle and laugh, admiring such a delicate creation that brought so much joy.

These cherished daydreams lifted my spirits and brought a quiet smile. The grace of God filled my heart, helping me calm the noise of my pain. My internal compass for self-belief and self-love was being evaluated and in the years that would follow, it would happen repeatedly. On each occasion I would rely on my faith to get me through, to be a light and strength. Step by step, moment to moment, light was strewn in my path to help me when life became dark. Dark with depression, dark with loss, dark because I chose to go there, thinking I could escape and dark because life sometimes takes you there because of hard things. My path, the one that only I could walk amongst the briars and thorns dared to test me. Dare to give me chances to outgrow the noise. Noise that in later years, I learned was mine to hear or carry for so long.

A phrase that has been entrenched in my soul created a framework for me to persevere despite doubts and disbelief. That phrase was: *Be still and know that I am.* In the latter part of my late forties and early fifties, I discovered what that really meant to me, and how it could change my self-belief language. The reference was God speaking and those words declared a powerful message on how to ignite your flame. I found a truth and it said, 'In the quiet, as I stilled the noise, the chatter, I would see who I am, as God sees me and knowing what to do. Knowing that I am loved, I am strong, and I am a beautiful ME. ... Believe in yourselves, in your capacity to do something remarkable. The work of the world is done by ordinary people who have learned to work in an extraordinary way.' I believe that we are all uniquely created and different is our own self brilliance. A brilliance that comes from experience, soul-heart languages, hope, faith and self-belief. How does this manifest in daily life. It starts with something as simple as kindness. I have found that kindness grows kindness. The kindness you grow within yourself reciprocates outwardly to others. Lastly find tools that work for you; that create divine connection.

The tool I was guided to was a combination of uplifting words crafted into a creation that seemed to be a universal message meant for me. These written musings become the silent stealth amongst the multiple layers of commotion. During the early days of my cancer treatment, I found that some things became less important, while others required my full attention. It was clear that my focus was on cultivating bravery, having courage and developing the resilience needed to thrive. I needed to be honest with myself about the internal language that would carry me through this treacherous expedition.

It was time to put my faith to work, realise it is not the destination – it is the journey and trust my intuition ... Writing was my new best friend. Each session of chemo I was armed with pen, paper, sketching supplies and a beautifully curated journal. This journal became my voice and a vital tool for healing. I realised I was not waiting for someone to come and rescue me; this was my time to save myself. I needed to look inward and discover a greater sense of empowerment and recovery from the pain that had troubled me for far too long. My body was finally speaking up about what I had put myself through.

This illness that was ravaging my body gave way to a passage of personal healing. It was about letting go of the past and learning not to bury or hide from it, but to heal instead. I chose to be a bloom in the desert, drawing nourishment from the life-giving waters of inspiration and facing my truth without shame, guilt or anguish. Stealth mode!

The cause and effect of seeing my life flash before me created a synergy for many delectable satisfying gifts that, in time, quenched the fires of fear, dispelled unbelief and unearthed my self-trust, a belief in my strength and resilience; and most importantly, when I had no hair, sunken eyelids, no eyebrows or lashes I was inside and out beautiful. A treasure that became what I call my heart whispers …

Whispers that guided my internal healing from an abusive relationship. To take the muzzle off my voice and speak the truth to myself that I eagerly sheltered myself from seeing. Healing from not being enough, a partner with shame. A deep-rooted vine that pulled at me often to keep me in check. Each of these wounds no longer served me and created commotion internally. To heal myself, meant. I could no longer remain idle or mildly discontent. This was my call to action because the very breath of life was counting on me to succeed.

To succeed I had to go to battle with a dark lord who was ever vigilant in his efforts to destroy. I stood at the threshold of a life battle. It is said that the pen is mightier than the sword, so I began to take the negative and turn it into positives. BATTLE became a source of light.

- B – Brave Belief.
- A – Accept.
- T – Total Surrender.
- T – Truth.
- L – Love & Live.
- E – Energy Exchange.

These words inspired hope and opened the possibility of joy, even in the face of my mortality right in front of me. They changed the noise, evened out the playing field and lifted a weary soul that was broken.

If that is true and I am a product of the conflict created by words, how can I redefine myself? We each have the opportunity and responsibility to respond in a way that brings love to ourselves and those we care about. I have come to realise that we often react to our life circumstances without considering the impact of our responses. When we respond out of anger, we cannot expect those around us to grow, appreciate or learn. Calmness creates a space for understanding, as it replaces noise with love. It has taken me many years to see past the pain caused by words and to find the peaceful things in my heart, anchored to who I chose to be.

If faith can move mountains, which mountains in my life could I move? By living through faith, we unlock the potential to embrace life at a higher level. I believe that through small and simple things, remarkable things happen. All you need is to hold onto hope the size of a mustard seed – no larger than a pinhead – to generate phenomenal and sustainable energy. This energy is something you contribute to with your thoughts and actions. Remember, thoughts are powerful. To believe is to see; with faith, you can drown out the noise and achieve anything you set your mind to, including overcoming the challenges in your life with powerful stealth.

The key to a better tomorrow lies in discovering the connection between your soul, heart and mind. When we heal, we achieve inner peace. This peace allows us to let go of what holds us back and become open to receiving joy, blessings, sunshine, hope and new opportunities. Opportunities are gifts that illuminate our path.

ABOUT MICHELLE

Michelle Lange is an everyday ordinary individual who wears many hats and seeks to do extraordinary things that inspire many. Hats that have arrived through her ability to see the good in life despite challenges. Michelle is an inspiring thought leader who has an ability to positively influence and empower others so that they see the world through the lens of their empowering selves.

Michelle's gift to the world is to be an inspiration. Her inspiring thoughts are harnessed through powerful stories and storytelling of her life experiences, learning and bringing the true potential of the possible rather than the impossible to her audience.

Michelle believes the written word and art have the power to connect, ignite a fire within, fuelling visual motivation to overcome the greatest of obstacles and get to the other side where a divine imagination resides. Hope is found when changing course to find a renewed energy to engage in your purpose and dream big.

Michelle's dared to dream and found it by becoming a coauthor for the anthology *Imperfectly Perfect Campaign Volume 1*. Michelle was able to pen insights with light, love and delve into the realm of personal growth, self-discovery and how she overcame monumental odds, being triumphant in getting to the other side with joyful celebration in her heart.

Through her etheric artistic creations, she captures the essence of energy, emotions, creating visual masterpieces that resonate with the soul so that the painting picks the person. Artistry became a part of her cancer journey as she dispelled the stress response cycle by getting creative.

Those who know Michelle love her spirit. A spirit that shares love, strength, courage in a very down to earth authentic way. True to herself with resilience tucked under her arm she forges new paths and thinking to be her imperfectly perfect best self. A self that hopes for the best in others and leads with faith in grace and goodness of God.

SANDRA SPADANUNDA
GUARDIANS OF THE HEART

'Family is not simply about genetics or DNA, it's about the love we have in our hearts and how we choose to share that love.'
– **Sandra Spadanuda**, *Rising Matriarch*, **2021**

Motherhood transcends genetic ties, encompassing a profound bond rooted in love, care and nurture. It's the selfless act of nurturing and guiding a child, regardless of biological connection. This enduring love knows no boundaries, embracing adopted children, stepchildren or those nurtured through fostering. Maternal love beyond DNA is a testament to the power of the human heart, to embrace and nurture unconditionally, shaping lives with compassion, support and unwavering devotion.

The protective instinct of a mother is a primal force that transcends species boundaries, shared by both humans and lionesses alike. It's a fierce and unwavering commitment to safeguarding the wellbeing of offspring, driven by an innate sense of responsibility and love. Whether facing physical threats or emotional challenges, mothers stand as fierce guardians, ready to defend their young with unmatched determination and courage.

BECOMING A FOSTER CARER: A JOURNEY BEGINS

My husband and I have never been the kind of couple to 'conform with the norm', and when it came to starting a family – instead of creating new life – we very consciously decided to 'foster' in the hope of providing a better life to children and young people in need. We had seen so much rejection, abandonment, grief and loss through our work, and we knew we were going to be a different kind of family.

As youth workers, we were both deeply immersed in the world of young people facing various challenges and adversities. We witnessed firsthand the impact of unstable home lives, neglect and abuse on the wellbeing and development of children and young people. We witnessed many teens trapped in a broken system where they were out of placement options, and these young people, children (in the legal care of the state) were often living it rough.

Through our work, we recognised the critical need for stable and nurturing homes for children and teens who were unable to remain with their birth families due to a variety of factors. We saw the profound difference that a caring and supportive environment could make in the lives of these young people, providing them with the stability, love, support and guidance they needed to thrive and flourish. This realisation ignited a deep calling within us both to step forward and offer a home for those we knew were all out of options and needed a safe place to stay.

Our workplace experiences with the foster care system enabled us to truly understand the need for caring, non-judgemental and dedicated individuals willing to open their hearts and homes to children and young people in crisis. Motivated by a sense of empathy and a belief in the power of love to heal, we embarked on the rigorous process, which involved extensive training, evaluations, preparation, meetings and interviews. Each step of the way we remained steadfast in our determination to offer stability, guidance and unconditional love to children and young people in need.

Youth workers are often naturally empathetic, patient and compassionate individuals, with a commitment to making a positive difference in the lives of young people, who we would often see continually let down and moved around. It was the youth worker in us both that ultimately led us to choose the parenting pathway of foster care. It was a natural extension of our roles as youth workers, allowing us to continue our venture of empowering and advocating for young people. In essence, our positions as youth workers served as a catalyst for our decision to pursue fostering as our chosen parenting pathway, providing us with the insight, skills and passion needed to embark on this journey of caregiving, advocacy and parenthood.

When our fostering journey first began in early 2013, we were clear about wanting to take in teenagers. They were the ones the system seemed to care the least about. They were not small, vulnerable newborn babies. They often self-selected their un-endorsed placements, often couch surfing and bouncing between hostel, to group home, to foster placement and back again. Even the department initially struggled to understand our desire to foster teens – instead trying to offer us babies and small children … But we stood our ground.

It wasn't easy. Teenagers can be hard work anyway right? But teenagers with a history of early childhood trauma, continually let down by a broken system, can be next level. There have been PLENTY of 'I hate you' moments, slammed bedroom doors and nasty name-calling thrown our way, but we never gave up. It wasn't an option to give them back when it got hard. To this day, I am still surprised and saddened by the ability of other carers, service providers or any kind of significant other in a young person's life, who give up on them so easily.

Our journey to foster was not without challenges, but it was fuelled by a deep-seated belief in the transformative power of love and the profound impact that a supportive and nurturing home can have on a child's life. Ultimately, it has been a journey driven by compassion, empathy and a steadfast commitment to making a difference – one child at a time.

The emotional and challenging journey of fostering is a testament to the resilience of the human spirit and the power of love to transform lives. It's a journey marked by moments of profound joy, heartache, growth and reflection, as foster parents, we must navigate the complexities of caring for children who have experienced complex trauma and adversity.

One of the most humbling aspects of fostering is witnessing the resilience and strength of those in our care, as they navigate the turbulent waters of their past experiences. It's a truly humbling experience to witness their courage and determination to overcome obstacles and rebuild their lives.

At the same time, fostering can be emotionally taxing, and as carers, we grapple with the realities of the childrens' trauma and the complexities of the foster care system. There are moments of heartache and frustration, as we confront the harsh realities of abuse, neglect and loss, and work tirelessly to provide a sense of safety, stability and belonging.

Saying goodbye to a temporarily placed child can be one of the most challenging aspects of the journey. Despite knowing that it's often in the child's best interest to reunite with their birth family or move on to a permanent placement, the bonds formed between us and them can be deep and profound, making the farewell bittersweet.

Throughout the emotional roller-coaster of fostering, as carers we rely on our resilience, compassion and support networks to navigate the highs and lows of the journey. It's a journey defined by love, sacrifice and the unwavering belief in the transformative power of care and connection to heal.

NURTURING LIKE A LIONESS: THE PROTECTIVE INSTINCT

As a foster mother, my experiences resonate deeply with the protective nature of lionesses. Both roles involve a profound instinct to safeguard and nurture the vulnerable, regardless of genetic ties.

GUARDIANSHIP

Just as lionesses fiercely protect their cubs from external threats, foster carers serve as guardians, providing safety for children facing adversity. Both lionesses and carers exhibit an unwavering commitment to ensuring the wellbeing and safety of those entrusted to their care.

A NURTURING INSTINCT

Like lionesses who nurture and teach their cubs essential survival skills, foster carers offer guidance, support and love to children in need. Both play a crucial role in growth and development, helping their charges to overcome challenges and thrive, despite past trauma.

EMOTIONAL BONDS

Lionesses form strong emotional bonds with their cubs, mirroring the deep connections foster carers develop with the children in their care. Despite potential heartache, both lionesses and carers invest wholeheartedly in these relationships, driven by a profound sense of love and compassion.

ADAPTABILITY

Lionesses demonstrate remarkable adaptability, caring for orphaned or adopted cubs as if they were their own. Similarly, foster carers embrace diverse backgrounds and experiences, offering unconditional love and support to children regardless of their biological lineage.

COMMUNITY SUPPORT

In lion prides, multiple lionesses often collaborate to care for the collective offspring, reflecting a sense of community and shared responsibility. Likewise, there are foster carers who connect, provide support and camaraderie, allowing carers to lean on one another for guidance, encouragement and solidarity.

Both foster carers and lionesses exemplify the timeless instinct to protect and nurture the vulnerable, showcasing the transformative power of love, compassion and maternal instinct across boundaries.

Challenges and Triumphs: Navigating Parenthood

Navigating the complexities of foster care presents significant challenges, each requiring patience, resilience and an understanding of the unique needs of the children in our care. We have fought (and still fight) more battles in their defence than any of them will ever realise or know. Behind many closed doors, in what seem like endless meetings, none of them knew about the continual arguments and debates we would have to defend them and advocate for them.

Even when they have thought the worst, we have always and unconditionally fought for their best outcomes.

NAVIGATING BUREAUCRACY

The bureaucratic hurdles within the foster care system can be daunting and ridiculously time-consuming. From endless paperwork and documentation to navigating regulations and protocols, as foster carers we often find ourselves grappling with administrative burdens, detracting from our primary focus of providing care and support to our children. Additionally, coordinating with multiple agencies and professionals involved in our children's case adds another layer of complexity, requiring us to have effective communication and advocacy skills to ensure our children's needs are adequately addressed.

DEALING WITH ATTACHMENT ISSUES

Many children in foster care have experienced disruptions in their attachments due to early trauma, loss or instability in their lives. As carers, we have encountered challenges in building and nurturing secure attachments, as they struggle to trust or form meaningful connections with caregivers. Addressing attachment issues requires patience, consistency and therapeutic interventions tailored to the child's unique emotional needs, often necessitating collaboration with professionals and support services.

MANAGING COMPLEX TRAUMA

Children entering foster care often carry with them a history of complex trauma resulting from abuse, neglect, exposure to significant family and domestic violence or other adverse experiences. As carers, we have faced the daunting task of supporting children through the healing process, while addressing the long-term effects of trauma on their emotional and psychological wellbeing. Managing complex trauma requires specialised knowledge, trauma-informed care practices and access to therapeutic resources to help children process their experiences, regulate their emotions and rebuild a sense of safety and trust.

SUPPORTING EDUCATIONAL NEEDS

Many children in foster care experience disruptions in their education due to placement changes, instability or other factors related to their life circumstances. As carers, it's been common for us to encounter challenges in advocating for and supporting the educational needs of the children in our care, from addressing learning difficulties and accessing academic support services, to navigating school transitions and ensuring continuity in their education. Providing consistent and tailored educational support requires collaboration with schools, teachers and educational professionals to create a supportive learning environment that meets the diverse needs of each child.

NAVIGATING TRANSITIONS AND LOSS

Transitions are an inherent part of the foster care experience, as children may move between placements or reunite with their birth families. As a carer, I have experienced the emotional toll of saying goodbye to children I have cared for, as well as the challenges of supporting them through their own transitions and helping them cope with feelings of loss and separation. Navigating transitions requires sensitivity, empathy and ongoing support to help children process their emotions, maintain connections and adjust to change in a healthy and resilient manner.

Despite these difficulties, our dedication, compassion and resilience play a vital role in providing stability, support and healing. By recognising and addressing the challenges inherent in foster care, we contribute to creating a nurturing and empowering environment where children can thrive.

Fostering comes with its share of challenges, but it's also filled with moments of profound joy and fulfilment that make the journey incredibly rewarding:

- Witnessing growth and development.
- Creating lasting bonds and meaningful connections.
- Celebrating milestones.
- Reinforcing a sense of love.
- Making a positive impact.
- Receiving gratitude.

The relationship of biological family and importance of connection.

Overall, the moments of joy and fulfilment in fostering serve as powerful reminders of the profound difference we are making in the lives of vulnerable children. Despite the challenges, the rewards of fostering in the form of love, growth and positive impact make the journey deeply worthwhile.

LESSONS LEARNED: WISDOM FROM MOTHERHOOD

LOVE KNOWS NO BOUNDARIES

Fostering has taught me that love transcends biology and genetics. I've witnessed firsthand the power of love to create bonds that are just as strong and meaningful as those formed through blood ties. Love in foster care is unconditional, resilient and capable of overcoming obstacles and challenges. It's a reminder that love knows no boundaries and can thrive in the most unexpected of circumstances.

RESILIENCE IS KEY

Fostering has shown me the remarkable resilience of the human spirit. I've seen children overcome adversity, trauma and loss with courage and determination. Their resilience has inspired me to persevere in the face of my own challenges and setbacks, knowing that strength and resilience can be cultivated, even in the most difficult circumstances. It has taught me that resilience isn't just about bouncing back from adversity, it's about growing stronger and more resilient as a result of it.

FAMILY IS DEFINED BY LOVE

I've come to understand that family is not defined by blood, but by love, care and support. I've seen how a nurturing and supportive environment can transform strangers into family, creating bonds that are just as strong and meaningful as those shared by biological relatives. Fostering has expanded my definition of family to include, not only those connected by blood, but also those connected by love and shared experiences.

EVERY CHILD DESERVES A CHANCE

Fostering has reinforced my belief in the inherent worth and potential of every child. Every child deserves a chance to thrive, regardless of their background or circumstances. My experiences have fuelled my commitment to advocate for the rights and wellbeing of vulnerable

223

children, ensuring they have access to the love, support and opportunities they need to reach their full potential.

GRATITUDE FOR THE JOURNEY

Fostering has taught me to appreciate the journey itself – the ups and downs, the challenges and triumphs, the joys and sorrows. I've learned to cherish the moments of connection, growth and transformation that make the journey worthwhile. Through fostering, I've discovered the true meaning of love, resilience and family, and I am grateful for the opportunity to make a positive difference in the lives of vulnerable children.

THE ENDLESS JOURNEY OF MOTHERHOOD

The journey of fostering has illuminated the universal nature of motherhood and the enduring bond that connects all mothers, whether human or animal. Despite differences in species, culture or circumstance, the essence of motherhood remains constant; a deep and unwavering love that transcends boundaries and defies definition.

I have witnessed firsthand the profound instinctual drive shared by all mothers to protect, nurture and care for their young. Whether it's the fierce protection of a lioness defending her cubs in the savannah or the tender embrace of a human mother comforting her child in the darkness of night, the bond between mother and child is a testament to the power of love in its purest form.

In the tapestry of life, the threads of motherhood weave a common narrative of sacrifice and unwavering devotion. It is a narrative that transcends species, language and culture, reminding us of our shared humanity and interconnectedness.

As I reflect on my journey as a foster mother, I am humbled by the universal truths I have encountered: the resilience of the human spirit;

the transformative power of love; and the enduring bond that connects all mothers, human and animal alike. In the end, it is this bond that sustains us, inspires us, and reminds us of the beauty and complexity of the human experience.

As I close this chapter, I want to leave you with a sense of hope and inspiration, knowing that the journey of fostering and motherhood, while challenging, is also profoundly rewarding. It is a journey marked by moments of joy, resilience and profound connection that transcend the difficulties and obstacles along the way.

In the world of fostering, I have witnessed the transformative power of love to heal wounds, nurture growth and ignite hope in the hearts of vulnerable children. I have seen the incredible strength and resilience of both the children in my care and fellow foster carers, who navigate the complexities of the foster care system with courage and determination.

Despite the challenges and uncertainties that come with fostering, there is beauty and meaning to be found in the small moments of connection, growth and triumph. Whether it's witnessing a child's first smile after overcoming adversity, or celebrating their achievements and milestones along the way, fostering is a journey filled with countless reasons to hope and believe in the possibility *of anything*.

So, to anyone considering the path of fostering or embarking on their journey of motherhood, I offer these words of encouragement:

Embrace the challenges, cherish the moments of joy and never underestimate the profound impact of love and compassion in shaping the lives of those in your care. Know that your efforts, however small they may seem, are making a difference in the world and leaving a lasting legacy of hope, resilience and love.

ABOUT SANDRA

A social entrepreneur; wellness advocate, award-winning author; speaker; professional youth practitioner and youth service consultant; fashion (runway and photographic) creative director and producer; experienced grooming and deportment educator; and public relations/media consultant, Sandra is described by many as a humble leader, change maker and social justice advocate, with a wealth of knowledge and experience spanning across the not-for-profit, local & state government and business sectors, working in the youth, community and social services sector of australia for the past twenty-six years. sandra is employed full-time as a public servant, working full-time, and undertaking various other volunteer roles within the community.

In 2015, Sandra co-founded Blue Beanie Projects, a registered health promotion charity aimed at reducing remote youth suicide rates and increasing regional & remote young people's access to professional, ethical & sustainable youth services. Blue Beanie work with young people to increase their social & emotional wellbeing, confidence, resilience, self-esteem & connection to community. Having lived & worked in some of Australia's most isolated & remote communities for most of her career, developing and implementing successful culturally appropriate youth service models, she is particularly experienced and a passionate advocate for service needs of young people & youth workers in remote areas; and improving funding, training & resources for youth workers.

'I am extremely fortunate to have shared some of my greatest passions in life with my husband Dave, who is incredibly supportive of me. Together we co-founded Blue Beanie Projects; we co-owned and managed Soul Café in Karratha; and the most treasured joy of both of our lives are our children. We made a very conscious and well thought out decision many years ago, to not have biological children. Together we chose to become foster carers. Through our work in community and youth services we saw the reality of children and teens without homes, moving between foster placements, group homes, crisis accommodation hostels and experiencing varying degrees of homelessness.

'It is what ultimately inspired us to become carers. We respect that this lifestyle choice is not for all families, but for us we asked why would we bring children into this world ourselves when there are so many children without homes and families already? People often ask us "why don't you have a family of your own?"; "don't you want to have your own kids?"; "why would you choose to take on other people's problems?" Our response is simple – our children, THEY ARE OUR OWN. We love them, care for them and will always be their mum and dad. You don't have to be biologically related to a child to call them your son or daughter. Family is so much more than biology, genetic makeup or DNA.

'As a mum, I raise my boys to be dreamers and believers; I want my boys to know that anything is possible for them and they can achieve anything they believe they can. We teach them every day, the importance of inclusivity, acceptance, understanding, empathy, kindness, speaking up for those who are silenced, gender diversity. The list is endless really, but the point is, each and every day we educate, mentor, guide, instil these very things into our children; all while balancing everyday life, work commitments, and above all keeping our boys connected to their Aboriginal culture, country and families. Educating them about Australian history and speaking to them of the truth of their ancestors, while continually reminding them of the resilience and courage of their people – those who walked before them for so many tens of thousands of years. Every day, building their pride, strength and ability to speak up even when their lips shake or their chins quiver. Teaching them to be advocates, social warriors and world changers.

'I love that these attributes and values are embodied not only in my youth work profession, but that I am able to weave them through my daily life, my friendships and with my family.'

MICHELLE WEITERING
A BELIEVER

When the phone rings at 2am you know it's not someone asking you for a cup of sugar. It doesn't matter what your week has looked like, how busy you were at work, how many projects you've juggled whilst running a smooth household. *Seemingly* smooth household – you try. Nope. As soon as that phone rings at that hour despite your exhaustion of the day, week or your entire life – you are immediately wide awake, as if you've just snorted a pack of whizz-fizz mixed with Berrocca.

You're reaching for the light switch as you hunt for your discarded bra and pull-on shoes and the dress you wore out the night before. You grab the car keys as you listen to the voice on the other end of the phone, informing you that your son has deliberately self-harmed and is currently on his way to the hospital via ambulance.

You're numb. Yet you feel everything. Your mind goes carefully blank as you force yourself not to go into overdrive. You're on auto-pilot mode now, robot-like as you get in the car and head safely towards the hospital.

'He's going to be fine, he's going to be totally fine,' you whisper to yourself every second as you draw closer to the hospital, praying for it to be true. You have faith. But you're human. You also feel the fear of the unknown. Finally, you pull up and park, then get out of the vehicle and quickly race towards the emergency entrance, taking deep breaths as you prepare for a battle of emotions.

Approaching the desk, you say your son's name and mention he should be arriving via ambulance. 'Yes,' the nurse informs you. 'He's on his way. Please take a seat and I'll let you know when he arrives.'

You thank the nurse politely then sit, cross your legs and pray to those you love … 'Please let him be alright.'

It felt like hours you were sitting there with your turbulent thoughts, but in fact it hadn't been too long at all when the nurse approaches you and says quietly, 'He's arrived and is with the mental health team. I can take you to him now.'

You nod, relieved to hear it and you hastily get to your feet, grateful your legs are holding you up as you follow her. You've been here before, to emergency. Several times over the years. From little worries to bigger issues; finding blood in your baby's poo, swollen tonsils, broken finger, a burst appendix and so on and so forth. But you're not heading towards the rooms that you normally would. No. You're being taken into the secure mental health ward, and into a large room that is filled with soft padded furniture.

You walk in behind the nurse and feel momentarily confused. She's made a mistake and brought you to the wrong room. This lost soul before you isn't your son. You turn away, then freeze, pausing for a moment before slowly turning back as the realisation hits you.

This *devastated,* injured soul is yours.

Yet, only fifteen hours ago when you last saw him, he had long silky hair. Now it's shaved short on a pale head. Fifteen hours ago his eyes were bright and filled with kindness and humour. Now, vacant dark pools are filled with utter grief and hopelessness. Those sad eyes aren't meeting yours. You calmly go to his side; you don't want to startle him or overwhelm him with your barrage of emotions. It's painfully obvious he has plenty of his own to deal with himself.

The nurse asks you if you're alright. You nod, forcing a smile you hope doesn't look deranged.

'We've given him diazepam for the moment - that will calm him. The doctors won't be in till 8am but the mental health team will be checking in again shortly. His wounds have been dressed and the bleeding is under control. If there's anything you need, just inform the team when they pop in.'

'Thanks,' you think you whisper, thinking it was an awfully long time between now and the doctors' shift starting, but that's the public system for you. And all in all – in *that* moment, you're grateful for the support your son is receiving.

The door closes and you kneel before your son, opening your arms as he falls into them, sobbing – 'I'm sorry, I'm so sorry …' His anguished apology breaks your heart.

'No, no. There's nothing to be sorry for. It's okay, love … it's okay. I love you so much.' You soothe, throat tightening as you gather his shaking body carefully in your arms, mindful not to hurt him further. His left arm is wrapped in a thick bandage from wrist to elbow and you are morbidly curious about the damage he has done to himself. *Your poor baby.*

You're so damn grateful you've been left alone together in that moment, so he can release his pent-up tears freely. You think about the journey he's had in the time you were away from him. The *one* night you'd been away from home to spend time in the city with work colleagues and then sleep at your girlfriend's house. The *one* night where he had been safe at home with his father and brother.

One.

Night.

Your world really can change in a heartbeat. *It reminds you again to live every day to it's fullest. Love unapologetically and with fierce joy. Tomorrow isn't guaranteed.*

His cries quieten before he leans back in the chair and becomes eerily despondent. You sit beside him without crowding him, hand on his knee as you silently let him know you are there. There are a million questions racing through your mind, desperate to ask him – but you know now is not that time.

As you sit in silence, your eyes wander around the room noticing the over-large furniture that looked like it could be in a *SpongeBob Squarepants* scene. Furniture that belonged to Patrick the loveable starfish. All velcroid together and squishy to sit on. You spot blood on the other side of the room and a pile of dried vomit in front of the other salmon pink couch. A small part of you is frustrated that your son has been placed in a used, dirty room – but your common sense knows the system. Perhaps the patient beforehand had a severe crisis and the care team hurriedly moved onto the next case; the filthy floor forgotten. Despite your silent guessed justification, it still frustrates you.

The staff buzz in and out of the emergency office like a scene from *Nurse Jackie* on mute, as you watch on with tired eyes. No matter what time it is when you're in a hospital, that time always feels warped. Especially anytime after midnight.

As you sit together in that large room, warped-time ticks by in the disturbing way that it does. You wish you could form a decent, constructive, supportive sentence from the frazzled words that are filtering through your head, yet you're worried that anything you might say could upset your son. You want him to know you're strong and in control and are nothing but a safe space for him. That no matter what is going on in his mind, he would feel, that despite his predicament, you were a solid, reliable piece in his crumbling world that you've always tried to be.

You exhaust yourself with your inner conversations and are grateful when a mental health team member enters and interrupts you to have an actual private conversation with your son. You stand out in the corridor, giving him the chance to extract as much information from your son in order to help him as much as possible. You have faith that the support from here on out is going to be exactly what your son and family need. It really does take a village, and not just in turbulent times. And not just a village. A community of knowledgeable and skilled individuals.

In your moment alone, you reflect on the past twenty-two years that you've had children. The utter highs and those lows that almost break you as a parent. This isn't your first experience of feeling utter helplessness. It hasn't been the first time you've been fearful of the possibility of losing your son. Although this knowledge doesn't make this experience any less frightening or heartbreaking. And in those times, you've always had support, guidance and love from your clan and community alike. You've done your part too, to gain insight and education in the field of mental health. Yet above and beyond … first and foremost. You. Are. A. Mum.

An unreasonable bite of guilt nips at your heart as you wonder if this would have happened if you'd been home. You wonder too, how much more you can bare and carry on as a sane human. You feel a numb coping mechanism settle over you at the odd hour, as if to protect you. Moments of your life, and every single battle you've experienced, play behind your closed lids like a movie trailer from a horror-thriller genre, with an unpleasant beat of comedy.

Although you've suffered plenty in your own personal story – you *know* it's given you the inner strength to quietly conquer anything that's thrown your way. Yet despite the demons you've slain your own past, *nothing* will ever compare to the pain of watching your children suffer ordeals that this life, this *era,* seems to be filled with for his generation. If only we could rewind time and dump us all back in the eighties.

How much heartache can a parent take? A lot, incidentally … and apparently it's all part of the job description. Ask any parent.

Suddenly it's your turn to talk to the gentleman with your son's consent, and looking back you know that Alan deserves a gold star for his role as a mental-health-whatever-his-full-title-is. He asks you if you know what bought the DSH on, and you say *no, you weren't at home when it happened.* Then you justify your answer, hoping not to look like a shitty neglectful mother because it was the *one* night you weren't home, not counting your shift work.

As a mental health and disability support worker who works up to sixteen-hour shifts, you *know* deep down that you're entitled to self-care, yet in that moment, after what had occurred in your absence, and in your total exhausted, shocked state … you wonder. Once the conversation is finished you ask Alan if there's a bucket and mop you can use.

He arches a brow and looks confused. You explain about the vomit and blood. He is mortified and moves your son to an identical, but extremely clean room … with apologies.

You spend several more hours with your son, who has been given another calming sedative, and before he slips off to sleep, he says in a broken whisper … 'I'm so ashamed, Mum … I feel so ashamed.'

As if your heart could break any more. The self-stigma and shame that attempted suicide can bring with it is a heavy thing to carry.

'No, love, you've done nothing to be ashamed of. I'm just so glad you're still here. I love you so much … sleep now … it's going to be okay,' you whisper, not wanting to ever let him go.

What else could you say? You know he's emotionally and physically exhausted. Not to mention the physical and mental pain he is going through. You know sleep is essentially what he needs right now. Once he drifts off, Alan, the kind gold-star-deserving-man, returns and saves you with a cup of tea. After he leaves, you cling to that hot cup like it could save you, taking tiny sips to make it last. The staff are too busy, and this will most likely be the last tea you'll get. You watch your son sleep, desperate to know what brought this action on. What broke him, or his heart, to this extent? Minutes tick by into hours and finally on the tenth hour, after ten staples, six stitches, too many steri strips to count and a follow-up conversation with the mental health team, you are on your way home.

For the next week CATT – Crisis Assessment Treatment Team – come to visit your son every day to make sure he is feeling safe, heard and supported. They are sensational souls completely qualified to be in the field they've signed up for. Not only caring, in every sense of the word, but also share several options with your son to see what services he may be interested in moving forward, to assist in supporting him.

Your son has selected to enter into a ninety-day service program with HOPE – Hospital Outreach Post-Suicidal Engagement. He has continued going to school at the David Scott School in Frankston, who also provide phenomenal wellbeing support.

Your pride in him has always been enormous. You've always said he was an angel born without wings. A sensitive soul, yes. Caring – always. Empathetic, passionate, gracious and mature. Has a great sense of humour, is hardworking and applies himself to everything he decides to have a go at. But watching him be so courteous to so many strangers that trickle through your backyard during a time where he's not eating, not sleeping and wearing his broken, shattered heart beneath his sleeve and bandages, well, *pride* doesn't cut it. He is the legend you've always told him he is.

Your beautiful, hurting boy *will* be okay. He's pulling air into his lungs which makes it possible for you and your little family to do the same, without falling to pieces. Sure, you're tired. *Hell*, you're exhausted. And even though you are, you can't sleep. That's the joy of trauma. And for an extra treat, there's even a touch of PTSD floating under the surface to keep it company. But your son is *alive*, and so you will honour *that* and *him*. You'll continue your *keep-it-together-mantra* and do what needs to be done no matter what. That's what you signed up for when you decided to have, and raise, children.

The answers as to why your son cut deeply into layers of his skin and muscle over sixty-three times with a razor isn't for these worthy readers. Yet, you want to share the courage it has taken your son to continue moving forward, with faith, that he *is worthy*. Faith that he is supported within his world of family and friends, teachers and peers. Faith that the mental health system in Victoria, Australia, will provide a comprehensive, supportive plan for him.

During this time that has nearly brought your family to its knees …
your son has felt cocooned by more than just a loving family; but by an
army of light and love that is impenetrable. That in itself, has given him
quiet confidence to move forward with stealth. You hold back your tears
of sorrow and pride when he holds his head high and sees his worthiness.
Finally … he sees what you've seen all along. You always had the faith
that he would.

Now … you can breathe with your heart in one piece. All will be
well. You have faith.

LIFELINE 131114

SuicideLine Victoria; Suicide prevention – 1300 651 251

Suicide Call Back – 1300 659 467

Beyond Blue Suicide Safety Plan – beyondblue.org.au

ABOUT MICHELLE

Mickey Martin is a romantic writer at heart who feels it is important to leave the reader with messages of hope and healing. Her books are filled with casts of colourful, resilient characters who thrive and survive hardships and trauma, allowing the reader to draw endless inspiration from memorable faces who have backbones of steel and hearts of gold as they go in search of their 'happily ever after.'

Mickey is also a non-fiction writer under her married name, Michelle Weitering. Here she seeks to write and make a difference, inviting the reader to question what more they can do to make our world a better place, with acts of kindness. As a mental health support worker, and advocate, she uses her writing to become a voice for those living and dealing with issues such as anxiety, depression, and other important social issues surrounding mental illness in order to raise awareness for mental health.

Mickey is celebrating her love for her home state, Victoria – stretching from the Western District, The Golden Triangle and The Mornington Peninsula, with her new series: *The Victoria Collection*.

Soul Keepers of Glenormiston was the inspiration behind this series, along with *Obsidian Souls*. This is her way of celebrating the beauty of

Victoria, and the memories she has made within each town. *A Chilling Summer in Inglewood* is set in the Golden Triangle, where her family have lived for five generations, and *Sweet Water Creek,* in Frankston. The gateway to the Mornington Peninsula, where she resides with her with her scrumptious, supportive husband, Jade and their two gorgeous sons, Jesse and Zane. Mickey is hoping to do for Victoria Tourism, what *Outlander* did for Scotland, with this collection.

Mickey is a multi-award-winning author, and shareholder with MMH PRESS, and is a member of the Romance Writers of Australia, Writers Victoria and the Peninsula Writers' Club, where she adores connecting with and supporting others on their writing journey. Mickey adores hearing from her readers, and you can connect with her on the following links.

www.instagram.com/mickeymartinbooks
www.facebok.com/michelle.weitering

KIRSTY DREDGE
TAKE THE TIME IT TAKES

'MUUUUUUUMMMMMM!' My peaceful bubble shatters into a million pieces as the sudden sounds of screaming and feet pounding down the hallway gets closer. At that moment, the cat pukes on the carpet, a car alarm shrieks loudly, a phone rings and my husband leaps out of bed realising he's going to be late for work.

I drag my bones out of bed, throw on some clothes, twist my hair up in a scruffy bun and step out into the eye of the storm. My twins wake up really early, so when I emerge there is usually already mess somewhere. Today, it's the latest version of their blanket fort using all six dining chairs, four stools, the entire linen cupboard and half the couch plus all twenty-three members of Zoe's impressive *Squishmallow* collection.

The first argument of the day follows shortly after breakfast; clean up the fort. But not wanting to ruin their handiwork, they team up and convince me they will get more English done from inside the lounge room fortress. So, to get things moving, I compromise the comfort of sitting up at the table with ample space and contort myself through the door (the legs of a dining chair), so we can get started.

After twenty minutes in the sweat-lodge, I'm desperate to come up for air so leave them to it and pack away the dishes, throw in a load of washing, tidy up, do the floors and feed the cats.

Housework part 1: done.

'Muuuuuummmm … What's next?' I crawl back into the parent torture chamber to start their maths lesson. They're starting to fidget, so after maths we take a yoga and snack (ahem, coffee) break before moving onto science, ukulele practice and a little Spanish, taking us through to lunchtime.

Homeschool: done. Now to start work.

I start my work day with lunch, eating at my desk so I can dive straight into my inbox and squeeze in some productive hours on the latest website project before I have to drive Zoe to dance. Today is also the day I put my big girl grumpy pants on and call my builder, who, for weeks, has not responded to emails about my house.

Work: done.

Now for the evening rush.

Being morning people, leaving the house in the afternoon is not a straightforward process for my girls. Getting them ready to go out is like herding cats, so by 3:30pm I start the process of reminding them to put some clothes on while I finish up at my desk.

We just make it on time. Zoe runs into her class and the timer starts for me and Aaliyah. We have one-and-a-half-hour to drive to the stables, feed the horses, then run into the fresh produce shop and stock up for the week, before picking Zoe up on the way home.

Horses, grocery shopping and dance: done.

Now home for dinner and housework part 2: shower, check in with work, read something and crawl into bed by 9:30 to do it all again tomorrow!

Not every day is like this. Some days I wake up early enough for a morning walk in blissful, reflective solitude. Some days I spend hours playing with or riding my horse, and on others I meditate, stretch and roll before bed. But even on those rare unicorn days, I am compelled to do something, no matter how small, towards my goals. If I don't do *something*, I feel itchy and uncomfortable in my skin.

Some days it takes every scrap of grit and determination I have just to roll out of bed and face the morning chaos. But I wouldn't give up a single thing … well … except building a house. Two and a half years in and we still don't even have a roof. I wouldn't recommend that stress to anyone. Say it with me: *buy established!*

If it wasn't for our builder messing us around with contracts, we would have never considered homeschooling.

Holding it together when my daughter is having a meltdown over some difficult maths problem is incredibly emotionally draining. Then there's staying up to date with the homeschool chat groups, spending my weekends planning out activities and then actually walking them through their lessons each day. But even with the emotional challenges and extra work, it has been the best thing I have ever done for them. They are more confident, happy little people, who have more than caught up academically and socially. They have stronger friendships than they ever did at school. Our homeschool community is incredible here in WA and I am so grateful to all the amazing families we have connected with.

And I couldn't homeschool without my business. The uncertainty of future income is relentless, but I love the flexibility my business allows me to have, working around my life, rather than living around my work. I absolutely adore my ever-inspiring clients who I am so blessed to work with. They are some of the most amazing business owners, authors and creators in the world!

Finally, I would be a basket case if it wasn't for my horse, Steve. He is a thoroughbred with a lot of baggage, thanks to his previous long and unforgiving career as a race horse. Although some days it's hard to find the energy to get in the car and it's been a roller-coaster for two years working through his many layers of issues, the time with him is my happy place. He has such a fun, expressive extrovert personality, you can't help but grin at his daily dance for dinner. At the end of a big day of tantrums, designing websites and client calls, a hug from Steve melts it all away.

It's a tangled mess of commitments, but it mostly works. To carry all of these huge time- consumers, I have spent a great deal of time experimenting with different tools that enable me to juggle it all without burning myself out completely. I'm still constantly changing things, but there are a handful of core values and philosophies that underpin everything else.

Take the time it takes …

In the immortal words of one of my horsemanship gurus: *Take the time it takes, so it takes less time.*

Ever since I first heard that phrase more than fifteen years ago, these words have been part of my life philosophy. It's making short-term sacrifices for long-term gain. It's spending the time, now, to set up automated processes in your business that save you time next week. It's decluttering your home and workspace so there is less to clean and keep organised. It's allowing your children to fail, working through the frustration of learning something new so they can do it for themselves later.

Living by this philosophy, I think, has contributed to my twins being such capable young people. People are often surprised to hear that they have been cooking, using the oven and cutting vegetables themselves since before age seven. They do the dishes (wash, dry and put away), they do laundry and clean their own bathroom – and these are not paid chores.

As I wrote that last paragraph, I was debating if it should be included; *What if they judge me harshly or think I'm neglecting my kids? What if they think it's too much for their age?*

My inner critic is telling me to find something else to write about, but my inner lioness is louder. She's roaring at me that I spend the time teaching my kids all of this for a reason. It's given them confidence, strength and coordination, and the small reprieve I get from doing *everything* for them is only a side-benefit. I take the time to teach them and get to enjoy the pride and joy on their faces when they prepare lunch for us all. Take the time it takes …

Every day in my business, I see budding entrepreneurs, wearing rose-coloured glasses, getting swept away in the overwhelming current of marketing hacks, productivity tools and business gurus online. They spin their wheels, working sixty-plus hours per week, doing all the busywork, with little to show for it at the end of the week. Burning the candle at both ends, always on the edge of complete exhaustion – no wonder they're constantly looking for something better!

Growing up, watching my parents run their engineering firm, working with clients in all different industries and having started multiple ventures myself, there is one vital key that all the success stories appear to have; a leader within the organisation who takes the time to plan and work out what comes next in a methodical, logical way (so it takes less time!). To avoid becoming another failed business statistic, don't fall prey to shiny object syndrome and allow anything to lead you off the path. Change is good, growth is great, but spreading yourself thin with too many tools, marketing channels or conflicting advice will only lead to overwhelm. Research, plan ahead and shut out the noise. Take the time it takes …

LEAN ON YOUR TRIBE

At around seven years old, I moved to Alice Springs in Australia's beating heart with my parents and my sister. Living seventeen hours up the road from my closest grandmother and with Dad frequently away on bush trips, meant that Mum was left alone with us kids … a lot. She's fiercely independent, but even the most reclusive hermit needs community sometimes!

I continued Mum's habitual independence until I had my kids. At first, I managed pretty well. I had twins, but I also had two arms and two boobs (my hat goes off to those with triplets!). My amazing husband has always been extremely hands-on and we have shared the job equally. But when they got up and moving, that's when things started to get tricky.

Taking them to the playground when Scott was at work was always more of a workout for me than them because they never wanted to go in the same direction. Thankfully, I had friends with babies around the same age, so we could get together and help each other out. I could not imagine attempting to go through those long days and sleepless nights again without my tribe.

You absolutely can have it all … but you cannot do it all by yourself! Whether your tribe is blood relatives or friends, lean on them fearlessly and without guilt.

Be prepared to go against the grain and never compromise your own values to fit in.

I have never been trendy or really cared what anyone else was doing. I homeschool, run my own business, use essential oils extensively in my low-tox home, brew kombucha and ferment my own kraut. Even with my horses, I go against the 'normal' and practice natural horsemanship techniques instead of the mainstream training methods.

While most people are accepting of these things on a surface level, if things get tough their advice is often to step back in line with mainstream. 'Kids driving you mad? Put them back in school! Business having a bad month? Get a J.O.B. Horse playing up? Send him off to a trainer. Feeling tired? Here's some chocolate, you deserve it!'

While they always have good intentions and just want to help, advice like that can be irritating and sometimes hard to know what to do. In the moment, flex those paws and stay grounded and in alignment with your own values. You've got this.

WORK WITH THE SEASONS, NOT AGAINST THEM

Human superiority has got us habitually thinking we can overpower nature. Artificial lights break our natural sleep cycles, modern agriculture has us eating tropical fruit in the middle of winter and being joined at the hip to our mobile devices twenty-four seven has our brains taking in new information all day long. We sit in the car to get to work, sit all day at the desk, sit in the car to get home, then sit on the couch to watch TV. We're more anxious, overweight and unfit than ever before in human history.

The underpinning truth is nature ebbs and flows. There is supposed to be phases of feast and famine, productivity and rest, growth and decay. Life flows better when you work with the seasons, weather patterns and your own internal seasons and cycles. Eat more seasonal produce and without trying, you'll get more of the nutrients you need, at the time of year that your body needs it. Work with your natural energy cycles; work when you're at your most focused and rest when you need to. For women, it's easier to do cardio during the high energy follicular stage of their cycle.

By tweaking your timing to live more in sync with your internal cycles and the seasons, you'll find everything takes less discipline and is considerably more enjoyable.

REST OFTEN AND DO IT MINDFULLY

Despite what we might like to think, humans are not machines. In my early twenties (before kids), I learned this the hard way. I had just opened my commercial office space in Berri, South Australia. I was so motivated that every waking moment was dedicated to growing my new business. I was in the office six to seven days a week and scarcely spending any time with my horse.

While I wasn't eating too badly, I was living on caffeine and my stress was off the charts, while I tried to prove to everyone around me, I could make it. At the end of my first year, I reached a point where it was really starting to affect my health. I credit my age as the only reason I didn't completely burn out.

After a series of uncomfortable tests, I was diagnosed with IBS, given a list of foods to avoid and sent on my way. Thanks for coming. At age twenty-two, I didn't want to live married to the toilet, so I set out to find a better solution. We closed up the business, moved back to Alice Springs and I started studying nutrition. Through my multiple studies in natural health, I adopted some new healthy habits that eliminated my gut issues.

Even over all the food, supplements and exercise, it's mindfulness and meditation training that's b e e n the most transformational for me. Working so many hours in the business, I would come home exhausted. So I'd get changed, see the sun for twenty minutes while I fed my horse, then collapse on the couch to binge through whatever show we were watching. Everywhere I went, my brain was being force-fed information, even in the car I was listening to podcasts. Always consuming something.

When I first started to meditate regularly, it was hard. Even five minutes of breathwork was awful, I hated it! But knowing something had to change, I stuck it out and after just a couple of days I felt myself being more resilient to stressors, able to sleep better and having more mental clarity.

So rest often, but don't do it in front of a device! These days we need to rest our mind more than our body, so turn off the screens, put down the book and go sniff some flowers.

Eat mindfully. Soak in a bath. Get a massage. Do the breathwork. My favourite is sitting out in the paddock watching my horse just do his thing. He's such a cheerful idiot I can't help but feel lighter in his company.

To recap; carefully plan and take the time it takes so it takes less time, lean on your tribe, do you without compromise, live naturally with the seasons and rest often. You've got this.

ABOUT KIRSTY

Kirsty Dredge is a professional website designer and digital creative. She grew up in the red centre, Alice Springs NT, and now lives in Rockingham WA with her husband and twin daughters.

Through her business Thorn Creative, Kirsty supports small businesses, start ups and authors to build and grow online through beautiful, functional and effective website design.

For a bit of fun, Kirsty also creates a range of digital products on her personal website kirstyjade.com, including digital planners, journals and other art projects.

When Kirsty's not homeschooling her twins, working on a client website or another digital project, you'll find her out exploring, or swinging in the hammock with her nose in a good book.

MEG PRICOLO
EMERGING
UNMASKED

I'd been married for nineteen years when I reached a pivotal point in my life; my heart and soul were telling me that something had to give. The hardest decision I've ever made. When I did leave my marriage, people were shocked. I had worn the mask of positivity for so many years, pretending everything was fabulous which, of course, was not the case. I lived a materialistic and addictive life, always trying to fill a void. Never feeling fully in control of my own decisions.

From about the age of fifteen, I had experienced significant periods of anxiety and depression, including three bouts of post-natal depression. My body was desperately trying to send me messages, but I didn't listen. Years after medical issues and finally surgery on my neck I again hit rock bottom and still refused to listen. My soul was trying to communicate with me for decades, but I didn't have faith in myself. I lived externally to everything; it was always someone else's fault.

I know any big change in life takes strength and courage, but at the time, I didn't believe I was being courageous, it just felt like an 'escape'. I always thought I was missing out on the life I felt I wanted, without gratitude for my life and abundances. Not living in the present.

The relationship with my kids was my priority, but it didn't show up that way at the time. I felt I'd ruined everyone's lives. Although I was making the change 'for me', I was still so focused on everyone else. Even when I'd made the decision and followed my heart's path, I was thinking of how everyone else was impacted, so my time was spent negotiating my thoughts about how to keep everyone else happy. Of course, I heard lots of negatives, the most common being, 'she's so selfish', but fast-forward to today, my kids, their dad and I acknowledge that it was 'the best decision I ever made' … for all of us.

The issue is that when you don't listen to your heart and soul, you stay stuck in everyone else's vibration. You can't do that. If you want to be satisfied in life, you've got to believe and live in the vibration of the person you are choosing to become.

I didn't truly understand it then, but I was stuck there, knowing I just had to get out. For so many years my mental health was compromised. I still have moments when I feel I could slip into depression, but I can honour that now and recognise it as part of the journey. Now in my fifties and having had a late ADHD diagnosis and being neurodivergent, I am finally beginning to put the pieces of the puzzle together and understand myself more. My focus is on my self-care. I recognise these thoughts more quickly now than in past years – they remind me to prioritise myself, my studies, my reflections and my journey of uncovering the darker parts of me that need light to shine on them.

I've come to learn the principles of how to raise my vibration. We are all going to experience times when it feels like 'everything's gone to crap. Everything's shit', but by living in love and authenticity I can see a way to move through what's holding me back. I can see the transformation in how I see things – the butterfly has emerged.

For so many years, I was closed off, living in the energy of others rather than my own. People called me a 'social butterfly', and for a long time, I believed that's who I was. But now, I can see the truth – I wasn't just adapting; I was reacting. Masking, as part of my autism, shaped the personality I created, a version of myself built for survival rather than living from my own choices and desires and being authentic.

But I am no longer that person. I've been through my cocoon phase, peeling back the layers, doing the deep, sometimes painful work of transformation. And now, I have emerged – not as a version shaped by others, but as the truest form of myself, unmasked and free.

I'm in control of my thoughts and I don't give that control to anyone else anymore. Of course, I still have doubts, but I know I have the tools to acknowledge the feeling, flip it and focus on what I want and who I want to serve. This continues to change my life, but it also changes other people's lives around me.

We're all human, and there are days when we must go into hibernation, as we know we are unable to make the best decisions for ourselves or others in that state. I don't make decisions or take action on those days. Sometimes, we need to ride them out and let them pass. Before these were days of hiding and fear, now they are a choice, honouring my boundaries, my strengths and myself.

I used to push and push to the point where it impacted my family's and loved ones' lives. I admit I'm not perfect in this area, as I'm still evolving in creating change. I do my best not to berate myself for it anymore. I've had conversations with my partner and family in just the last few weeks to remind them that when I am in these transitional times not to take it personally if I shut myself away. It's not their behaviour or anything they have done, it's all about me and what I feel I need to do, in the moment, to achieve my goals. I am reminded that I am not responsible for others' happiness. We must all prioritise ourselves if we want to bring our best self to any relationship.

All mums would know that we want to put our kids as the number-one priority, but we can't give them our best self unless we prioritise ourselves first. When I started to prioritise myself, I felt I was getting backlash and judgement from others, but then I recognised that the judgement was my own – no-one else's.

Once you align with your values to create the life you love, your kids benefit from your high vibration and happy self. We can't compromise all of ourselves for motherhood, if we do, we're showing our kids how to compromise themselves. By taking action towards fulfilling ourselves, we're showing them to fulfil themselves, because they learn more from our actions than they do from our words.

I've seen the difference this has made with my kids, particularly with my eldest, who's on the autism spectrum. He has to learn differently because his mind is wired differently. I've had people say crazy things, like, 'He'll grow out of it,' or, 'There's so much that he can't do,' but I have faith that he can find more than one way to achieve his goals. We keep moving forward because we don't know our greatest triumphs until we've achieved them. There's always judgement until success happens.

It's the little things together, even the negative ones, that make us unique. It's the specialist knowledge we accumulate over time, and every adversity brings with it the seed of greater or equivalent benefit. All that I went through, the lessons I learned from that, is exactly why I'm here now and why I am able to serve others.

How wonderful that the things I'm changing in my life are healing down through my hereditary line. During a meditation, I saw the line start to light up and it kept lighting up as it got closer. I felt my grandmothers acknowledge that I was the one changing the repetitive cycle. Instead of going round and round teaching our daughters to behave the same way throughout generations, my actions continue to create a positive wave of change.

When I see my daughters and some of their behaviours, even my nieces and nephews, I can see how they are acting on their genetic programming, but that too now is beginning to change. When my kids see me in a low vibration, they say to me, 'Come on, Mum, you know better than that!' Particularly my middle daughter, who's turning twenty-one this year, she is very aware and tuned in to her own psyche. She has never studied personal awareness and or self-development. She's picking up on it because I've allowed that opening. What an incredible gift.

And that's what I'd like to leave you with now. The gift of awareness that you can change your life with stealth and faith. You can align with your highest vibration and create the life of your dreams.

When I left my marriage and my mental health improved so dramatically and I began developing a positive mental attitude, my mum came to me one day and said, 'Wouldn't it have been fantastic if you'd have had YOU now, back then?' It's about adopting new principles for life, even when you don't think you are ready. I could have found these life principles earlier, but I wouldn't have accumulated the knowledge I needed and the experiences I had to create my uniqueness as it is today.

Change can, but doesn't always, happen overnight. It takes courage, self-belief and faith to get you there. I wish you love, light and growth as you progress on your journey.

Big love.

ABOUT MEG

Meg Pricolo is a powerful storyteller and advocate for personal transformation, drawing from her own journey of self-discovery and resilience. Megan bravely chose to listen to her heart and soul, embarking on a courageous path that would ultimately lead to profound personal growth and healing.

A Mum, neurosparkly queen, transformation coach, mentor and healer. Meg from an early age grappled with anxiety and depression, challenges that were compounded by the responsibilities of motherhood and life's unexpected turns.

Her journey included overcoming post-natal depression, confronting medical issues, and embracing a late ADHD and autism diagnosis, all of which continue to shape her understanding of herself and the world around her.

With a unique blend of vulnerability and strength, Meg continues to inspire others to embrace their true selves and pursue the life of their dreams.

WENDY SHANNON
MAKING SPACE FOR GRIEF

I sat in the hospital corridor, in a daze, watching as the cleaner navigated his machine back and forth across the floor. Every now and then, I got up from the chair, walked to the window and looked out into the cold February darkness. My head spinning from the events of the last three hours.

My daze was suddenly interrupted by two people walking towards me, dressed in scrubs. I stood to meet them and as they drew closer, I observed their faces appeared sullen. Blank. I began to feel edgy, more worried than I had been. They sat down beside me, introducing themselves; one a nurse, and the other, an ICU consultant. The nurse cupped my hand in hers, in a comforting manner, a gesture as a nurse myself, I was all too familiar with. The consultant began to explain what was happening. This was the beginning of a life-changing situation for me and my family.

On 12 February 2021, I took my daughter Rachael, to the emergency department at our local hospital. She had developed a 'bug like' illness that week, something that wasn't new to her. She was born with Noonan syndrome, a condition recognised in 1969 by Dr Jaqueline Noonan, who discovered that certain characteristics put together, resulted in this syndrome. Rachael was described as being at the mild to moderate end of the spectrum. She had short stature, heart disease, mild learning difficulties and due to a weakened immune system, caught infection easily. So this time, it was nothing unremarkable. Her father and I managed it as we did any other infection – with an antibiotic and a huge helping of TLC!

I'm a nurse and was at work on 12 February 2021. During my afternoon break, I checked in with Rachael's father to see how she was responding to her antibiotic. He told me, 'There's not a lot of change, but her hands and feet are freezing and her nails are a funny dark colour.' With Rachael's cardiac history, I was immediately alarmed, so I asked permission to leave work and went to her. She was lying on the couch, pale and lethargic, and yes, her nails were blue. The medical term is cyanosis. Not wanting to wait a minute longer, I drove her the short distance to the hospital myself.

Rachael was triaged, seen within minutes, and taken into the resuscitation area. I sat across the corridor in the waiting room. I knew this was serious. With my nursing background working in critical care, I was acutely aware Rachael was being treated with an urgency, as I could hear the alarms sounding on the monitors she was attached to. The alarms meant her vital signs were not within normal parameters. I sat nervously, waiting for information. I had already given Rachael's medical history to the doctor and a senior nurse came out every so often to update me. One thing I will never forget her saying was, 'We're so glad you brought her in.' Due to COVID-19, hospitals had significantly restricted people entering the building, so I advised Rachael's father to remain at home and I would keep him updated.

Three hours later, Rachael was transferred to the intensive care unit. I accompanied her, along with the medical team, and as she disappeared through the door of ICU, I bent over and kissed her, reassuring her. 'I'll see you shortly, once they get you settled. Dad is on his way, and we are going to stay with you. Love you, darling. See you soon.'

So there I sat outside in the corridor, worried and scared, repeating to myself, as a 'glass half full person' … *This is going to be alright.* It had to be alright. There was no negotiation. That was … until the consultant and nurse met me.

Rachael's father arrived as the nurse and consultant were speaking. I'd called him to come in. We were ushered into a room just inside the intensive care unit. We learnt that Rachael had suffered a cardiac arrest, and her life hung in the balance. We sat there speechless, numb, unable to compute the information that had been relayed to us. This had to be someone else's nightmare!

Time passed, and a different consultant came into the room. With a glimmer of hope, he told us Rachael had been resuscitated but was now on life support. We were told she was being treated for sepsis, and the next twenty-four hours were critical. Harry, her older brother lives away, and from that moment on, he was in the room with us on Facetime.

Through the night, her father, my sister and brother-in-law, who had also arrived, took it in turns to sit with Rachael. Due to the information being relayed to us by the medical team, Rachael was going into multi-organ failure. We made the most difficult decision of our lives. We signed a 'do not attempt to resuscitate' order, meaning, if Rachael had another cardiac arrest, no further attempts would be made to revive her. The medical team were uncertain if she'd suffered brain damage during a prolonged resuscitation after admission to ICU. Far too much was against her. She looked vulnerable lying there. I felt sick to the pit of my stomach. There was nothing I could do to help her. I could see the numbers on the monitor were out of sync. Rachael was struggling, and I didn't know how much more of this invasive assault her little body could take. Time to re-evaluate. For Rachael's sake.

We spoke to the medical team again. We asked questions. Was there any chance of survival? We were told she was so critically ill, it was highly unlikely. Despite the cocktail of drugs and being on artificial ventilation, Rachael was not responding to treatment. Another massive decision. We asked that Rachael be taken off life support and let nature take its course. We had to let her go. From that moment on, we never left her side. We talked to her, told her we loved her, and to go and *join the other angels.*

On 13 February 2021, twenty-four hours, almost to the minute, from admission to hospital, Rachael lost her fight and left us. She was twenty-seven years young.

Losing a child is something no parent should ever have to face. It's the wrong way round … not the proper order. You don't bury your child. But here we were. Faced with something we never imagined happening. The loss of a beautiful daughter, sister, niece, cousin, friend. We were devastated beyond comprehension. Hearts broken. Dreams shattered. Plans ruined; a family in turmoil. For me, as a mother, I had no idea how to even begin to process this. How was I to come to terms with losing a life that was carried, given birth to, guided, nurtured and loved unconditionally for twenty-seven years? The straight answer is, you don't. There is no sugar coating it. There is no blueprint, no time line, no 'one size fits all' for grief. I have worked in a nursing career, spanning forty years, and have seen many things during that time. I have grieved my own parents' loss, but losing Rachael catapulted any grief I felt during those events to another level.

During the days following Rachael's death, the feelings of numbness, shock and disbelief were overwhelming. I went through the motions of the funeral on autopilot, but it was in the months that followed, that I truly got into the 'business end' of my grief.

I returned to work six weeks following Rachael's death, throwing myself into it, putting all my energy into caring for others. I parked my grief, but underneath, I was struggling. I wasn't sleeping or eating well. I was experiencing brain fog, muscle pain, nausea and tremendous fatigue. I was crying a lot and was thankful for face coverings! It was coming up to the first anniversary of Rachael's death, and I was reliving every moment. It was torturing me. I felt empty, lonely and broken. I kept it to myself, and not wanting to burden my family and friends, I plodded along, getting deeper and deeper into my grief.

By January 2022, I was physically and mentally exhausted. As usual

I was going to work, but, one day, *something* suddenly hit me. I can't explain what it was, but that day was my turning point. I was in a state of panic. I couldn't focus on my work. I thought I was going crazy. I got into my car and drove home. To this day, I have no memory of that journey home. My mind and body had completely shut down. I called my doctor, fully believing I was about to be admitted to a psychiatric hospital to treat my madness. My doctor listened to me sympathetically and reassured me, 'No, Wendy, you are not going crazy – you are having a severe grief reaction.' I remember being relieved at this diagnosis, but many of you will know, as I now have learned, that grieving a loss such as this, or any impactful loss, can make you think you are going mad.

I have discovered that grief is exhausting and debilitating. It hurts … physically, mentally and emotionally. There are various narratives on how grief can impact us; the train coming hurtling down the track at breakneck speed; the huge tsunami sucking you under. And you have no control. There is no warning when a grief reaction is going to trigger. It can be a thought, or sight of something memorable, that can completely change my day. I personally describe my bad days as 'horrible'. I have also come to realise that grief is an ongoing process. You travel back and forth through the stages of denial, anger, bargaining, depression and acceptance. I honestly don't know if I can ever accept Rachael's death, how she was so quickly taken from us, at a point in her life where she was blossoming into a beautiful young woman. She led her life with quiet dignity and grace. She loved children and was a qualified child care worker. She was a Scout leader. She volunteered at our local football club. She was a shopaholic; hoodies, socks, pyjamas were her favourite purchases, and indeed, hid many a bag in her room after being in town with her lifelong friend Meave. She was living her best life! She was also a little sister. She worshipped and adored her older brother Harry, who was hugely supportive of her. She was resilient and determined, and these characteristics would have helped her progress in her life. How ironic she will never need them now.

Following what I would describe as my 'cathartic' moment in January 2022, and discovering that I wasn't actually a mad woman, I made a conscious decision to find a way to grieve that would somehow *serve* Rachael. Besides, I was in a living hell; there had to be a more gentle and respectful way of living with my grief. And so began the process of self-care.

I researched and discovered the practices that work for me – and it didn't happen overnight. I was aware self-care included outings like a spa weekend, a manicure or a facial, which are all beneficial, but, in the face of my grief, I came to learn, self-care is so much more. Self-care is about looking after your body physically, emotionally and spiritually. Adopting a mindset of self-care takes patience and resilience. Self-care is not being selfish. It's about carving out space, finding the tools and reframing the way you heal and deal with the impact and devastation of grief.

My day starts with breath work, meditation and journalling. I find this puts me in a positive frame of mind for the day ahead. I read affirmations and more recently, daily stoicisms. I never thought I would get into philosophy, but if anything, I am learning on this journey, that whatever helps smooth the soul, has to be a deserving space for Rachael. This greatly comforts me.

I love to walk in nature, look up at the vast sky, and feel the air on my face. This is my favourite space to reflect on the many things I miss about Rachael, and I tell her that during my ramble. I tell her I miss being her mum and her friend. I miss her smell, her presence in the house; everything that was Rachael.

Some days, it's just about being still – and breathing! I am learning it is also okay to say 'no'. If I get an invitation, and I don't feel up to it, I politely decline saying, 'No thank you. Not today.' This response leaves the door open for future plans to be made. Though self-care can still be challenging. On my 'horrible days', it takes extreme effort and I have to 'dig deep'. But I always do something, even if it's a walk around the garden for five minutes. I have given space to my healing.

Aside from my self-care practices, we, as a family, acknowledge calendar anniversaries. The 'firsts' were excruciatingly painful. Mother's day, Rachael's birthday and Christmas. The grief calendar is vastly different. First day at school, first tooth, learning to swim.

On Rachael's birthday, we have a family meal, eat birthday cake and sing 'happy birthday' to her. At Christmas, Rachael has her own tree with all the decorations she either bought or made herself. It stands proudly in our hallway for all to see. I've developed a memory garden, and my sister made me a comfort blanket out of Rachael's favourite hoodies and T-shirts. Keeping Rachael's memory alive is very important to my family and they give me a huge source of comfort.

You don't 'get over' or 'move on' from grief. You make space for it, and you eventually grow your life around your grief. Making space to grieve well enables me to think and feel more positively about Rachael's life. Her many achievements, despite her health challenges, and rather than ask 'why', I turn it around and think 'what and how'. What she did in her twenty-seven years, and how she never complained. It doesn't always work, but I know I have Rachael's back forever.

Grief has become part and parcel of my life. I have become another version of myself. On the surface, I look and sound the same, but intrinsically, I can barely recognise the person I am now. I know I will be grieving for the rest of my life, but by creating that space for self-care, it is helping me to heal. More importantly, it is giving Rachael the attention she so richly deserves, and with the help of an amazing family, friends and community network, I am very slowly and tentatively *adapting* to a life without Rachael, in the physical sense. However, I know that spiritually, Rachael will never leave my side, and I love that comfort.

Today, I am living and growing my life around my grief. I recognise and embrace grief for what it is; life-changing, heart-breaking and impactful. I practice the self-care interventions that work for me, to help me on my journey of healing and hope. It is a journey that has many bumps in the road – sometimes potholes, but it is a journey for life.

ABOUT WENDY

Wendy Shannon is the founder of The Grief Lens, and set her business up as a grief advisor following the death of her twenty-seven-year-old daughter Rachael in February 2021. Rachael had assisted living needs and following a very short illness, sadly passed away in hospital. This followed the heartbreaking decisions not to attempt further resuscitation and to switch off life support, all within twenty-four hours.

Setting up The Grief Lens in Rachael's honour is enabling Wendy to give support to grieving parents and runs her business both on and offline, details of which we'll give to you at the end of this podcast.

Wendy grew up in Co Fermanagh, a rural area in the west of Northern Ireland with three siblings, one brother and two other sisters. She was raised in a working class family, and describes her parents as loving and hardworking, and her childhood as happy, free and 'never going without'.

Wendy is a registered general nurse, with over forty years experience in the field of orthopaedic nursing, critical and high dependency care and in the past five years, she has worked in the field of dementia, palliative and end of life care.

Wendy describes herself as a compassionate and caring person, and firmly believes that it is her career in nursing has enabled her to 'master her craft', enhancing and building on those core qualities that Wendy states are fundamental to her business in helping those navigating the grief journey.

Wendy is a TEDx speaker, having taken to the 'red dot' in June 2022 in her home town of Enniskillen in Co Fermanagh, Northern Ireland. She describes this as one of the proudest moments in her life, where she delivered a powerful message on coping with and navigating child loss, a talk for which she received a standing ovation.

Wendy has co-authored a book which is part of the Karen Weaver *Hear Us Roar* anthology and docufilm series, and is currently writing a memoir on her personal experience of navigating life after her precious loss. Wendy has also been nominated for a 2024 Women Changing The World Award to be held in London in May.

On her 'downtime', Wendy volunteers at her local sports/football club and she is a fundraiser for the British Heart Foundation, a cardiovascular research charity in the United Kingdom which funds medical research related to heart and circulatory diseases.

As a grief advisor, Wendy is now on a mission to get people talking more about grief and it's physical, psychological and emotional impact on grievers and the wider family and community. It is hoped by having these discussions, it will allow us to understand more about grief and loss, how to tread the journey, how to honour grief, and most importantly, that 'you are not alone'.

Facebook: The Grief Lens
Instagram: @the_greiflens
Email: thegrieflens@outlook.com
linktr.ee/the_grieflens
ted.com/search?q=Wendy%20Shannon

FLEUR CHAMBERS
HEALING WITH
A HEARTFELT PAUSE

I spent much of my late thirties and early forties searching the medical world for answers to my physical pain. Doctors, specialists, physiotherapists, osteopaths, chiropractors, scans, X-rays and a myriad of gadgets, all provided little relief. This mysterious condition manifested as daily pain in my skull, eyes, neck, shoulders, back, arms, hands and hips. Some days, the pain felt dull and deep, like a familiar ache. Other days, its expression was sharp and swift, often catching me off guard and taking my breath away.

There were times when I was certain something in my physical body was broken, torn or out of place. At other times, the pain had an emotional element to it, almost as if sadness was finding a home in my physical body.

During this time in my life, I also had much to celebrate and be grateful for. My three gorgeous boys (then five, six, and eight years old) were happy and healthy. I had a loving husband, a supportive social network, and was in the process of an exciting career reinvention, moving from the not-for-profit sector to the mindfulness and meditation space.

But there were moments when the pain overshadowed all these positives. It felt like there was a sheet of glass between me and the life I loved and valued. This negative cycle of pain and fear was all pervasive. It took charge of my thoughts, actions, emotions and, at times, my identity.

Seven years ago, at the age of forty, I was formally diagnosed with fibromyalgia – a chronic pain condition that results in your nervous system getting caught in a state of constant 'wind up'. In other words, my nervous system was *stuck* at a nine out of ten … all the time. This was not a relaxing place to be! My brain responded to this permanent state of agitation and arousal by sending signals to my body to produce pain – and the cycle of stress, pain and fear took hold.

My recovery (or healing, if you prefer that word) was, and continues to be, filled with experimentation and humour. There was a stint on medical marijuana which my kids objected to as I ate every sweet thing – or 'special treat' as we call them – in the pantry.

There was past life healing (apparently, I used to be a man and was still carrying the wounds of being left at the altar by the love of my life, hundreds of years ago). There were acts of solidarity as my kids and I chanted together in supermarket queues. Did you know, it's almost impossible to sing and feel pain at the same time?

There were changes to my diet and way of life. I embraced a gluten-free lifestyle, became vegetarian and meditated so frequently, it felt more like a spiritual boot camp than relaxation. I even tried juggling to rewire my brain. In case you are wondering, this experiment was unsuccessful.

My all-time favourite was a bizarre car chase between me and my loving mother. Distressed after a doctor's appointment, I had a 'small' breakdown in the car park. My mum tried to calm me down, but instead of allowing her words to soothe me, I jumped in my car and sped off like a middle-aged maniac. She was so concerned, she followed me … and I just couldn't shake this seventy-year-old speedster! When I finally got out of the car and saw her pull up behind me, I laughed and cried at the same time. It was a ridiculous situation, but one that has been etched in my mind as a moment of deep healing – a time when I knew, that despite my erratic behaviour, I was not alone.

As I look back at this time of great physical and emotional pain, experimentation and growth, one simple practice stands out; the practice of listening to the wisdom of my heart. It was, and continues to be, the most effective, transformational and healing practice of them all.

Given that I (and so many of us) have grown up being taught to prioritise thoughts over feeling, our head over our hearts, I realised that as an adult, I actually knew very little about this part of me. So, I began to forge a relationship with my heart by first getting to know its physical capabilities.

Take a moment to consider that your heart will beat around 100,000 times today, thirty-five million times this year, and over two billion times in an average lifetime. All day, every day, it pumps blood with vital nutrients around our bodies. In one day, your heart helps blood travel up to 19,000km across your body. Over a lifetime, the heart will pump one million barrels of blood. Pretty incredible don't you think?

It also has the most powerful electromagnetic field in the body. It's about sixty times greater in amplitude than the electrical activity generated by the brain and can be detected nearly one metre away from the body. This means that people and pets in your immediate environment can be affected by the state of your heart. Maybe this explains why you feel so good in some people's company and not in others?

But the human heart is more than an effective pump that sustains life. It's also a source of wisdom, intelligence and truth that we can use to experience more balance, creativity, healing and purpose in our lives.

The heart is the gateway to compassion, gratitude, joy, peace, fulfilment and happiness. It has a strength that can guide us towards greater resilience and courage. When we begin to see our hearts as a place to access inner guidance and wisdom, our world becomes more vibrant and interesting. We make more aligned decisions. We listen with more compassion. We live from our values. We act courageously. We may even heal from mysterious or often 'incurable' conditions like chronic pain, autoimmune disorders, disease, anxiety, depression, stress, loneliness and so on.

During my recovery from chronic pain, I developed a practice I call the *heartfelt pause*. Whenever I feel myself getting busy, overwhelmed, fearful or caught inside my head, I'd take a few deep breaths and imagine them landing in my heart. If I was on my own, I'd place my hand on my chest and feel the warmth of my own skin. Amazingly, this simple physical gesture of placing my hand on my chest was enough to bring me down from my mind and relax my nervous system.

From here, I would open up to any arising emotions. In truth, these emotions had probably been there for a while, I was just too caught inside my head to notice them. I would offer these emotions (the overwhelm, fear, guilt, distraction or worry) my attention. I would notice where they found a home in my body – often across my back or in my belly. I would offer them my non-judgemental awareness. In these moments, I chose acceptance over resistance. It felt surprisingly good.

After just a few weeks of doing this short practice each day, I began to feel totally different. I was less stressed and more grounded and at ease. Excited about this new world that was emerging for me, I took the practice one step further. I began to ask my heart this simple question: *Heart, what message do you have for me, what would you have me know?*

My heart responded immediately (and had quite a sense of humour too!). Here are some of the things my heart has said to me over the years.

You are tired, have a rest.

Drink more water, your organs are thirsty.

Stop taking things so personally, not everything is about you.

Be kind to your body.

Stop eating meat.

Forgive, forgive, forgive.

When I began to live less from my mind and more from my heart, I had fewer pain flare ups. I felt less fearful. My mind wasn't in overdrive, worrying about my next pain episode. Interestingly, committing to these simple heartfelt pauses created a ripple into many different aspects of my life, not just my chronic pain circumstances. I felt closer to my children and husband. There was more fun and joy in our home, greater creativity at work, more flexibility when plans changed and increased compassion towards strangers and people who pushed my buttons.

Committing to these heartfelt pauses a few times a day is a powerful way of softening the incessant, and often self-critical, mental chatter and dropping into a more grounded and wise way of walking through the world. Another way to do this is to reflect back on the times in our lives when our heart has been cracked wide open, and get curious about how we can take these feelings into our everyday lives. Let's explore this together now.

REMEMBER AND REIGNITE YOUR PEAK EXPERIENCES

After knowing my now-husband for just one month, we set off on an adventure, travelling from Australia to Patagonia. Three planes, two trains and four boat trips later, we found ourselves in a remote part of Southern Chile, surrounded by soaring mountains, bright blue icebergs and golden grassland sprinkled with tiny yellow wildflowers.

As we travelled through a mighty fjord in an army-grade inflatable, dressed in oversized waterproof pants held up by braces, I realised we had bypassed the romantic dating phase in our relationship!

The water was cold and perfectly still. The sheer cliffs on either side took my breath away. I remember a wave of awe and wonder washing over me, bringing with it a sense of peace and timelessness. The land felt prehistoric and sacred. I imagined seeing a Neanderthal man wandering the side of the mountain in search of food. In that moment, linear time dissolved. We stepped into 'soul time', the home of deep connection, intuition and oneness.

That night we camped beside the Grey Glacier, a thirty-two-kilometre stretch of the Southern Patagonian icefield. This glacier was more than eighteen thousand years old, its colour resembling a precious stone. Our guide told us the glacier could be seen from outer space – a sparkling blue mass.

I remember being tucked up in our tent, all warm and cosy in my sleeping bag, mesmerised by the soundscape. Hearing the iceberg groan, shift, crack and fall away into the lake, it was as if the Grey Glacier was alive. I imagined her breathing, expanding on the inhale, contracting on the exhale. I felt into the miracle that she had been doing this for thousands of years.

Energised by the life force radiating from the glacier, I got out of the tent and gazed up at the night sky. The bright stars sparkling against the endless darkness spoke to the depths of me. At that moment I felt small, insignificant and humble. I also felt part of the mystery.

Seventeen years later, I look back on that day with gratitude, knowing it was what Abraham Maslow defined as a 'peak experience'; moments that fill us with intense wellbeing, a feeling of wonder and awe, reverence, humility, surrender and presence.

Put simply, peak experiences open our hearts. They encourage us to see life as it is; a miracle. In these moments, we wake from the trance of busy-ness, the incessant chatter of the mind and realise just how precious life is. Our daily complaints and ruminations about the heavy traffic, our demanding boss or our aging body feel small and insignificant. Peak experiences are like a lightning bolt of perspective, illuminating our desire to live a more aligned and heart-centred life.

But we all know, that often, these peak moments and the internal shift they create, don't last. We return from an awe-inspired holiday and before long we are complaining about our endless inbox and the dirty washing. We bring our newborn baby home from the hospital and the feelings of unbridled love and connection get buried by fatigue and overwhelm. Living an authentic and aligned life includes using these peak experiences to guide the way we live, love and interact with life.

That night in Southern Patagonia seventeen years ago, I connected with the mystery contained in the night sky and the life force radiating from the Grey Glacier. My perspective expanded as I began to understand that everything in nature contains the same universal energy. My heart cracked open as I realised I was part of the mystery of life.

I realised that when we connect with this sense of aliveness, our troubles feel smaller, we experience more peace and our sense of possibility magnifies. I've used these gifts many times throughout my life, in times of challenge, in ordinary everyday moments and in my meditation practice.

In the weeks after I had COVID-19, I often found myself awake at night, my heart pounding and my mind racing, wondering if I was ever going to fully recover. Desperate for some reprieve, I would go outside and shift my gaze upwards to the night sky. Immediately the anxiety would soften and my perspective would expand. My tiny racing heart felt so small yet also held by the universal energy of love and compassion.

I also weave the night sky into my early morning trip to the bakery for the kids' school lunches. Each morning, I pause, look up and smile at how life can be domestic and filled with routine, whilst also blessed with mystery.

And finally, the experience of moving from linear time to soul time whilst cruising through the fjord in Southern Patagonia has been a memory I have taken with me and weaved into my meditation practice.

Perhaps as you've been reading this your own peak experience has come to mind? Maybe you've reflected upon the birth of a child or grandchild, or a wilderness adventure that left you feeling awestruck and deeply aware of what really matters to you. Can you pause a moment now, and bring the details to mind and heart of a peak experience you've had?

Now ask yourself these three questions.

- What gifts did this moment give me?
- What did this moment reveal to me about how I want to live and what's important in my life?
- How can I bring the learnings and good vibes from this peak experience into my everyday life?

You might like to write these answers down, or just take a few deep breaths and imagine them landing in your heart.

Peak experiences and heartfelt pauses are just two of the many ways you can awaken your heart each day. Get playful and curious as you cultivate your own unique relationship with this wisdom centre. Remember, the heart is the gateway to greater love, wisdom, creativity and purpose. It's there to help you make the good times feel great, and the setbacks less stressful!

ABOUT FLEUR

Fleur Chambers is a multi-award-winning meditation teacher, creator of *The Happy Habit* app, bestselling author and philanthropist. Through her guided meditations, courses and books, Fleur is helping people all around the world say yes to their entire lives, even the challenges and setbacks.

With proceeds from *The Happy Habit* funding grassroots projects in some of the poorest communities around the world, Fleur is using meditation as a tool for social change. *The Happy Habit* has provided a permanent source of drinking water to over sixty thousand people.

Often referred to by her students as gentle, curious and warm-hearted, Fleur reminds us that there is strength in softness and that we are safe to be ourselves.

ROBYN VERRALL
ENTERING YOUR HEART TO EXIT YOUR MIND'S NOISE

When I step into any room, whether surrounded by people I know and love, sitting in a business meeting, or entering a crowded event – I pause. I take a moment to steady myself, aware that nerves can accompany me in every corner of my life. Even when I'm the one leading others into the room, guiding them forward with confidence, I am quietly scanning and observing. My eyes instinctively seek out the person standing alone, their posture echoing how I sometimes feel inside.

I make a choice not to walk away from people standing alone at events because I value connection, inclusion and creating a sense of belonging. My leadership roles and advocacy for women in agriculture, demonstrate that an understanding of the importance of making others feel heard and valued. Approaching someone who is alone reflects empathy and a desire to foster supportive environments where everyone feels welcome, are qualities that align with personal and professional values. It's a natural extension of your commitment to creating spaces where voices are acknowledged and people can thrive.

Without hesitation, I make a beeline toward them. I introduce myself, not with rehearsed small talk, but with genuine curiosity. I ask why they are there and if they know anyone in the room. I listen – really listen – to their answers. I want to show genuine interest in the person's experiences, ideas and values, encouraging deeper dialogue. This approach builds trust, creates stronger relationships and often leads to insightful exchanges that can inspire growth and collaboration. Thoughtful questions open doors for others to share their stories, feel valued and engage more meaningfully in conversations. It reflects my commitment to fostering environments where voices are heard and ideas are respected – something small talk rarely achieves. This intentional focus allows me to craft thoughtful questions, ones that move beyond the predictable, like 'Where do you work?' or 'What school did you attend?' Instead, I aim for questions that invite authenticity and connection.

Small talk is also necessary, but it is sometimes awkward and can quickly lead to silences. There is nothing worse than being in a person's presence and yet feeling unseen and unheard. There needs to be a connection and rapport must be built from nothing, to trust and confidence, in the formation of the relationship as soon as practical. Otherwise, thank them for talking with you and excuse yourself. Remove yourself from the situation. Finding common ground to have more meaningful conversations is intentional. It sharpens my focus on the individual in front of me, anchoring me in the present moment. It quiets the distracting noise in my mind and gives me clarity and purpose. This, to me, is stealth: the secret art of entering the faith of your heart and leaving the noise of your mind behind.

Stealth is not about blending in or becoming invisible, though that can be useful in some circumstances, it's about moving with quiet confidence and intentionality. It's understanding that true power doesn't always come from being the loudest voice in the room but from being the most attentive listener. In mastering this art, I've come to realise that genuine connection holds far more influence than any speech or presentation. It's the soft, steady strength of presence – choosing to engage meaningfully rather than merely performing. It gives the speaker and the listener time to pause and connect, while opening the area for others to join in with conversation.

This approach has opened doors I never imagined and introduced me to friendships that span cultures, industries and socio-economic backgrounds. By focusing on others and patiently discovering common ground, I've built bridges in spaces where I once felt unseen. I've sparked meaningful collaborations, forged lifelong connections and contributed to charitable causes and business ventures that resonate deeply with my values. Opportunities I once only dreamed of, have become reality because I dared to listen, engage and act with intention. Stealth is an internal discipline, one that demands self-awareness, mindfulness, and emotional intelligence. This form of stealth is not about hiding from others but about quietly understanding and guiding oneself.

When engaging with people on all levels, I manage my thoughts, emotions and reactions. I consciously pause to observe internal chatter and external stimuli without jumping to immediate responses. This mindful stillness fosters deliberate and authentic actions, empowering me to navigate life's complexities without being overwhelmed by mental noise. Like a shadow that moves silently, inner stealth allows me to progress through challenges with grace and intention.

Where I once would quietly slip out of events at the earliest opportunity, now I find myself staying until the end on many occasions. Though I do sometimes leave early if I feel I want to, I remain to be fully present at the event, to stay immersed in conversations and to enjoy the company of others and, more importantly, my own. I've learned that many people are simply waiting for someone to notice them, to extend a hand and invite them into dialogue. In those moments, stealth becomes a powerful tool; the quiet strength to make others feel seen while staying firmly anchored in my own purpose.

There is a liberating freedom in this quiet confidence. It allows me to move through both personal and professional spaces with grace and assurance, ensuring that every interaction is intentional and every connection is genuine. This is the path I choose; a life of purposeful presence, guided by the steady rhythm of my heart and the unwavering clarity of my mind.

One must also trust in the faith of one's heart and this is not always easy. It's like falling in love with something you know isn't right but holding on anyway, to save face, to avoid failure or simply out of fear. Many people refer to toxic relationships as 'twin flames,' believing they are destined connections when they are often the consequence of ignoring their own intuition and not having faith in their heart.

Toxic relationships are never what they seem. People wear disguises – charming exteriors, whispered promises, and the illusion of love or friendship. But beneath the surface, they corrode, chipping away at confidence, distorting reality, and leaving scars that only the heart can truly feel.

The real damage isn't always in loud fights or obvious betrayals; it is in the slow erosion of self-worth, the manipulation so subtle it feels like self-doubt rather than deception. Gaslighting twists truth until reality itself becomes a battleground. Ghosting – a silent, deliberate withdrawal – leaves questions unanswered, wounds unhealed, and a heart searching for closure where none exists.

I have witnessed this firsthand – I have been this person, abandoning my inner voice, silencing my instincts in the name of love, loyalty, or fear of being alone. The warning signs flicker like distant lightning, but I ignored them, dismissed them as overreactions or my own insecurities. And that is the stealth of toxicity – it creeps in unnoticed, wearing the mask of care, companionship, or even necessity, until it tightens its grip.

But the heart knows. Even in the silence, in lying awake in the dark, pondering the relationship in the confusion of doubt, feeling that ache – a knowing. The hurt settles deep, not just from the actions of others but from the betrayal of self, the realisation that the truth was always there, whispering, waiting to be heard.

Breaking free requires all the courage one can find – the courage, to trust one's own voice again, to reclaim boundaries, to walk away even when every manipulative thread tries to pull one back. It means learning that love does not suffocate, real connection does not manipulate, and silence should be a refuge, not a weapon.

Healing from toxicity isn't just about leaving; it's about rediscovering oneself, finding strength in the heart's quiet wisdom, and never again letting someone else's shadows darken the light within

The heart symbolises intuition, passion and the very core of our beliefs. To have faith in the heart means to trust one's inner convictions, allowing them to guide decisions beyond what logic alone can explain. This trust is rooted in authenticity, choosing to act based on my personal values and emotions, rather than succumbing to external pressures or societal expectations.

Faith in the heart empowers us to pursue paths that may seem irrational but are deeply meaningful. It is a quiet, inner form of stealth, a guiding force that influences our actions and decisions in subtle yet powerful ways. This faith fosters resilience, fuels innovation and leads to a life of deeper personal fulfillment. Trusting the heart doesn't guarantee an easy path, but it ensures one that is rich with purpose, growth and authenticity. This can be as simple as remaining single for a while or changing a job that doesn't align with us.

Contrasting the heart's quiet guidance, the mind often generates noise; an incessant stream of thoughts fuelled by fear, doubt and societal expectations. This mental noise manifests as overthinking, anxiety and self-doubt, clouding judgment and paralysing decision-making.

Quieting the mind is not about silencing all thoughts but about discerning which thoughts serve and which hinder. This discernment is a stealthy practice, subtly shifting focus from mental noise to one's inner truth. Think of all the wellness advisors, sessions and opportunities offered in the form of assisting one's mental health.

Merging with heart and mind, harmonises the heart and mind. It involves listening to the heart's quiet wisdom while engaging the mind as a supportive tool rather than a controlling force. This balance fosters intentional, authentic actions. It's about living one's beliefs demonstrated by action.

Listening to the heart over the mind is about tuning into your inner wisdom – the quiet knowing that exists beyond logic, fear, or external expectations. While the mind examines, rationalises, and often creates doubts, the heart simply knows. It speaks in feelings, instincts, and subtle nudges, guiding you toward what truly aligns with your values and purpose.

To listen to the heart, you must first create space for it. Silence the noise – whether it's from others' opinions, societal pressures, or even your own overthinking mind. Pause. Breathe. Ask yourself: *Does a decision bring peace or unease? Expansion or contraction? Excitement or dread?* The body responds to truth – trust those signals.

The mind is not the enemy; it is a tool. Instead of allowing it to dominate with doubt or overanalyses, use it to support the heart's wisdom. When the heart nudges you toward something, let the mind figure out the steps to bring it to life. This is where harmony happens – where thoughts and emotions work together rather than against each other.

Living from the heart doesn't mean ignoring logic; it means aligning your actions with what truly matters to you. It's not just about what makes sense – it's about what at the deepest level. It's about trusting yourself enough to move forward with courage, even when the mind hesitates.

Stealth and heart together create a life of authenticity. You act not out of fear, but from conviction. You don't just say what you believe – you embody it. Every choice becomes intentional, every step guided by the quiet, unwavering wisdom of your own heart.

Making sure that I bring my authentic self to all situations and lowering the internal chatter, involves cultivating mindfulness, trusting my intuition and engaging logic when appropriate. Meditation for stillness and gratitude journaling, where I can write three things each day I'm grateful for, (these being people, events, opportunities and or happenings). Reflective journaling and reflection also allow me to sit in my own thoughts and start and end my day. Sometimes I am aware that I need to sit in solitude, as it gives me balance which helps me to move through life with clarity and grace.

My favourite saying is, '*Find what you do and do it on person*' – a quote attributed to Dolly Parton. I take this and live it. I do not worry if my actions aren't socially acceptable. I do help people; I will say hello and ask them if they need anything (elderly, homeless and those looking distressed). I was in a shopping centre recently and there was a gentleman caught up trying to get his backpack off. He was very distressed and the man sitting at the table next to him, with his family, told his children not to look. I did not walk past, I put my bag on his table and helped by lifting it over his head so he could get unravelled. He thanked me, I walked on. There was no reason why I couldn't help; there was no reason not to assist, so I did it.

STEALTH OF HEART IN HARD CONVERSATIONS

The other night, I sat with my women friends discussing the 'hard conversations' – those moments when we must talk to loved ones about difficult but necessary life changes. We spoke about asking someone to stop driving, encouraging them to move to safer housing, or planning for aging in a way that preserves dignity and security. These topics can be uncomfortable, yet they are essential for ensuring safety and wellbeing.

I was surprised when someone suggested these conversations should be approached with subtlety. My instinct is to be direct and honest – after all, these discussions aren't just about personal preference; they can save lives and prevent heartache down the road. While honesty is crucial, I began to see that delivering truth with care, patience, and timing can make all the difference. It's not just what we say but how we say it that shapes the outcome.

These conversations can be painful for the receiver, touching on loss of independence, fear of change, and the reality of aging. Yet, avoiding them only leads to greater difficulties later. Discussions about wills, funeral arrangements, and end-of-life care may feel uncomfortable, but they provide clarity and peace, ensuring that families can work together rather than be left scrambling in crisis.

This is the stealth of heart – knowing when to speak boldly and when to soften our words, ensuring that love and understanding guide our honesty. It's about balancing truth with compassion, offering support rather than control, and helping our loved ones navigate life's transitions with dignity and respect. Hard conversations aren't just about telling someone what they need to hear; they're about listening, guiding, and walking alongside them with care.

The mind's noise stems from the ego's need for control, validation and certainty. It seeks logical explanations, over-analyses outcomes, and fears failure. While logical reasoning is essential, excessive mental chatter can overshadow the subtle wisdom of the heart. It's lying awake at night asking oneself questions and coming up with the ifs, buts, hows etc.; a continuous repetitive negative thinking that exacerbates stress and leads to anxiety. To stop the chatter in the top paddocks, mindfulness practices such as meditation, journalling and deep breathing help quiet the mind. By observing thoughts without attachment, individuals create space for heart-led decisions. Quieting the mind is not about silencing all thoughts but about discerning which thoughts serve and which hinder. This discernment is a stealthy practice, subtly shifting focus from mental noise to one's inner truth. A profound element of inner stealth is learning to detach from the opinions of others.

The phrase, *What you think of me is none of my business*, encapsulates the liberating practice of not allowing external judgments to dictate one's self-worth. This mindset is an essential form of psychological stealth – moving through life unseen by the critical eyes of others; not because they aren't watching, but because their gaze holds no power. Many people, me included, have spent years burdened by the weight of others' perceptions.

I remember constantly worrying about what others thought of me, replaying conversations and over-analysing interactions. This cycle was mentally exhausting, feeding insecurities and paralysing growth. It wasn't until a close friend shared an experience that I began to understand the futility of this mindset.

She told me how her ex-partner had spoken poorly about her to their mutual friends, going so far as to text them directly with cruel words about her. Some of these friends had forwarded the messages to her, leaving her hurt and shaken. My immediate instinct was to ask for details – to know exactly what was said, to understand the depth of the betrayal. But then something shifted within me.

I realised that knowing these words wouldn't serve her or me. It would only deepen her pain, fuel unnecessary anxiety, and give power to someone who no longer deserved a place in her life. Instead, I looked at her and said, 'Please don't tell me what he said. I don't need to know. You are my friend, and I trust and value you. His opinion of you does not define you, and I refuse to let his words have any influence over how I see you. More importantly, the person who sent that message to you is not a friend. Forwarding such negativity is hurtful and harmful, and I won't be party to it.'

In that moment, I saw the weight of his words begin to lift from her. She didn't need me to dissect the insults or react with anger – she needed someone to affirm her worth, to remind her that she was more than the narrative her ex tried to create. And I understood something profound: other people's words and opinions are reflections of their own insecurities, bitterness, or unresolved issues – not a reflection of the truth. We don't have to carry them, entertain them, or give them space in our minds. By choosing not to engage, I was choosing peace, and more importantly, I was choosing to stand by my friend in the way she truly needed.

I have stopped people telling me what they think about me or my business. If anyone wants to 'share' their opinion of me, with me, I walk away and do not ponder what I'm missing out on. Protecting my mental space is a priority. This act of stealth – choosing not to engage with negativity – allows me to preserve my peace. It is a conscious decision to remain unseen and untouched by judgment.

Merging stealth with heart and mind true inner stealth harmonises the heart and mind. It involves listening to the heart's quiet wisdom while engaging the mind as a supportive tool rather than a controlling force. This balance fosters intentional, authentic actions.

MERGING STEALTH WITH HEART AND MIND: MY JOURNEY

In my leadership role in agriculture, I have learned that true change doesn't come from force alone – it comes from strategy, patience, and authenticity. My heart tells me that ensuring women have a voice at decision-making tables is essential, that fairness and inclusion matter. But I also know that simply demanding space won't create lasting change; it can eve create resistance.

Early on, I pushed harder, I called out inequalities more directly. But over time, I have realised that my mind needed to work alongside my heart. Instead of trying to break down doors, I built relationships. I mentored and mentor younger women, gained allies, and proved my value through action. When I faced resistance, I learnt not to react emotionally – I responded with clarity and confidence. I asked questions that made people think rather than putting them on the defensive.

I share stories and data to highlight the importance of diversity, making the case for inclusion without alienating those who hadn't yet embraced it.

Through this balance, I have created real impact. I have secured seats at influential tables not just for myself but for others, not by overpowering others, but by showing up with intention and purpose. My heart fuels my mission, my mind refines my methods, and together they drive meaningful change. This is the stealth of heart – aligning passion with wisdom, emotion with intellect, and purpose with action.

In farming, true mastery comes from balancing knowledge with intuition, much like a skilled martial artist anticipates movement not just through logic but through deep, embodied understanding. Experienced farmers don't rely solely on data and technology – they develop a feel for the land, reading the seasons, sensing changes in the soil, and knowing when to act even before the signs become obvious.

Similarly, agricultural leaders who balance strategic thinking with emotional intelligence create lasting impact. They don't just push for innovation or policy change from a technical standpoint – they listen, build relationships, and inspire trust. We understand that real progress in agriculture isn't just about adopting new methods; it's about engaging people, respecting tradition while embracing evolution, and leading with both vision and practicality.

Creative problem-solving in farming also mirrors this balance. Farmers and agribusiness innovators often enter a 'flow state,' where intuition guides decision-making. Whether it's timing a crucial harvest, handling livestock with an unspoken understanding, or making business choices that feel right even when they defy conventional wisdom, success comes when the mind quiets and the heart leads. This harmony between knowledge and instinct allows farmers not just to survive but to thrive in an ever-changing landscape.

I truly believe in the power of trusting the faith of the heart while quieting the mind's noise. It requires mindfulness, emotional intelligence, and intentional action. By mastering this inner stealth, I navigate life's complexities with authenticity and purpose. Choosing what is right, offering kindness without expectation, and moving with quiet conviction is truly liberating.

In a world saturated with distractions, opinions, and external pressures, the ability to move silently within oneself becomes a powerful tool. It is in this stillness that we hear the quiet truths of the heart – the unwavering wisdom that has always been there, waiting for us to listen. When the mind's noise subsides, clarity emerges. Decisions become grounded, actions become purposeful, and life unfolds with deeper meaning.

This practice of inner stealth is not about retreating or disengaging – it is a strategic advance, an artful way of living where the heart leads with courage and the mind supports with focus. It is a path of quiet strength, of moving through life with intention, wisdom, and unwavering faith in what truly matters.

ABOUT ROBYN

Robyn Verrall is a dynamic force in agriculture, an influential leader, and a master connector, bringing people and ideas together to drive meaningful change. More than just a successful farmer, she is a passionate advocate, business owner, keynote speaker, and the recipient of numerous awards, including co-creator of a Gourmand 'Best in the World' award-winning cookbook.

As the 2022 South Australian AgriFutures Rural Women's Award winner, Robyn founded Harvesting Potential Ltd, a non-profit organisation dedicated to empowering women and girls through scholarships, mentorship, and economic opportunities. Her work extends to providing affordable food solutions and supporting First Nations families through Harvesting Potential Inc. Her unwavering commitment to gender equity and leadership development has led to her sponsorship of girls in leadership programs, instilling self-worth and confidence in future generations.

In recognition of her dedication to gender equity, Robyn was honoured with the 2024 National Recalibrate Gender Equity Award for Individual/CEO. She is also the South Australian Skills Commission Chair for Agribusiness, Food, Wine, Beverage, and Racing, further solidifying her role as a key voice in shaping the future of these industries.

Adding another chapter to her career, Robyn has recently joined KMD Books as a partner, leading the charge in stories that speak – bringing rural women's stories, First Nations yarns, and food traditions to the global stage. This exciting venture continues the strong literary legacy built by Karen Weaver and her team.

A true champion of women, agriculture, and gender equity, Robyn Verrall is making an indelible impact, ensuring that voices from all walks of life are heard, valued, and celebrated.

SHEENA McGORMAN
PRACTICE POSITIVE IN ANY NEGATIVE SITUATION AND ALREADY YOU WIN

First of all, it's so important to take some time for yourself. What do you enjoy doing? Maybe even try new things – sometimes these can turn out to be the best for us and exactly what we were looking for.

Be OPEN! If I hadn't been open to meditation, journaling, working on my mindset and setting goals, I don't believe all that I have achieved would have been possible at all.

Being grateful – gratitude is everything. Coming from an attitude of gratitude enables us to see the good in every situation. I know some pretty bad things happen to some people, some worse than others, and I do get that, but there is always something good to come out of any situation if we look hard enough.

Strengthen your relationship with the universe and, trust me, it will strengthen all your relationships. Notice when something doesn't sit well with you … and remove it. When something is toxic to your mind, it can really hold you back from your path of fulfilling your goals and dreams.

I like to bubble wrap myself at times – you know, that gut feeling you get when something isn't right and it's out of your control. Simply remove it … and this does become easier the more we do it. There will be lots of emotion around it, especially if its someone close to you, but in the long term you will have to do it anyway, so don't prolong these things. Holding on to things those don't serve us, is what holds us back and diminishes our dreams. Go with your gut always … its' never wrong.

Mind your mind. If you are unable to cope with something, mentally notice that sometimes, when things become too hard, we explode. Learn how to control these emotions so you can avoid that explosion. Some of us have partners and children, and we must also consider their thoughts and emotions, so it can be harder, but the more you become aware, the better and quicker the problem will be resolved.

What is it you desire?

Have you had some time to think about this? Are you ready to accept the guidance necessary to see this through?

It's so important to know what it is you want to achieve in life, personally and spiritually, in mind, body and soul. Take some time to gather all those feelings and make the decision … the universe will take care of everything else to help you achieve them and send you the ideas and opportunities to make this happen.

You see, we are all programmed from the first day we begin our journey in life. All our habits, good and bad, were inherited. When we start to create our own ideas and notions, we may have to work a little harder in some areas to remove some limiting beliefs. These beliefs will try and pull you back and stop you in your tracks, because owe are stepping outside of our comfort zone … and that's a scary place to venture, isn't it? We so don't like it out there. This is such a hard place to overcome, but with your desire to make those changes, becoming stronger, growing that muscle of feeling the fear and doing it anyway, you will make this happen in the small consistent steps you take each day.

One thing you don't need to worry about is the *how*. Trust the universe and it will happen. You will get guidance and signs if you ask for it. Don't ignore the signs, as this is what will move you forward.

Negative thoughts = Negative Outcome

Positive thoughts = Positive Outcome

It all begins and ends in your mind.
What you give power to, has power over you.
– Leon Brown

… but only if you allow it.

So many of us think life happens to us when, actually, life happens for us.

> *'What we think about comes about.'*
> **– Buddha**

Think about this, when something bad happens or something we are not happy about, we give it bad energy and we start to imagine the worst, thinking things like, *What next? Things are not working out for me,* but we never consider our thought pattern. We are responsible for what happens in our minds – we create it.

As an example, when the car might not start for some reason and we kick the tyre and get mad, we make up all sorts of scenarios in our head. The next thing we know, it's been towed away and there is more problems with the car than you ever thought possible!

But what if we were to see the good in things that moment and that the universe is working for us?

Then we take the attitude of, *Oh well, there's a reason the car isn't working.* You then find another solution, and nine times out of ten, the next time you try to start the car, it starts no problem. The universe was just working in your favour and didn't want you travelling on the road at that time, for some reason or other, simply protecting you!

With this viewpoint, everything seems a lot better, doesn't it? I challenge you to try that the next time a situation arises and see if it improves the outcome. I *know* this to be true because I've been practising myself for some time and always have a much better outcome.

For me, during my time of practising this attitude, I have been able to see the lessons and blessings presented to me in these scenarios and situations. So, what does that mean?

For example, if someone does me wrong and I'm hurt or feeling angry about it, in the past, I would often retaliate and take it out on others – normally the people I'm closest to.

But I have discovered that by practising gratitude and noticing the lesson, asking myself, *Why does this happen with certain people or why do people make me feel this way?* the blessing appears and you realise you are grateful you are not like them. You would never want to make anyone feel like that so you remove yourself from that environment or those kind of people, to protect yourself and your mind.

I find that by sending them love, even when they upset you, this will help to clear the path in our mind, allowing us to move on from it, without giving it any energy in return. You no longer feel the anger and this helps you to clear the upset from your mind. It allows you to move on.

'Remember, where focus goes energy flows.' – *James Redfield.*

You will also bubble wrap again and not allow such people in, nor will you entertain a negative attitude from anyone, regardless of who they are. Initially you will find this hard but it will become easier for you.

We all need to find a way of dealing with people and emotions, especially our own, remembering we never need to tolerate any of that upset.

If I question how someone makes me feel down or upsets me, I ask myself, *Would I do that to them?* The answer is always NO, so I don't tolerate been treated this way. Again, this has taken time and working on myself to discover and change this. I also try to understand why this person might have treated me this way, or what the intention was. We don't always come up with the right answer, but it allows me to address the situation, move on and clear the thoughts from my head. It's so powerful.

There is something built into us, which makes us think bad things about ourselves, or not accept compliments.

I'm not good enough, I don't like this (or that) about me. I am not confident enough.

We are programmed this way, and it's something we all need to work on to change our thoughts. We have no limits when we are small children. We have great imaginations, and a no-giving-up attitude, but something happens as we grow. Suddenly, we procrastinate about everything we do, with that little voice in our head telling us we can't do it.

Why is that?

It is what we are made up of. It's our past generations and how we've been brought up. This goes back generations and is passed through each generation, as we inherit little bits of everyone who's been before us.

The best news is, we have the ability to change the habits and thoughts passed on to us. I decided I would, and I work on myself every morning. first thing, I get up earlier than I need to, before the rest of the house awakens, and I start my morning with a 6am mindset call and gratitude journaling, writing my goals. I end with a guided meditation. This only takes thirty minutes and it is the best thirty minutes of my day. This working on me, and being crystal clear of what I want to become, has been key to my success, with the power of gratitude and manifestation.

Being grateful and affirming it each day, is so powerful. Not only does it make me grateful for life, but for all the amazing things so many people take for granted. If I'm being honest, when I started this, I had no idea what I was doing or if I was doing it right. Now when I write my gratitude's I can tell how grateful I am, as practice really does make perfect.

Sometimes bad stuff has to happen for us to realise just how lucky we are and to truly value life and how precious it is. We can make an impact with our children, our grandchildren and great-grandchildren, and also everyone we cross paths with, by sharing a little smile or a hug (I am such a hugger). It's warmer than a handshake and you can leave a long-lasting impression, as we don't know who might need it. Nobody knows what people go through on a day-to-day basis. Everyone is so busy, they don't have time to be present, everyday rushing into the next. A day becomes a week, a week becomes a month and so on. Nobody has time to care for themselves, so how can you care for others? Just like nobody has time to be sick and they forget to look after their health.

We must make the time we all need for ourselves, otherwise we cannot care for everyone we love.

You can start today by looking after your mind daily. My practice has actually given me more time, better relationships, better time management, more openness to things, more willingness to learn and to discover myself, but most of all, more passion to help others. That's my biggest passion; helping others.

I now go after the bigger goals because I have the faith and trust in myself, my thoughts, my actions and my reactions. I know anything is possible. I can achieve anything I put my mind to.

How do I help myself get to there?

I started to realise the importance of what I was feeding my mind on a daily basis. Listening to the news, reading sad stories in the papers and magazines; all of these things have a major effect on our thinking.

- Many people start their day opening their eyes, angry that they have to get up, still feeling tired. Yet life is a gift, we should get up and embrace every day.
- Many people start the day scrolling aimlessly through their phone, seeing stuff that might upset them – that's how they start the day.
- Some people get up late, causings them to rush through everything in the day, which is stressful, and effects not only you but everyone around you.

Awareness is key so change. Start your day with positivity by creating a morning routine. Let the positivity flow everywhere you go and watch what happens.

Listen to something positive and uplifting – there's plenty of free stuff on YouTube.

Get a journal and write:

1. Five things you are grateful for that you have in your life.
2. Five things you are grateful for that you really want in your life but you don't have just yet. Write them like you have already achieved them, as we can trick our minds into believing just that.
3. Write a goal as if you have it achieved. This can be a short-term goal or long-term goal … you decide.

Finally … listen to a guided mediation.

I listen to health and wealth power meditation daily – and I love it.

It's a powerful practice to think of your goals as if they are already achieved. Trust the process and don't give up on this because it works. It takes a little time to get into it but it's so worth it. I still practice this routine five days a week and it has helped in so many areas of my life – I'm so grateful.

When you discover that everything is working for your higher good, you see everything so differently. You will be presented with different opportunities and you will show up as a different person altogether. What's best about that, is that you will lead by example, down through your children.

Remember, a good mindset is key to everything we do, because if we don't have that right, we cannot do anything right.

I've heard it be said that my attitude to mindset is 'a bit airy fairy'. In fact, I was once one of those people. I didn't realise then that ego is the thief of success, just like procrastination is the thief of time. However, we continue to entertain them. When I became more open was when I started to strive forward. A closed mind is open to nothing, so we all need to be more open. If we want things to change, we have got to change just. If we want things to get better, we have to get better. When we become more open to things, we can overcome and achieve absolutely anything.

And when we have faith that all is working for our greater good, we must not expect it to all happen by sitting back and waiting. We must take the action and visualise exactly what we want to achieve. This will present ideas to us and we must act on them accordingly in order for it to come about. Remember not to worry about the *HOW*.

'If you can see in it in your mind, you can hold it in your hand.' – *Bob Proctor*

The universe presents things to you and you must receive by taking action.

ACTION = REACTION

The universe can do its bit, but you must also do yours, while trusting the process. Choose to see the positive in every outcome. You will achieve more when you believe in yourself. This will encourage you to dream bigger and push yourself a little more each time. It's so powerful.

Think of all the things you want to manifest into your life, but not the things you don't want! Find a buddy to do this practice with daily, to keep you accountable

Energy is everything – knowledge is POWER.

ABOUT SHEENA

I am Sheena and I am a dedicated mother of five and a proud nanny to one, with a passion for helping others transform their lives. I believes in the power of living a healthy lifestyle to not only improve physical well-being but also to cultivate a positive mindset and a more optimistic outlook on life. Through my guidance, I empower individuals to become the best version of themselves, embracing healthier habits that fuel personal growth, confidence, and a better attitude towards life's challenges. With a nurturing spirit and a commitment to wellness, I like to inspire others to thrive in both body and mind.

KATE FISHER
DEFYING THE
INSURMOUNTABLE

What would you say to your child if you were told you only had ten minutes to say goodbye to them … and then they would be taken away to die in a room without you by their side?

What would you do if you were dependent on the kindness of strangers to anonymously take time out of their day, to donate a part of themselves, to keep your child alive?

What would you do if you identified a creative solution to a social problem? One which had the potential to not just keep your child alive, but save the lives of people all over the world?

Sometimes courage comes when we feel at our weakest, at our most hopeless, broken and defeated. This is my story, of how when I barely had the strength to muster a whisper, I found the courage to roar.

When a flower doesn't bloom, we fix the environment in which it grows, not the flower.

My first step in leading with courage was cultivating an environment in which I could bloom! This has meant surrounding myself with people who have overcome adversity, people who show kindness, generosity of spirit and are passionate about making the world a better place for people to live in. If I am the flower, I bloom when I am not just standing alone, but surrounded by flora of all different shapes, sizes, viability and potential. I lead by not just working towards my goals with passion but also by recognising and building the capacities of those around me, so that as a collective, we can have a positive impact.

I've had to lead with courage in so many different ways in my life: whether it be developing public health policy for a national portfolio; advocating for disability funding or accommodations for my children; completing my final years of educating while couch surfing with no fixed address as a homeless teen; advocating for myself as a patient while undergoing fertility treatment and sixteen surgeries for endometriosis and adenomyosis; or for my daughter with a life-threatening health condition. Every one of these experiences taught me something new about leadership.

I learned that the best leaders come from a place of authenticity and vulnerability. I've led with the greatest courage when I've been able to strip back my ego and lead with a sense of purpose. For me, that vulnerability came when our youngest daughter was diagnosed with a life-threatening health condition at just three years old. Seronegative paediatric autoimmune encephalitis is a condition for which there is no cure, however treatment is possible with intravenous immunoglobulin infusion (IVIG), which is made from donated human plasma. At her sickest, Marleigh was spending three days out of every two weeks receiving that treatment, and it was the only thing that would stop her having life-threatening, prolonged status epilepticus seizures, the longest of which lasted thirty-nine hours. Marleigh will be dependent on blood products for the rest of her life, as for her, blood products are lifesaving when she has an acute relapse and life-preserving for every infusion in-between.

The best parents become who their child needs them to be.

I've always practised an attachment parenting style. This has never been more useful than when my child was living in and out of hospital, for years on end, with a life-threatening condition that has no cure, and was robbing her of her physical and cognitive abilities. As the mother at the helm of a family with additional needs, I had learned with each child, as their needs emerged, that the best parents become who their child needs them to be. This has meant changing the way we ate when our children and I were diagnosed with a rare form of genetic diabetes, maturity onset diabetes of the young (MODY2). I had to show my love through restricting the foods we previously enjoyed, constant monitoring of blood glucose levels and lining the kids up to administer insulin injections.

I've become the mother my children needed by learning about neurodiversity and how best to parent children with attention deficit hyperactivity disorder and autism. I've learned how to advocate for my children to have appropriate accommodations made in their school and community settings, how to secure funding for them through the National Disability Insurance Scheme, access the best supports for their early intervention, and to support their independence into adulthood. Not just so they can cope, but so they can thrive.

I've navigated infertility, IVF, recurrent miscarriages, delivering and caring for a premature baby, a birth that left me with a permanent physical disability, the death of one of our identical twins during our pregnancy, while carrying them both to term and birthing them both. I've been to my own baby's funeral, holding one of the twins in my arms while looking at the tiny shoebox-sized white coffin of the other. My breastmilk soaking my dress and flowing as freely as my tears as I battled to manage the oversupply of milk that my body was producing in anticipation of feeding two babies, rather than just the one surviving twin.

I've learned how to manage seizures at home, administer seizure rescue medications and optimise my child's ability to continue breathing on her own until an ambulance arrives. I've become accredited as a service dog handler, passed a public access test with Marleigh's seizure alert and autism support service dog and become responsible for his ongoing training.

I've done most of the above while pursuing a career that I loved, undertaking postgraduate study, volunteering and contributing to my local community, all while loving my husband and making our home a place filled with joy, where we feel safe and connected, and trying to be a kind and supportive sister, daughter and friend.

Because to be the mother my children need, I need to be engaged in pursuits of my own, that stimulate me in ways outside my home and my domestic responsibilities.

We are a collection of our experiences; our best-laid plans take us on adventures we could never have dreamed of.

When Marleigh was at her sickest, we lived life in a fourteen-day cycle. The first three to four days were spent in hospital receiving IVIG and other medications to optimise its effect. This would prolong her life for ten days at a time before her immune system would, again, start to identify her healthy brain cells as foreign and attack them, causing brain inflammation and terrifying seizures that threatened her life, leaving her with devastating deficits. Before she became sick, Marleigh was a happy, strong, healthy three-year-old who frequented playgrounds, tended to her veggie patch and her chooks in our backyard, loved her weekly playgroup, sport and dance lessons. Within the space of a year, she was using a wheelchair, unable to feed herself, regressed back to nappies and was learning how to use a speech device to communicate. Each time she would have a prolonged status epilepticus seizure, she lost more skills. For a while, she didn't recognise us as her parents. She would then spend months in hospital, undergoing extensive rehabilitation, and even regain some of the skills she had lost, only to have another massive and prolonged seizure, ending up in another helicopter being emergency airlifted to a paediatric intensive care unit in an induced coma on life support, to start the process all over again. IVIG was the only treatment that worked. No amount of science or medical technology can preserve her life without this treatment and blood can't be made! The kindness of Australian blood donors keeps her alive!

I've shown the greatest strength when my 'roaring' has been a barely audible whisper …

I've been told, more than once, 'It's unlikely your child will survive the night.' I've been given ten minutes to say goodbye before she was taken away from me and put into a COVID-19 insolation room without me. We were prepared for her to die, surrounded by strangers covered from head to toe in protective equipment; strangers who were the most incredibly selfless medical professionals, risking their own lives and the lives of their loved ones to care for our daughter. These were the health professionals who managed the right medications to help her overcome the pneumonia that resulted in a sepsis, all the way from the paediatric intensive care doctors and nurses to the phenomenal PICU administration staff to the play therapist who would, in the months to follow, help Marleigh to tell her story that she 'went up through the roof into the clouds but then the rainbows brought me back to my mummy'.

I've experienced the feeling of utter devastation and frustration at the injustice of my child being the one afflicted with this horrible illness. That's what I've wanted to 'roar' at – to scream and spew violent, toxic hate. But instead, I've recognised there is no point in investing my energy in things I can't control. I've redirected that energy into dedicating my life to being a blood donation advocate. When I commenced this, I thought it would be Marleigh's legacy project. A thank you to the Australian blood donors who gave her more time and improved her quality of life. I couldn't have imagined she would reach the age of eight, achieve remission and be part-time at school, with only a distant memory of using a wheelchair and a speech device.

Adversity can give clarity to our mission and purpose.

Saying goodbye to Marleigh, even though she survived, has been life-defining for our whole family. It's made us all reflect on our priorities; not just what we want the legacy of Marleigh's illness to be, but what impact we want to have during our lifetime. It's made us realise that the future isn't promised … for anyone.

Before Marleigh became unwell, I didn't know that Australia experiences persistent critical blood shortages, or that one in three people will need blood during their lifetime, yet only one in thirty Aussies are blood donors. This means that much of the blood required to treat Australians is purchased from overseas. Before my child's life depended on people donating blood to preserve her life, these facts were just another headline I scrolled past because I didn't think they were relevant to me.

My blood donation advocacy movement is a creative solution to a social problem. I've created a variety of platforms through social media, my podcast and my book, where those who have needed blood (or their loved ones), tell extraordinary tales of survival to thank blood donors and to encourage new ones. This creativity in storytelling aims to address the social problem of not enough people donating blood to meet the demand of those who need it to preserve their lives. I never want a family to have to say goodbye to their loved one because not enough people have donated blood to save their life.

'What do you want to do when you grow up?' or 'Who do you want to be?'

I am a mother at the helm of a family with additional needs. We share a long list on various physical and neurodevelopmental disabilities and complex medical conditions, however, I refrain from using the terminology 'special needs child' to describe any of our children, as I don't think it fully reflects the impact that an injury, illness or disability has on a family. There is no doubt the disability and health challenges my family experience have a social, economic and emotional health impact on us all. It's significantly impacted my career trajectory but it hasn't changed my commitment to using my skills and experience to make the world a better place for those around me.

There is nothing unique about the challenges I have faced and re-evaluating my priorities and the contributions I wish to make. Everyone will face personal adversity at some stage in their lives that will likely influence their productivity. I encourage people to think about what they would like to do first ... or next. Maybe we need a greater focus on the impact we wish to have, rather than the job title we wish to hold.

Embracing career manoeuvrability and combining my education with my personal and professional experiences has allowed me to position myself as Australia's primary blood donation advocate. My work is being recognised as having an impact on blood donation rates all over the world. Most importantly, I know I am doing everything within my power to ensure that if/when Marleigh has an autoimmune encephalitis relapse, there will be enough plasma in Australia's reserves to make her treatment possible.

Blood donors don't just keep people alive, they keep families together. If you are a blood donor and ever listen to an episode of my podcast or read my book, you can wonder if you were the one who saved, prolonged or improved the quality of life of the person in each episode or chapter. Every blood donation has the ability to save three lives. If you can't donate blood, please join me as a blood donation advocate. Share a social media post, download or recommend the podcast or buy a copy of my book. You never know when it will be you or someone you love who will be reliant on the kindness of an anonymous blood donor.

I will end this chapter in the same way that I end every one of my podcast episodes, by leaving the final words to Marleigh, who always says: *'Thank you for my plasma!'*

ABOUT KATE

Kate Fisher is Australia's primary blood donation advocate. She is the founder of Milkshakes for Marleigh, where she is on a mission to end persistent critical blood shortages in Australia and around the world. Kate has a number of family members who have received blood including her daughter Marleigh who will be dependent on blood donors for life.

Kate is the host and producer of *The Milkshakes for Marleigh* podcast where she tells the survival stories of blood product recipients. This is her creative solution to the social problem that not enough people donate blood. Only one in thirty Australians donate blood and yet one in three will need it in their lifetime. Kate is on a mission to change that, while thanking as many blood donors as she can along the way.

In 2024, Kate published her first book called *Milkshakes for Marleigh* which tells extraordinary tales of survival thanks to Australian blood donors. Like the podcast, the concept of the book is that if you have ever been a blood donor, you can read a story in the book and wonder if you were the blood donor who saved their life? It is her most recent tool in her blood donation advocacy.

Kate is a mother at the helm of a family with additional needs. Kate has four children, three of them are living and like her, they have various complex medical conditions, physical and neurodevelopmental disabilities. She is helplessly in love with her husband Geoff and adores navigating their crazy, challenging, joy filled life together.

Australians can add their blood donations to the The Milkshakes for Marleigh Lifeblood Team, which allows Kate to track donations made by people who have been inspired by her blood donation advocacy and Marleigh's story. This group of donors have saved the lives of over five thousand Aussies in the last three years! Those outside Australia can share their stories and blood donations via the Milkshakes for Marleigh social media channels.

Website: milkshakesformarleigh.org
Instagram: Kate Fisher @Milkshakes_for_Marleigh
The Milkshakes for Marleigh Book:
kmdbooks.com/milkshakesformarleigh

Please book an appointment to give blood today and if you are in Australia, add your donation to The Milkshakes for Marleigh Lifeblood Team!

LAURA ELIZABETH
EMBRACING THE JOURNEY

As I write this chapter, I'm reminded of the winding path that has led me to where I am today. It's a path marked by challenges, struggles and moments of profound growth. In sharing my story, I hope to illuminate how my experiences as a single mother, navigating divorce and battling anxiety and depression, have enriched my role as a mentor, educator and healer.

I've spent years grappling with facets of my identity that didn't fit the image I wanted to project. Each time I levelled up in life, it came at a cost, feeling compelled to shed another layer, burying parts of myself in the process. How can I positively impact the world if I don't have it all together?

However, I've realised that by rejecting these aspects of my identity, I've inadvertently shut out opportunities for meaningful connections and lucrative ventures to facilitate real change and impact. What if, instead of shunning these parts of myself, I embraced them as integral to my identity? What if every experience, every twist and turn, contributed to the rich tapestry that is me, Laura, right now?

It's time for a shift in perspective. What if I viewed my past not as burdens to be discarded but as stepping stones that have sculpted my resilience and added to my unique skill set? With this new approach, I can fully embrace the complexity of who I am.

Yes, I'm an author and publisher. Yes, I specialise in sex education and empowerment for women and couples. And yes, I'm a devoted single mother of three. But I'm also the kid who endured bullying, the person who sings wildly and out of tune in the car and shower, and sometimes, the person who cries at romcoms. Embracing all these aspects allows me to offer my true, authentic self to the world.

LIFE EXPERIENCE

My journey as a single mother has been challenging and rewarding over the past eight years. Balancing the responsibilities of parenthood, while pursuing my devotion to being of service, has taught me invaluable skills in multitasking and time management. Juggling school pickups, basketball practice and bedtime snuggles with deadlines and client meetings has honed my ability to prioritise and organise my time effectively. But the greatest lesson I've learned as a single mother is the depth of unconditional love. Every sacrifice, late night and scraped knee is a testament to my unwavering love for my children.

Navigating divorce was one of the most challenging chapters of my life. It forced me to confront my fears, insecurities and the reality of burning life, as I knew it, to the ground and starting over. But through the pain and confusion, I discovered a reservoir of resilience within myself that I never knew existed. I learned to adapt to new circumstances, find strength in vulnerability and embrace the unknown with courage and determination. Divorce taught me the importance of self-reliance and independence, empowering me to stand on my own two feet and forge my own path forward. I learned to say yes to more and pivot when it didn't align.

Yet, it was in the depths of anxiety and depression that I faced my most significant challenges. The weight of daily responsibilities and the relentless pressure to keep it all together pushed me to my breaking point. But through therapies, mentors, self-reflection and support from loved ones, I found the courage to confront my demons head-on. I learned to embrace my vulnerability, to practise self-compassion, and to seek help when I needed it most. In doing so, I discovered a new-found strength within myself that allowed me to weather life's storms with grace and resilience.

These are just a few experiences that have profoundly shaped me, moulding me into the person I am today. They have taught me the importance of perseverance, compassion and empathy. They have instilled in me a deep appreciation for the complexities of the human experience, and a profound gratitude for every triumph and setback. They have equipped me with the wisdom and insight to guide others on their journeys of self-discovery and healing.

TRAUMA AWARENESS

My personal journey has provided me with a profound understanding of the lasting effects of trauma on mental health and overall wellbeing. Having faced my own battles with anxiety, depression and the upheaval of divorce, I intimately understand the intricate layers of pain and struggle that accompany traumatic experiences. These firsthand encounters have cultivated within me a heightened sensitivity to the silent wounds so many carry with them.

Through the lens of my own trauma, I've gained a deeper appreciation for the complexities of human suffering. I've come to understand that trauma isn't confined to a single event but can manifest in a multitude of ways, infiltrating every aspect of a person's life. The lingering sense of fear grips your heart in moments of vulnerability. The persistent doubt whispers in your ear, convincing you you're not worthy of love or happiness. The invisible scars dim the surface of even the brightest smile.

This awareness has profoundly shaped my mentor, educator and healer approach. It has instilled a sense of empathy that transcends words, allowing me to sit with others in their pain without judgement or condemnation. It has also cultivated a deep understanding of the intricate web of emotions that underlie every individual's journey, enabling me to offer support and guidance tailored to their unique needs and experiences.

Additionally, trauma awareness has heightened my commitment to creating safe and nurturing spaces for healing and growth. Whether I'm leading a workshop, facilitating a somatic therapy or bodywork session or simply engaging in conversation with a friend in need, I strive to nurture an environment of trust and acceptance where individuals feel seen, heard and valued for who they are.

My journey through trauma has been a catalyst for profound personal and professional growth. It has taught me the importance of bearing witness to the pain of others with compassion and understanding. It has reminded me that healing is a journey, not a destination and that each step forward is a testament to the resilience of the human spirit and the identity we build upon along the way. Most importantly, it has reinforced my belief in the transformative power of empathy and connection in healing and recovery.

DISCERNMENT AND BOUNDARIES

Through these challenging circumstances, life has been a masterclass in discernment and setting healthy boundaries. When faced with adversity, I was forced to confront what mattered and prioritise accordingly. This process honed my ability to discern between what is essential and merely noise. This skill has proven invaluable in my personal and professional growth.

As a mentor and educator, I draw upon these experiences to guide others in cultivating their own sense of discernment and establishing boundaries that honour their needs and priorities. I understand firsthand the impact blurred boundaries can have on mental and emotional wellbeing. I'm passionate about empowering others to create and embody healthy boundaries that support their growth and happiness.

Central to this process is cultivating self-awareness and tuning into our innermost thoughts, feelings and desires. By encouraging introspection and reflection, I help individuals clarify their values, goals and boundaries. Together, we explore what truly matters to them and identify areas where boundaries may be lacking or need reinforcement.

Most importantly, I emphasise the importance of self-compassion when setting boundaries. I remind individuals that it's okay to prioritise their own needs and wellbeing, even if it means disappointing others or stepping outside their comfort zone. I recognise that boundaries are not a sign of weakness, but rather an essential aspect of self-care and self-respect. In doing so, I believe we create a ripple effect of empowerment and transformation, extending far beyond ourselves.

DETERMINATION AND RESILIENCE

Regardless of whether life has challenges, I've always focused on pursuing a better future. Where I am today is a testament to the unwavering power of determination and resilience; two qualities that have carried me through even the darkest times.

When faced with adversity, I chose to harness the power of determination to propel me toward my goals and aspirations. I've learned that resilience isn't just about bouncing back from setbacks; it's about embracing the challenges we face and using them as catalysts for growth and transformation. Each stumble has been an opportunity for me to dig deep, tap into my inner reservoir of strength, and emerge stronger and more resilient than before.

As a healer, my role is more than providing solace and comfort to those in need. I see myself as a living example of the transformative power of determination and resilience. By sharing my experiences, I inspire others to tap into their strength, persevere through their challenges, and embrace the journey of self-discovery and healing.

True healing begins when we acknowledge our pain, confront our fears and refuse to let adversity define us. By embodying all parts of our identity with the qualities of determination and resilience, we empower ourselves to transcend our limitations, break free from the chains of our past and step boldly into the future.

WHY EMBRACE ALL ASPECTS OF IDENTITY?

Embracing all facets of our identity is crucial and transformative. Our struggles, triumphs and everything in-between contribute to the tapestry of who we are, adding depth and authenticity to our being.

Acknowledging and honouring our struggles is the first step towards cultivating self-awareness. When we confront the challenges we've faced, whether, in my case, it's the pain of divorce, the demands of single parenthood or the battle with mental health, we gain a deeper understanding of ourselves. We uncover hidden strengths, unearth buried emotions and confront the vulnerabilities that make us human. Through this process of introspection, we cultivate a profound sense of self-awareness that extends beyond the surface level and delves into the depths of our psyche.

But self-awareness is just the beginning. Embracing our struggles opens us to compassion and empathy, which are essential for building meaningful connections with others. When we recognise the pain and suffering we've endured, we become more attuned to the struggles of those around us. We develop a heightened sense of empathy, allowing us to connect with others on a deeper level, to share in their joys and sorrows and to offer genuine support and guidance.

We can break down the barriers that separate us from one another. When we share our stories authentically and open up about our experiences, both triumphs and tribulations, we create a space for vulnerability and connection. We invite others to do the same, building a community that transcends the boundaries of race, gender and background.

Embracing all of our identity means acknowledging the messy, complicated, beautiful tapestry of human experience and finding strength and resilience in our shared humanity. To co-create a world where authenticity, compassion and empathy reign supreme, where we can truly see and be seen, support and be supported, love and be loved.

CREATING THE PERFECT RECIPE FOR AUTHENTICITY

Authenticity is not about presenting a polished facade to the world – far from it! It's about embracing our entire selves, flaws, scars and all. When we dare to be vulnerable and acknowledge and embrace the struggles that have shaped us, we unlock the power of authenticity.

Embracing struggles allows us to integrate our experiences into our identity and become more authentic mentors, educators and healers. When we share our stories authentically, we invite others to do the same. Our vulnerability becomes our strength, our scars become our badges of honour, and our willingness to show up as our true selves inspires those around us to do the same.

As mentors, educators and healers, authenticity is our greatest asset. It allows us to connect with others on a deeper level, build trust and rapport, and create meaningful change in the lives of those we serve. It is what makes us relatable. Being honest about our imperfections shows others that being human is okay.

Integrating our struggles into our identity and claiming all the parts of us is the key to authenticity. It's what allows us to show up as our true selves and create meaningful change in the world. *All of you* matters. All parts of your identity add value to the lives you enrich and deepen your capacity to help others.

When we embrace all aspects of our identity, including the parts that society may deem as undesirable or imperfect, we unlock a wealth of wisdom and empathy that can profoundly impact our work as mentors, educators and healers. Our personal struggles provide us with a unique perspective. We can offer guidance from a place of authenticity and create genuine connections built on trust and understanding.

Our willingness to embrace our struggles and share our stories authentically is a powerful act of self-acceptance and empowerment. It sends a powerful message to others that they are not alone in their struggles, that their experiences are valid, and that there is hope for healing and growth.

In this way, embracing all aspects of our identity becomes a personal journey of self-discovery and acceptance and a profound opportunity to make a positive impact in the lives of others.

So, there will be no more deleting parts of ourselves with every win.

Instead, celebrate the entirety of who you are, constantly adding the new pieces that make up your magnificence and helping to inspire healing, empowerment and transformation in the lives of everyone around you.

ABOUT LAURA

Laura Elizabeth, a trailblazing change maker and front runner for elevating the pleasure frequency of the planet. Bestselling Author and publisher, Director at Tikl and expert trauma informed space holder, energy worker, somatic bodyworker, sacred women's medicine code keeper and exorcist (to name a few).

Dedicated to creating intimate experiences for conscious humans ready to step into a deeper layer of understanding and healing of themselves. I stand with you as you remember to embrace and embody your sensuality, reclaim your voice and own your personal power.

A passionate solo mother of three, leading by example, smashing goals and living with purpose, Laura hopes to be a positive influence for her children to reach their full potential and inspire others to do the same.

www.lauraelizabeth.com.au
www.instagram.com/the_lauraelizabeth_official
www.facebook.com/eroticmaven

TEENA RAFFA-MULLIGAN
A LEGACY OF LOVE

As a child growing up in Western Australia in the 1950s and 60s, I thought all families were like ours. The four of us – Dad, Mum, me and my younger brother – lived in a small asbestos house in a quiet street in a working-class suburb south of Perth, surrounded by similar homes built by the State Housing Commission after the war.

Dad rode his bicycle to and from the Fremantle leather tannery, where he worked as a labourer, until he could afford to buy a car. Mum stayed home to care for all of us and keep house. It was a simple life focused on family. There wasn't much money but the bills were paid on time and there was always food on the table. Everyone else we knew seemed to live much the same sort of life.

It wasn't until I was older that I realised there was something different about our family. The ideas my brother and I were being exposed to in those early years were unusual for that era and in that environment. For our dad had experienced a spiritual awakening early in his marriage that changed his life and, of course, ultimately ours as well. It has without question been the strongest influence on the direction I took in my life and the person I became.

A little background here. My father, Joseph – Joe to all his family, friends and colleagues – was the son of an Italian fisherman who came to WA at the start of the twentieth century from Sicily and was one of the pioneers of the State's crayfishing industry. Once established here, he decided it was time to marry and raise a family, so he returned to Sicily, married my grandmother, brought her to Australia, and they settled in Fremantle in view of the sea that was his livelihood. It was a close migrant community that retained many of their homeland's traditional values, and the children grew up between two cultures.

Dad was one of seven children, five sons and two daughters; the only son who didn't become a fisherman. He was baptised in the Catholic religion but by the time he reached his teens, he had become, in his words, 'an atheist who looked to science for the answers to the riddles of life and the universe'. His foray into theosophy and philosophy led him to the books of Krishnamurti and Paul Brunton, which set him on a path of self-discovery and spiritual awakening, and he experienced a life-changing revelation in his early twenties. As he put it many years later, 'In a blissful moment of discovery, the God the Bible speaks of, the Allah of Mohammed and the longed-for Nirvana of the Buddhists came into my life.'

From that moment on, spirituality was the foundation of his life and his interactions with others. Throughout my childhood the tiny kitchen, in that modest house in the suburbs, was a hub of discussion about the meaning of life and the importance of self-discovery if we wish to live together in peace and harmony. A procession of family, friends, acquaintances and strangers, who happened to cross Dad's path, sat around the table over the years.

Mum served tea, sandwiches, cake and biscuits as the conversation rose and fell in that welcoming space. There was much laughter … and often tears, for some came especially to speak with Dad about their troubles. They knew he would listen without judgement and sensed he might have insights to offer that would help ease their way through life's difficulties. With those who were open to it, he shared his own spiritual journey and the message that what had touched him and transformed his life so dramatically was there for anyone who cared to seek it.

I grew up hearing that message and accepting dreams, visions and insights as a normal part of everyday life. In an era when most children were still expected to be seen rather than heard, I was free to have a voice. I was encouraged to question everything, and most importantly, to question everything I thought I knew about myself and the world in which I lived.

'The answers are within you,' Dad said, and those words resonated with me from the start. I never doubted the truth of them and readily accepted there was a greater power than us and a deeper meaning to this experience of living than there appeared to be on the surface.

'Look inward,' he said. So I did, observing my thoughts and emotions, the working of my mind, and from the age of fourteen, I considered myself a committed spiritual seeker, setting out on my own path of self-discovery.

When my children arrived, they grew up hearing the same message I had heard as a child, and their upbringing has helped to shape the parents they have become. For a man who believed he was nothing special, Dad's influence has touched many.

Unlike me, Dad never set out to become a writer, but his experience led him to put pen to paper, to encourage people seeking truth to turn their attention inward, rather than looking for answers to the meaning of life in the outside world. Some would describe Dad's inspired writing as 'channelling' and this description could easily be applied to it, for he never took to pen and paper with a clear intention of writing or any conscious decision about what to write. He always spoke of the writing as 'coming through' him.

Over the years, he also wrote countless letters on topical subjects to newspapers and became quite well known in his local community. However, most of Dad's writing was only shared among family and friends and did not find a wider audience because he wasn't driven to seek publication. I always felt that making his work available to other spiritual seekers was my role, although I didn't take any practical steps to do this until 1999.

At that time, Dad was experiencing the greatest challenge of his life – caring for my mum, his beloved 'blue-eyed girl', as she slipped ever deeper into Alzheimer's disease. I wanted to do something to lift his spirits, so I published a collection of his essays about Jesus as a small paperback called *Beyond the Cross*. He was touched by the gift but it was not a time for celebration.

Mum's decline was rapid and shocking to us all. Within three years of being diagnosed, she was bedridden and totally incapacitated, unable to speak, walk or care for herself in any way. Dad spent hours every day at the nursing home, feeding her, holding her, letting her know she was deeply loved. It was a time of heartbreak for us all and I felt the loss deeply, for not only was I saying a lingering goodbye to my lovely gentle mum, I'd lost Dad too. His spirit was crushed and his heart badly broken. It took me by surprise. This deeply spiritual man, who'd been such a powerful influence on my life, seemed lost.

After Mum died, I expected Dad to pick up his pen again and continue the writing that had been interrupted so brutally by the demands of caring for a wife with Alzheimer's. It didn't happen. Not long afterwards, he was diagnosed with cancer and instead spent his final years in quiet contemplation and communion with nature.

I knew he planned to entrust me with his collection of manuscripts and we'd talked of it often.

Writing was one of the interests Dad and I shared, though our focus was different. While he only wrote when the compulsion arose and was convinced it was coming from a higher aspect of consciousness, my own writing was with conscious intent. Surrounded as a child by my extended family of English and Italian relatives who willingly shared their stories with an eager listener, I had known from an early age that I wanted to be a writer. I began writing for children and seeking publication from the age of twenty-one when our son was born, and spent my working life as a journalist and editor.

Often following a family meal at my parents' place, Dad would duck out to the sleep-out he now used as an office and return with his latest spiritual piece for me to read. There were frequent phone calls to seek my opinion on a letter to the editor or to report on the latest publication or response by other readers of the local paper.

Dad wrote everything by hand. Initially I typed his work for him. However, once I started doing regular freelance work for magazines and newspapers, I bought myself a new typewriter and passed on my little portable Olivetti to Dad. He'd had a work accident many years earlier that left him with parts of his fingers missing on one hand, so he built up the typewriter keys with cork and taught himself to type. When I graduated to computers, my husband and I eventually convinced Dad to make the switch too.

An orderly man, he filed printouts of all his writing in ring folders, complete with indexes, and by the time he died in 2010, these collections filled two bookcases, and all his original handwritten manuscripts were stored in boxes. There was also a box of floppy disks, for although Dad graduated from a typewriter to a computer, he never saw the need to update, especially when there were more important things to deal with in his life. Fortunately, my son-in-law had access to a computer where he worked that he could use to copy the files from the floppies to small disks.

There was no room at our house for Dad's two bookcases (I'd already brought home Mum's Singer treadle sewing machine, the His Master's Voice Radiogram and Dad's other bookcase from their lounge room), so during the process of clearing out his house for sale, I packed all the files and manuscripts in boxes. For months afterwards there was barely room for me to move in my office as I slowly sorted through more than a dozen boxes that, along with Dad's writing, also included half a century's worth of receipts and family records.

I knew from the start that publishing Dad's work would be a slow process. Although I retired from my part-time job at the local paper several months after Dad died, I was still busy with my own writing, plus volunteering with a community arts group and later the local writer's centre. The publishing scene had changed dramatically since I'd produced that small copy of *Beyond the Cross* ten years earlier, and it excited me how easily authors could release print-on-demand (POD) and digital (e-book) formats of their work.

While the process of publishing this way looked straightforward and I was sure I could navigate my way through it easily enough, getting the first of Dad's books to readers took far longer than expected. First, I had to convert all the individual document files from his ancient word processing program (Word Star, for those with long memories) to Microsoft Word. Because the files were already on a separate disk, it made sense to release a new, updated edition of *Beyond the Cross* first. This was released in 2014, followed by *The Silent Guardian*, a manuscript that had been accepted for publication by a Queensland spiritual publisher before Dad's death but had never gone ahead. Then came *Beside Still Waters*, a beautiful collection of Dad's essays that touches on the universal search for meaning and inspires readers to reach out for the still waters of the spirit.

I also started a blog called *Towards the Silent Heart* to post some of his many spiritual articles.

Sea Song Publications was established in 2018 as the next stage of the publishing process and the first six titles were released of what I was now calling *The Kitchen Table Philosophy Series* because throughout my life, that's where our family shared so many in-depth conversations about the importance of self-discovery and the meaning of life. In 2021, I released a digital boxed set of this series, but publishing more of Dad's work has been on hold for the past few years.

Some health and family issues, as well as the global pandemic, led me to experience a period of personal reflection. I stopped writing. For the first time since I was a child, I didn't have a head full of stories insisting on being written, and it took me by surprise. Outwardly, I was still involved in the writing community, for I continued to publish manuscripts I had on file, present workshops and talks and do some freelance copyediting and proofreading. But as far as I was concerned, my writing days were over and I came to feel at peace with that. Unexpectedly, towards the end of 2023, I began to write again, starting with a few nature poems and several non-fiction personal experience pieces for anthologies. Coupled with this has been a renewed excitement about possibilities for the future, and sharing more of Dad's work is part of that. I'm planning a podcast … a newsletter … audiobooks … the release of additional titles. He left such a wonderful legacy of spiritual writing, which although it wasn't written recently, has just as much relevance for today's troubled world as it did when he wrote it.

Publishing Dad's books has never been a business venture for me but a labour of love. It isn't about notching up sales figures, but reaching those readers who will find his words speak to them inwardly. I'm committed to sharing his writing in the same spirit he offered it, along with all the guidance he provided to the many people who sought his support in times of trouble: from one heart to another in love.

ABOUT TEENA

Teena Raffa-Mulligan grew up in an English/Italian family in Western Australia, surrounded by natural storytellers whose tales about their lives captured her imagination. Books also opened a window into the world of make believe and her ambition to be a writer was born at an early age.

Teena writes quirky, whimsical books for children full of warmth, gentle humour, heart and hope. Her publications range from picture books to middle grade and YA novels, exploring themes of family, friendship and the need to belong. Many of Teena's poems and short stories for children and adults have appeared in magazines and anthologies and her writing life has also included a long career in journalism. She is passionate about the importance of story in our lives to inspire greater empathy and understanding between people.

Teena shares her home near the beach with a sometime surfer and a golden Labrador with anxiety issues and a toast obsession. When not writing or encouraging people of all ages to write their own stories, she likes to fill her life with family time, sunshine, birdsong and flowers.

CAROLE GOODMAN
WHERE IS MY MUMMY?

On the 23 February 2019, sitting at a business conference in Brisbane, I knew something was 'missing;' there was this *something* I did not know. I looked around and saw the faces of those with whom I had journeyed with for so many years, as if in a time warp, and I knew there was MORE. The realisation was that few of us were achieving the results in our lives that we had worked so hard and long for, and worst still, none of us knew WHY. I developed a burning DESIRE within me to seek and find the answer.

There was something we did not know, something we were not being told, something beyond our grasp I could not put my finger on. I walked away from that conference, slipped out of the world I had known all my life and began the search.

I was sick and tired of the limitations in my life. I wanted to be, do and have so much more and I was determined to find the answer.

Whilst I did not know WHAT, I knew a door had opened; a door that no man could shut.

I did not know then what I know now and that is:

'What you are seeking is seeking you.' – Rumi

And so, my journey began.

This was a pivotal time for me as I also realised that not just myself, but many others like me, were stuck. I looked around and could see those like me, *doing the hard work* but not getting the results they wanted. YES, there was something 'missing'.

My search for a fuller understanding was prompted by a deep sense of isolation. I began to feel myself separating from those around me; my friends, family and business associates. I felt very alone.

To the outside world, I had everything. I had been born to a deeply religious father, who had converted to Catholicism at the age of thirteen. My mother was an alcoholic with a troubled past and left when I was young. It was my father who raised my sister and me, and for that, I am eternally grateful.

My husband and I raised our children within an Ecumenical Covenant Community for twenty years and, with this background, I believed everything I was taught; I was taught never to question.

I had been married to my soul mate for over fifty years. We had retired early, travelled extensively all over Australia in our caravan, as well as overseas to wonderful countries, including Nepal and Antarctica. I was regarded by my family and friends to *have it all* and now was the time, at the age of seventy, to settle into 'old age thinking' and bring out the knitting and puzzles, accepting I was in my twilight years.

At this time, I felt more isolated and misunderstood than I had ever felt. I was starting to speak *a second language*; a language that my family and friends did not understand. I withdrew more and more into myself.

Worst of all, I felt I was being judged as *greedy*, because to the outside world I did *have it all.* But, somehow, I knew within me, this was not enough; I was not satisfied. I knew there was MORE. I could not settle, as there was something calling me on. Just what that *something* was I wasn't sure, but I knew I had to find it.

Little did I know then, but a book that had been put into my hands in June 2014 – *Think and Grow Rich* by Napoleon Hill – was going to my guiding light. I picked up this book again in 2019 and began to read it, over and over again. Looking back, I still did not understand this book, but I just couldn't put it down. Now, it is one of my most treasured possessions.

One morning in February 2021, I stumbled across a man on YouTube called Bob Proctor, who was being interviewed by Lewis Howes. During this conversation, Bob mentioned his beginnings with *Think and Grow Rich* and how it had changed his life back in 1961, when he was twenty-six years old.

So began my journey with Bob Proctor. I listened on YouTube as he explained about the '11 Forgotten Laws of the Universe'.

I was intrigued, as I had never heard of this sort of talk before. And so I listened, even transcribed these Laws 'word for word' into a Word document on my computer. Yes, I was so intrigued, Bob Proctor had caught my attention and I wanted to know more.

I continued to listen to Bob Proctor and his words rang true for me. Little did I realise then, that 'this truth would set me free'. I saw that there was truth in what he was saying and I made a decision to find out more.

I chose to sign up for a five-day seminar given by Bob Proctor and on the completion of this, I knew this was where I was meant to be. Right then and there, I made the *decision* to begin the twelve-month coaching course offered by the 'Proctor Gallagher Institute' (PGI).

As Steve Jobs quoted, 'You can't connect the dots looking forward; you can only connect them looking backwards.'

This is so true for me, as it is only now looking back that I realise the *truth* that had been hidden from me for so long; the *truth* of 'who I am' and what I and every other human being is *born to be*.

The greatest discovery for me through my twelve-month journey has been the realisation that I am a *thought-evolved being*. It is my 'mind' that governs what I choose in my life and who and what I believe I am; what I am capable of being, doing and having. I now also realise, through an understanding of physio cybernetics, how I have been controlled, through my past conditioning, passed on through genetics and the environment in which I grew up in; my parents, grandparents, teachers, the church, society and all other well-meaning people. I have been conditioned into believing 'who I am and what I am capable of' and more importantly, 'what I am *not* capable of'. I have awoken to the monstrous belief that I have always lived by, and that is of 'earning *my place into heaven*'.

I understand, now, that everyone living with that belief were just doing their best with the knowledge and understanding they had in their own lives, but it crippled my spirit and governed my life for all of my seventy years.

Many people walk around like zombies, not because they don't care but because they don't THINK. They don't question what they are taught to believe.

We think about what we are going to wear, what accessories would match our outfit. Then we may think about what we are going to cook for dinner that day or what holiday we might go on … and so on and so on; constant repetition every day. Yes, this is all necessary but it is not real 'deep' thinking. We don't consider the 'thinking' that controls our life. More importantly, we don't think about what will shape the precious life of the children in our care that will influence their behaviour and beliefs for their lifetime.

There are only a few short years to shape the thinking of our children, which will ultimately control their lives forever.

Can you imagine the difference it could make in our societies if each and every child grew up knowing they are loved? Or how having a great self-image and self-love of themselves can impact their life. What if they understood who they really were and what they are capable of?

I believe if every child knew their worth and felt (yes that feeling) that they belonged and saw themselves as beautiful in their skin, knowing they have the potential to reach for the stars, we would not have the problems we have in our society today. It really does start with US.

What is self-image? It is the way we see ourselves. It is the way we *feel* about our beautiful selves. It is the way we interact with others. It is how we navigate this world. YES, our self-image is the barometer we use to live in our world. We can never underestimate how important our self-image is. A great self-image will carry us to the moon and back – a poor self-image will keep us stuck and unable to move.

If our children grow up with a healthy and beautiful self-image, odds are they will never need to 'follow the follower', which in my opinion, is the downfall of so many of our young people today. They have never been taught to THINK. They often follow the follower, who does not really know where they are going.

I have shared these thoughts extensively in my book, *Where Is My Mummy?* It was written from a burden I have carried in my heart over many years.

I studied a bachelor of human services, graduating in 2002 at the age of fifty-three, and found myself drawn to corrections, where I witnessed the devastation of incarcerated women, not knowing who they were and the power within them. They had lost their families and their children.

However, it would be many years later before I came to understand *who I was* and how true freedom is brought about through a healthy self-image, which has the power to change our lives and that of our children. When I did discover the power of a healthy self-image, I knew what it was I was born to do. I felt compelled to make this understanding my purpose, my legacy, and bring it into the world NOW, before it's too late.

I cannot express my gratitude for having found this material; the unique understanding of Bob Proctor who understood how our minds work; the conscious and subconscious workings of the mind. Through this understanding, my life has changed. The subsequent growth beyond all understanding that comes when one opens oneself to this awareness; the understanding of the workings of the mind and who we really are is the lost treasure; *it is the secret.*

This revolutionary understanding, taught by Jesus, and so generously and lovingly understood and passed on by the giants of the past, now operating in my life, is by far one of my most precious gifts.

For now I know; THE KINGDOM ON EARTH IS NOW. It is not in some 'far off' place where I arrive at after I die, after living a life where I have to struggle to be 'good enough' to enter.

Life is meant to be lived. God's gift to me is more talent and ability than I could ever use and my gift to God is to live this life to the best of my ability.

This journey with Bob Proctor has been like peeling the layers of an onion; sometimes difficult, sometimes exhilarating, and at other times, not wanting to let go. At times, I wanted to sit in my misery; I did not always want to let go of the paradigms that had controlled my life up until then. These were challenging times because at these junctions of my life I could choose to hang onto the old paradigms that had controlled my life for seventy years. I could keep blaming others for my mistakes and not take responsibility for my own choices.

It was like wearing a comfortable old coat; I did not always want to let go. But I also knew I can never sit still, as spirit within me is always calling me on to be better today than I was yesterday, to become my 'better self'. I finally became free when I understood that my old paradigms were controlling my life, by wanting to *keep me safe,* but they were, in fact, killing me.

I am so happy and grateful that I stumbled across Bob Proctor at a time when I was searching for something I knew not what. I am grateful now that I understand I am the creator and maker of everything in my life; that I am totally responsible. I now take full responsibility for my life; good bad and indifferent. All the blaming, shaming, fussing, fuming, grief, worry and doubt is a thing of the past, as I now know who I am and the power within me. I am truly aligned with the Divine.

I love how Lisa Nichols describes 'my journey' on Page 182 of *The Secret:*

Every single thing you've been through, every single moment that you've come through, were to all prepare you for this moment right now. Imagine what you can do from this day forward with what you now know ... Who you are, what you do, begins right now.

So now it is my turn to ROAR.

I now know my purpose. I now know what I was created to do. I know my legacy is to pass onto every woman, in every corner of this incredible world, the understanding of *who they truly are* and the understanding of who this beautiful unique creature really is that they have brought into this marvellous world, as well as the responsibility that lays before them to give their child every opportunity to grow up with the most beautiful healthy *self-image* and understanding of *'who they are'*; to realise they are not alone but have the choice and a power within them to make *'their world'*; not their parents world, not their mates world, not their media's world but *their* world.

Yes, I was born to add value to this beautiful, wonderful world, so now it is time to HEAR ME ROAR.

ABOUT CAROLE

Born on 25 November 1949, Carole Josephine Goodman nee Burnham was born and raised in the western suburbs of Sydney, New South Wales, within a dysfunctional home, where her father was in the army and her mother an alcoholic, leaving when she was seven years old.

She was educated at St Jerome's Primary Punchbowl and spent some time at St Martha's Girls Home in Leichhardt before finishing her education in year ten at St Felix Catholic High School in Bankstown.

Study was always something she enjoyed and she further studied theology at the College of Theological Studies Banyo for many years, then completed a bachelor of social sciences (human services – corrections) in 2002, as well as recently studying under the Proctor Gallagher Institute of Personal Development.

Her marriage of fifty-four years, mother to her three children and grandmother to her seven grandchildren are to her the greatest achievements of her life.

Her passion today is in being an advocate for women to know who they are, their uniqueness in being a mother and the legacy they share in the raising of our teenagers of tomorrow.

Her motto is, 'It is never too late to learn – it is a lifelong experience.'

MICHELLE GARDINER
DON'T LET THEM TAME YOU

'You were wild once, don't let them tame you.'
– Isadora Duncan

Deeply inspired by dance, movement and human anatomy, this quote captured me on every level, many years ago, at a time when I was outgrowing layers of myself quicker than I could name them. Isadora Duncan, the creator of contemporary dance, found her way as she broke out of the norms of ballet by defining a more modern, free-flowing and bare-footed variant as a substitute for those who craved something more for themselves and the world of human expression.

And so, I find myself being invited to write a piece in a book with the title *Hear Us Roar*, with a lioness on the cover and the undertones of the terms *stealth and faith*. Out of all book titles, my journey into the entrepreneurial world, and life itself, most strongly resonates with the lioness. I feel deeply connected to the essence of the lioness and what she stands for. This is as much as I define entrepreneurialism as being spirit, life and change, wanting to breathe and birth itself through human form, often in bold and sometimes outrageous ways.

Recently called a 'small, petite, diminutive woman,' I appreciate that this is how I may be perceived. What underpins this, and what the world may at times undermine, is an uncanny sense of intuition, resourcefulness and bravery … a readiness to leap when the moment calls for it. What the world, this world, has taught me in recent years, is the profound magic that happens when we are open, willing and expansive in the way in which we walk through the fire that the world labels 'risk'.

When I tune into the lioness, the word *prowess* comes to me. Prowess is defined as having particular skill or expertise in a given activity or field. It is also about having exceptional bravery. And when applied to the lioness, she is inviting us to both claim the power that belongs to us, as much as she demands that we take up our true place in the world.

As an essence and energetic resonance, there is something vitally regarded in the prowess of a woman who boldly stands on higher ground, who holds the position of matriarch of the pack. And at the same time, not a single word is needed or able to define her – for she is here to be seen, felt and noticed in her dignity, in an essence that truly is her own. She just is who she is, and she is moving in the ways that she was put here to move. With no banter, no ego, nothing more than a genuine knowing of *this is who I am and what I am here for*. Often silent in her roar … and so she is.

I often share about the *Charlie's Angels* moments in my work.

'And what are the *Charlie's Angels* moments?' she asks!

You know that part in the movie where there is a giant ball of flames that explodes? The one where you hold your breath because you know the Angels must get through it … somehow. Because that's what movies are for. Yet our innate human nature is to jump to 'they are done for!' and 'what now?' Yet, what actually happens? Just when your breath is about to release and your heart is pounding … the flames separate, and we find Drew Barrymore, Cameron Diaz and Lucy Liu dressed in black leather as they strut right on through the middle of the perfectly parted flames, towards us, yielding the kind of piercing gaze that could slice their opponents in half.

This moment is exactly what it has all been for, the moment where there is not a single ounce of doubt that they are here for something that can only be defined in paranormal terms.

THIS is the true visual of a lioness; a woman on purpose. The moments that ask us to rise into our boldest, fullest versions of self without a single guarantee of success are what we are here for, as much as the moments where we are deeply nourishing the pack. If we truly want to live fully, it would serve us well to choose a huge mission in this world. The kind where we come to see challenges as opportunities, to know ourselves far more deeply and to connect more fully to our integrity and the medicine we were put here to both embody, hone and share. The kind that cracks our hearts, minds and being wide open … over and over again.

'Your spirit must always be stronger than what you want to create,' Mama Ati shared with me. I was sitting on the concrete floor of a temple in a rural part of Bali with this female priest who had only met me as this ceremony began, an hour prior at sunrise. She continued to share with me, 'I can see that you are a woman who wants to do big things. And you can. But you must always protect your spirit first and make sure that it is big enough first.'

It was early in the pandemic and all I knew was that what wanted to come out of me was far bigger than me, and that it wanted to involve women from around the world. I had no frame of reference for how the human vessel I owned would navigate this longing and mission.

To speak of the hero's journey (or heroine's journey in this matter) is to speak to those who create and co-create us along the way. I am a firm believer that if something is not aligning for us, where it is tied to our purpose for being here, our job is to dig deeper within ourselves, as deep as we think we can go, and to use what we find as our launch pad to rise higher. Each and every time, the answers are waiting within, as much as they are scattered throughout our everyday existence. This time in Bali taught me the powerful and profound lessons of nature and the world around us in a way that affords me a deep understanding that part of my role here is to move between worlds, sharing deep wisdom found within these different realities and to use them to inform the whole of what I offer humanity.

To have faith is to know that everything we need is within and around us. To use faith is to have the foresight and openness to use and enact what comes to us. Faith, I believe, is an active process between ourselves and the unseen spirit world that we choose to interact with. I believe we are vessels put here on Earth to walk, talk and interact in ways that contribute meaningfully, improving the overall existence of humanity. We are all here for change and impact. Whether we like it or not, we are constantly changing and each and every action has an impact that either encourages humanity forward, or not. We have complete power of choice in each and every moment. The more we grow and expand, the greater the range of choice we have to play within.

Stealth as a concept is, as I connect with it, about having quiet confidence. It's about approaching leadership with mindfulness and intentionality, and in having the capacity to hold the big vision in the same light while we attend to the tiny details in unison. It is the way we are able to be with both the things that are going wonderfully, in the same moment as the parts that are falling apart or are completely foreign and unknown; the things we are calling in that do not yet make sense to us. I see it as being a balance of self and our role in the world amongst all of these parts in any given moment. It is in seeing ourselves as being an employee to our creation and mission in this world. Once our body of work exists outside of us, it guides and informs us on where and how it wishes to exist. Once we reach this point, there is power in our releasing and allowing this thing to be as it chooses.

My journey of founding *The Aspire Series* and *55 FACES* truly began in the deepest moments of nothingness I have ever experienced. Stuck in Bali mid-pandemic, I now understand that my entire 'old world' in Australia had to be removed before I not only found myself in a space of nothingness where every single door felt not only shut, but deeply overwhelming. I was left with no choice but to create from scratch.

Feeling deeply depleted, and as if I had concrete on my feet, I asked for universal intervention. I asked for something to carry me forward. What came was a simple idea. A social media experiment. Something to show up for until the next step presented itself. I did not expect this thing to be the seed of my next mission. I did not expect it to become a series of books, a global women's leadership, change and impact summit, a mentorship program and the entire evolution of who and how I am in the world.

From this place, I discovered a depth of creativity I never imagined possible for myself, and the understanding that this, creativity itself, is the true essence of change. In order for change to occur, we must be open. Open to our ideas and concepts flipping on their head, as much as we have to be okay with pissing people off along the way. Creativity is fuelled by braveness backed by getting our kicks out of shaking things up a bit. If we are not prepared to have these things happen, then I question whether we are really creating change. Change happens on the outside of the box labelled 'status quo' and often alongside the terms 'letting go' and 'surrender', at times seen as modern day rebellion in a world of 'fix it now and fix it quickly.'

As I share these words, I wish to refer back to the deep inner trust and knowing that we can hold anything that presents itself. It might shock us to know that we WILL live through ... and most likely grow into ... whatever comes our way, including the fire of retribution brought on by our own creative juices when they run through our arteries, pumping for us to put them to immediate and prolific use, for them to live and breathe in the world outside ourselves, so that the world, too, can respond and feed us and our creations.

We each have our own version of *Charlie's Angels* and when we decide to go for it and put our everything behind it, the universe MUST move the puzzle pieces and align them so that we come out on top, or somewhere far closer to it. This I know for sure. There is both deep power, patience, love, graciousness and a ferocity that is deeply grounded in humility found in these spaces. With our head held high, we get to strut right on through because we cannot be given a mission and purpose that we do not have the heart to fulfil, no matter how perfectly or imperfectly the end product presents itself. And this mission is only ever going to be the expansion of our human selves, the parts we love and also the parts we don't.

As the woman who leads, our power is banked in the ways that we merge the strength, conviction and fortitude of the *Charlie's Angels* moments with the devotion and heart of the mother and creator. We find ourselves in a time where we get to redefine what this means and how we use it. Never before have women had the capacity and power to do what we can do today. Never have we had the choices and the voice. What we do today matters because it is the groundwork for what every generation of women who come after us will springboard off.

The story we create matters, because our story will become THEIR baseline. Our story is not ever going to be the greatest story. It IS the new baseline. For ourselves. For other women. For our community and for society. WE get to carry the new baseline story with what we have at our disposal in this very moment. And as women, I hope we each see the privilege that lives in that, more than we focus on what is yet to unfold.

And so I return to the lioness. Why does she matter? She matters because she is me. She is me as much as she is you. She is the woman we have been, the woman we are, and the woman we are yet to become. And we get to define and redefine her over and over again. She is the woman of indescribable passion and determination who holds her head high with an air of mysticism that has her stand out from the pack and those who surround her, regardless of what she is presented with.

This woman, she is timeless as much as she is the babe of the yet-to-be-written story of her very own time. For this woman, there is no 'finding her voice', because she knows all too well that her voice is already uniquely defined and embedded as her own. And it just is. It is evidenced in every single move she makes in this world. And every single move is the change in itself.

This lioness, in womanly form; she is calmness, grace and protection as much as she is ready to pounce when the circumstances beckon it from her. It is her deep attunement with nature and spirit which informs, guides and directs her. She is excellence and mastery in everything she does and for this, her reputation is that of integrity. Not the kind she claims for herself, the kind that is widely known outside and far beyond her. Her voice, spoken or not, quiet or loud, it does not matter … for she silences a crowd with her presence alone. This, the lioness woman, she has answered the call of the feminine leader that is asked of this time.

As I complete this piece, I feel called to draw your attention to a quote I wrote many years ago as I began *The Aspire Series*. It speaks to my own experiences of finding and defining my own within the story I now call my current reality, and I suspect, the next reality that I step into. I believe that you, too, will see yourself and your own journey within it.

'If ever the world gives you a reason to shy away, remember that you are in fact being given the greatest opportunity to step back with a stronger, wiser, bolder and more expansive heart than ever before'.

… and always remember, do not let them tame you.

Love,

Michelle x

ABOUT MICHELLE

Michelle Gardiner is the founder and director of *The Aspire Series*, including Aspire Société, the Aspire Summit and 55 FACES. These are a movement for women who are dedicated to pioneering social change and impact as well as a methodology in facilitating change work.

Michelle spent over fifteen years working in the Australian child protection and community sectors, supporting children, young people and families through some of their most vulnerable life experiences. Through hearing many life stories, Michelle became most passionate about raising the aspirations of women, which has greatly inspired her work with *The Aspire Series*. This passion parallels Michelle's own experiences of working hard to define her own voice and to use this to build a life that she, too, is proud of.

It is Michelle's intention in creating *The Aspire Series*, that as women, we can become more connected and heart-centred leaders and use one another to become the best that we can be, for ourselves and the future women who model themselves on us. From this place, we can truly influence change and shift the dynamic of both our local communities and global society.

MICHELLE GARDINER

Michelle holds a bachelors of social and community welfare, graduate certificate in mental health science (child psychoanalytic psychotherapy), she is a yoga teacher (500 hours – Moksha Yoga Academy), a certified life coach, is undertaking her masters in narrative therapy and community work, and has a background in leadership and empowerment program facilitation and trauma informed practice. Michelle also carries significant non-for-profit board member experience.

Michelle lives between Bali, Indonesia, and Melbourne, Australia, and is enthused by dance, yoga, chasing the sun, exploring and learning about people, arts and culture.

KEZ WICKHAM ST GEORGE
BE SEEN. BE HEARD. BE KNOWN

My background is in education and the arts. In my early forties I majored in abstract arts and curating of exhibitions. When the joy of the above dimmed, it was time to move on, choosing a more holistic career.

Choosing an education in aromatherapy, it was soon discovered I had a way with descriptive words, encouraged to place my written contributions in a monthly newsletter. This led to writing articles for a local Auckland newspaper and holistic magazine. With my diploma in aromatherapy, I set up a hand and foot massage business, where my clients would often tell me their stories. The alarm went off, with me asking, *Why is this person's story not being written into a legacy of sorts?* With my upbringing being around my Maori and Irish decedents, who were natural storytellers, and being of an inquisitive nature, their answers saddened me, as they replied, 'Because it's not important.'

To expand my education within a holistic field, I was drawn to art therapy, where I majored in the specified units of art, philosophy and communication. Here, the importance of storytelling was made very clear, as it combines all the arts. Learning that ancestral and multiculturalism stories were organically blended by intermarriages, it all came down to a genetic code in the art of delivering cultural information from the DNA of their ancestors.

When I was offered a teaching role in (Esol) English for speakers of a different language, my skills in art therapy and community storytelling

KEZ WICKHAM ST GEORGE

proved important. I began to understand the power of building corridors of communication between many countries, the power of storytelling, which I had always found fascinating, began to unfold. It was around this time I decided to post morning motivation quotes on social media. If I learnt anything in the years I had spent in the holistic field, it was this: *our spirit responds kindly to motivation.*

It seems the international stage agreed with me; it was time to bring those stories together. I was invited to speak internationally in Bali, Japan, Ireland, London, New Zealand and Australia-wide. I spoke on cruise ships and local tourist boats, in State libraries and local parks, plus, I received the call for creating workshops on creative writing. Success means different things for different people. To me it means this; to author or co-author a book is not only an amazing passport to many new corridors. It's like a business card, only more powerful. When you use the title of *published author* anywhere in the world, it instigates an interest.

In retrospect, to become who I am today would not have happened without the opportunities offered and the many friendships gained. My cup is full knowing my contribution to the writing world has given many authors the opportunity to shine. My advice is to write your story, or join an anthology, leave your legacy for others to follow, there is no time like the present.

ABOUT KEZ

Kez is a highly gifted writer, a bestselling award-winning author and a global writer's consultant. She is passionate about championing people from diverse backgrounds to tell their stories and write with passion. As a leader in her profession, she has spoken nationally and globally, sharing her wisdom and knowledge about the process of writing, editing and producing all forms of written communication. Kez contributes to a number of regular magazines, sharing her insights. She has also coordinated and compiled a number of anthologies. Across her Western Australian community she is known for her work empowering people to write, heal with art therapy and gives back via her volunteer work. Kez has co-produced and co-hosted a weekly international show, highlighting the work of authors and artists across the world. She has since gone on to produce a short film from the prologue of her trilogy *Scribe*, shown across theatres in Australia. Kez is consistent, dedicated along with her incredible creative energies and refreshing idealism.

ROSIE KEANEY
BREAKING FREE

What if I am judged for being me? What if I am shamed for not fitting in? What if people don't like me because they cannot accept who I truly am? Does this mean my only option is to be something or somebody I am not? And continue to live an unfulfilled life of wondering what ifs? What if I could be who I wanted to be? What if I could live the life of my dreams with no limitations?

Now, don't get me wrong, I am very blessed in my life. I have a husband, four beautiful children, two fur babies and a community of family and friends who I would die for. Yet, I have always had this burning desire for more. It's a bit like an itch that doesn't stop; the urge to do more, to want more, to dream more became stronger and stronger. I often wonder how beautiful the world would be if we were able to be exactly who we were meant to be!

Do you remember when you were a child, when everything was so carefree? You watched life pass you by without a care in the world! No matter what would be going on around you, you always believed in the greater good, nothing was a bother. Life can be so beautiful, and we all have the potential to tap into the universe's infinite power, however fear will often hold us back. During certain life experiences and challenges, we can become so paralysed and overwhelmed by fear (false evidence appearing real) that we decide to give up at the first hurdle and retreat to our comfort, avoiding the discomfort of the unknown.

A colleague had a beautiful message for me today. She reminded me of the age-old saying, 'Feel the fear and do it anyway.' This is something I most certainly needed to be reminded of. How powerful. Do you receive messages and signs at precisely the right moment in time? Do these messages send tingles down your spine as they resonate with your exact thoughts and feelings? There are no such things as coincidences, only synchronicities.

Full transparency, this healing journey is not always as it appears to be. When you feel like you have put in the work, self-reflection, self-care, self-awareness *because it is* all it is all about the *wonder of* self, the moment another challenge arises, you start to wonder; *What is this all about? Why do I feel like this is never going to end?*

These past two years of my life have felt like I've been taking two steps forward and two steps back. I have been pushing myself to step out of my comfort zone and face my fears, by saying yes to more opportunities, even though I was terrified. I decided in January 2022 that I wanted to change my life. I was sick and tired of feeling stuck. I just needed to take a chance, a leap of faith, and the only person capable of making those changes for me, was me! I needed a wakeup call – there was no knight in shining armour coming to rescue me!

My awakening began in 2018. I had closed the doors to my business overnight, as I was expecting my fourth child. It was one of the most difficult decisions of my life, but equally one of the most importance decisions I've ever made. I hit my rock bottom. I felt like an empty shell. I had lost *me*.

Looking back five and a half years later, what I did not realise is that I experienced PTSD as a result of the action I had taken that day. I had become overly anxious; my self-esteem and confidence had nosedived. I no longer recognised myself in the mirror – nor did I want to. It wasn't until several years later that I had an epiphany, realising that my breakdown had led me to my *breakthrough*.

This was the beginning of my spiritual journey. Finding my true north and facing my fears was one of my greatest battles. I truly did not see how my negative thinking patterns and habits were impacting my life and keeping me stuck. Looking back today, I am so proud of the journey, but it was extremely difficult for me to appreciate the steps I was taking in my life, as I felt like I was starting all over again.

At that time in my life, I had no hope and no sense of purpose. Everything had changed. It was as if my world had been turned upside-down, only I couldn't see that back then. I was so focused on caring for my newborn that I disregarded my own feelings and emotions, as it felt too much to handle at the time.

I was a perfectionist. I had a great way of convincing myself that whatever my intuition was guiding me to do, it was best to ignore it as that option would not be safe; it was too dangerous. Just like an elastic band, anytime a new opportunity presented itself, I would retract back to my comfort zone, as my overthinking and catastrophising thoughts had taken control. The safest option seemed for me to retreat to the safety of my home.

My home was my haven. It was a case of *batten down the hatches* and stay in my safe place where I found comfort from those who love and support me. I had become so reliant on being within those four walls, that I resisted leaving the house more and more. I was safe there; no-one could hurt or harm me. I consciously decided that my *safe place* was the best place for me to remain. Having a newborn gave me the perfect excuse to avoid every opportunity to leave the house as I felt safe. I never again wanted to experience the emotional pain I had experienced.

To give you a synopsis of what life was like for me prior to 2018, it had become a comfortable routine of regular patterns. I woke up, got the kids ready for school, went to work, went home, cooked the dinner; every day felt the same. Sometimes I dreaded the monotony of day to day life where others may have felt it to be familiar and safe. Was I truly happy? Looking back now, I don't believe I was. I was happy to be a mum and a wife, but I wasn't feeling fulfilled. I wasn't living my purpose. It wasn't my dream.

Can you relate to how some years feel like you're just waiting; waiting for next Valentine's day? Mother's Day? Easter? Summer holidays? Halloween? Christmas?

For me, it was like my life was on repeat. A hamster in a wheel scenario, everything predictable, so much so that I couldn't even see the bigger picture. There was a world of opportunities out there for me, but I was a prisoner in my own mind. I started to question if there was more to life; *What if there was more to life than working nine to five?*

What if the life you are living right now could be transported into the life of your dreams? Whatever you are passionate about, you have the power within you to follow your dreams – you just have to believe to make it happen.

My comfort zone was keeping me safe. It was my safe haven, as everything felt familiar and at ease. The comfort zone is characterised by minimal emotional and mental stress, as tasks and situations are within our ability and understanding, providing us with a sense of control. Because I felt safe, I had limited feelings of anxiety or stress; I felt protected from the outside world. But I now know that was not reality, I was actually trying to escape reality.

Our emotional wellbeing can be drastically impacted during challenging times. Feelings we get can consume us. Overcoming our negative thinking patterns, challenging our unhealthy habits, becoming awake to our thoughts, emotions, feeling and behaviours, will be extremely triggering.

I was one of the lucky ones. I had so many loving and supportive family members and friends who helped me through my most challenging time. The right people will always show up for you. They will guide you back towards the light. I will be eternally grateful to all those who helped me, especially my husband, Nick, and my younger sister, Dean, who were there through my darkest days.

So, my question to you is: Why do we struggle so much to shine a light on our true selves? If you could only see the beauty within you, you'd understand that it's clear for the world to see.

There will have been times when you were silenced, ridiculed or taken for granted, and it's in these moments you need to be a champion for yourself. The words of others can negatively impact how you feel about yourself, so it's important you protect yourself from negativity.

We need to surround ourselves with positive and uplifting influences. If you don't step away from the negativity, it will eventually consume you and you will then start to enter a downward spiral of disbelief. When you have been challenged, this can lead to self-doubt of your own personal beliefs and values, especially if you have been continuously knocked down by the words and actions of others.

In these times, you will feel trapped, as if you have no way out. You may start to doubt your own thoughts and beliefs. It can feel like you have the weight of the world on your shoulders; *surely life isn't supposed to be this difficult?* Well, I am here to guide you, from my own personal experience, to let you know you do have a voice and you do have a choice.

In time, you will begin to feel stronger. Reach out for help, as with support, you can recover. You need to have faith in yourself, as you are stronger than you know. The more difficult the situation the more significant the change will be in your life. You will not be the person you used to be, you will be changed for the better. There could be a deeper meaning to this situation too. By digging deep, you can sometimes discover something incredible about yourself you may have never realised before. It might just be leading you to the new path you always wanted, but didn't know how to take those first few steps, opening new doors of opportunity to help you live the life you were meant to lead.

You are only human and we are all massively impacted by the negative behaviours of others. If you can work on your self-awareness, self-love, self-control and self-healing to understand more about you and who you are, your triggers, getting more comfortable in your own skin, making the changes you need in your life, then you will grow in confidence to combat the negativity and become more resilient.

Once I had started to step outside of my comfort zone, my very first step was to prioritise *me*. All those years, I had become accustomed to believing that prioritising my needs was selfish. This is most certainly not true; a limiting belief of sorts. By prioritising the needs of others over our own, we are refuelling from an empty vessel.

We must look after ourselves in order to best serve others. Once we learn to truly take care of ourselves, priortising self-love, our personal boundaries and being truly grateful for who we are, then we will notice the shift in our reality. When you become awake to who you truly are, you start to question everything; you wonder why you do the things you do. You even start to question your very being.

You will begin to see you are being confronted by you, as you are the one in control. Sure, we can be hurt by the actions and words of others, however, we are catching ourselves on the hop!

Before we put that item of food in our mouths PAUSE, before we react to a harsh comment or judgement PAUSE, before we react on our feelings and emotions – PAUSE.

People often remain within their comfort zones to avoid the discomfort of the unknown and the potential stress of failure. However, staying exclusively within this zone can limit personal growth, skill development and new experiences. The comfort zone is a useful concept in understanding behaviour in various fields, including psychology, education and personal development, highlighting the balance between comfort and challenge needed for optimal performance and growth.

I realised the only person who can make things different for me, is me, and that I already have what it takes to make the changes in my life. So why is it so hard to leave the comfort zone? It nearly feels like trying to walk through the sphinxes in *The Never Ending Story!* Do you remember that movie? What a classic!

You don't need to have all the answers, you just need to trust; trust that what you are being guided to do is the right course of action for you. As much as this scares the living daylights out of you, you know deep down that you will feel so much better when you start to believe in yourself. By taking tiny baby steps, you will soon start to see that the change isn't that scary after all and what you have achieved as a result of facing that fear is far more rewarding than staying in your comfort zone.

It takes daily practice to leave our safety net and if you don't try, how will you ever know? Transformation and self-belief takes time and you need to do the work. If you have a big vision, how do you get closer to it? You take one step at a time, step by step, day by day. When you start to step out of your comfort zone you are showing up for yourself. Watch how that fear can change to excitement and the impact this will have on your life.

So how do you stop the same cycle replaying? You can change your life when you start to take action. You begin to imagine the endless possibilities by thinking outside of your comfort zone and question what is it that makes you happiest? What is it that you are passionate about?

Is there something that you have been putting off because of fear of failure, fear of judgement from others? Or not having faith in your own abilities?

This is where you have to go deep, a friend asked me a crucial question a number of years ago; 'Rosie, what do YOU really want?' Automatically I thought of what others would think I should do, I started to consider what would make other people happy.

As lucky and as blessed as I am in my life, and as good as other people's intentions are, we are the ones who only truly know what we desire. By waiting for other people's permission or their approval. we are responsible for holding ourselves back. That day I had a realisation; it had to be something for me, something that lights me up from the inside out, just as it should be for you; all of our passions and talents are unique to us.

I began 2022 with courage and the faith that I was going to continue to trust my intuition and enhance my self-belief. We can all turn our pain into power, no matter what you have been through. We all deserve happiness and fulfilment in life, so trust that inner knowing of who you truly are.

Always follow your dreams; they are meant to guide you. Follow your curiosity, as your inner child knows how. Even when fear shows its ugly head and it terrifies you, say *yes*, as you are stronger than you know. Of course, there will be days when you will feel helpless and hope may leave your side, but it is only temporary, everything in life is; there will be good days and bad days.

Reach out as well, as there is always someone there to guide you. Look for the signs, push yourself out of your comfort zone on a daily basis and keep questioning. To question is how we grow. Keep wondering, for there is so much opportunity waiting for you. Keep believing, trusting and taking the action.

Remember, on those days you want to give up, you are almost there. Don't give up – give yourself some self-love and keep following your intuition. Your spirit knows the way. You are amazing just the way you are! Keep being YOU and celebrate every step!

ABOUT ROSIE

Rosie Keaney is not just an event manager – she's a catalyst for inspiration and transformation. A captivating motivational speaker and TEDx speaker, Rosie empowers audiences to dream big and reach for the stars, inspiring individuals to unlock their full potential.

Balancing her role as a wife and mother of four, Rosie understands the importance of finding harmony between family life and personal aspirations. A published author and contributor to *Unstoppable Stories, Mental Wealth, The Voices of 7* and excitedly her fourth collaborative contribution to *Hear Us Roar Book & Docufilm Lioness Edition* where Rosie shares her wisdom and insights on resilience, empowerment and personal growth.

An intuitive life and business coach in mediumship, Rosie guides others on a journey of self-discovery and spiritual awakening, helping them connect with their inner wisdom and higher purpose. Rosie is also a dedicated tropic ambassador, committed to promoting wellness and natural beauty, empowering others to embrace a healthier lifestyle.

In additional to being a published author, Rosie also utilises her gift for writing, in sharing her experiences and insights on her personal blog *The Journey Within* offering readers a glimpse into her inner world and spiritual journey.

Rosie's background as a former project manager and business manager at Toddle In, along with her role as her current role of wellness development manager has equipped her with invaluable skills in leadership, organisation and wellness development.

Join Rosie Keaney on a journey of inspiration, empowerment and personal growth, and together, let's dream big and make our dreams a reality with Dream Big Events!

You can contact and follow Rosie on:

IG – @rosemariekeaney

FB – Rosie Keaney

LinkedIn – Rosie Keaney

JULIE M PHIE
THE FOREVER
SPIRITUAL GIRL

It came to me all of a sudden in February 2024, while sitting on my couch in my home in Queensland – *The Forever Spiritual Girl*; a book I wanted to write. Two other titles came to me at the same time, and that I had to do a series of three books.

I felt my late Grandma Chesher (Maureen) was with me. At the time, I was grieving a few losses in my life, including losing Grandma in January 2023, she was 89 years of age. I was also super happy with where I was headed that year. 2024 felt different to all previous years. Like, finally after forty-nine years of being on this Earth, I had come into my own self, fully and wholeheartedly; no-one was going to stop me or what I want to do with my life. I mean, turning fifty really starts to give you a new life perspective. At this age, you start to hear about old school friends passing away, which is such a shock, as I still feel like I'm in my twenties.

It's been a long time (too long) of people pleasing, of worrying about others and putting them before myself. Though I certainly don't regret anything or anyone I've been there for, or helped in my lifetime. They have all led me to where I am today.

Most of us have been raised to believe that the road to a happy life is paved with pleasure and that the pursuit of pleasure is the path to fulfilment. But as we grow up, we begin to realise that life is not always easy or pleasurable. In fact, much of it is difficult and painful. We all experience loss, disappointment, illness, aging, and eventually, death. We encounter stress, anxiety and fear. Life is a constant of navigating the ups and downs, the ebbs and flows. Life can't and won't always be the same; it can never be good all the time. Change is inevitable, and it is how we handle that change that makes us live a more fulfilled life.

And yet, we continue to cling to the idea that happiness is found in pleasure and the avoidance of pain. We try to avoid our painful experiences, by numbing ourselves with drugs or alcohol, distracting ourselves with TV or social media, or obsessing over our work or our relationships. But the more we try to avoid the basic reality *that all human life involves pain,* the more we are likely to struggle with that pain when it arises, thereby creating even more suffering. I have seen this so much in my life as a psychic medium, yoga instructor, personal trainer, medical intuition practitioner, retreat facilitator, and also working with people living with disabilities. I've seen much suffering, in all forms. I lived with it for so long and didn't even realise I was directly affected by someone else's pain, whether it be my family's adversities when I lived at home, or in my marriage.

True happiness is found in the simple things, the little moments spent with our loved ones, or out in nature. Once we accept that life is sometimes painful or a struggle and acknowledge that without judgment and a willingness to be present in the moment, we can take action for ourselves in line with our own values and goals. Only then will we find joy and meaning in everyday life. I mean, I actually had a great upbringing. I always felt life was pretty good, despite any chaos around me. Even back then, I felt the angels were with me, guiding me. I had an unwavering faith that everything would be okay. I felt super optimistic, positive and happy, as I always wanted to make the people around me feel happy, smiling and comfortable. Even if they weren't that way towards me.

As a young child, I felt a little different. Although no one would know at the time, other than the fact I was sometimes slow, late, or just seemed off with the fairies … haha… I literally was though. I remember feeling so connected to everything; the Earth, the universe. I felt so loving positive and happy, all the time, about so many things, especially my family and friends. I loved them all … no matter what … unconditionally. I would massage my mum and dad's feet when I was young, just to ease their pain or stress of hard work. Even back then, I was practicing medical intuition … I just didn't know it.

I would stare out the window of our childhood home in Redcliffe, Queensland, where I grew up and I would dream about so many things; big things. I would stare at the moon, stars and sky for hours and hours after I was told to go to bed. I would think about the infinite possibilities of what I could do with my life. I felt there was always something out there greater than me and could feel an energy or universal force guiding me in some way. I felt messages coming in.

I have a very loving family and am blessed to have had the simple seventies and eighties childhood of no technology, and lots of wild, free adventuring as a child and teen. But don't get me wrong – super disciplined as well. Dad was very strict and made sure we all grew up with respect for everyone and everything, and that we learnt to be independent. Dad is very passionate about his family, loving and supportive. He's the one you go to if you want to have a deep and meaningful about life or any struggles you might have. Dad (Ray) was the eldest child of his siblings, so he was always the responsible one that had to get things done. He moved homes quite a bit when young, due to his father being in the Army. Dad worked for his father in wholesale travel in Redcliffe, and eventually became the managing director of the travel business. Dad was on the board of so many things, the Margate Chamber of Commerce, back then he helped start the plan of the Railway line in Redcliffe. He organised Margate having Christmas lights each year, as at the time only Redcliffe Main Street had lights. He was the manager for my brothers Soccer team and was even asked to go into politics. No wonder I am involved in so many things in our community and have a volunteering spirit. But mum has always helped people in need and not asked for anything in return. She fostered kids after school when I was growing up. She was a cleaner, did peoples ironing, and Mum worked in disability for years at a special school & they all loved her there. Actually a lot of my family members worked at the Woody Point Special School, including myself, my sister in law, my cousin, & my mums twin sister. Mum also should have been a counsellor or psychologist she's a great listener of people's issues, and offers great advice without telling you what to do. As a child I remember mum leaving for work early and dad taking us to Suttons Beach Redcliffe for a swim in the ocean before school, then home to wash the sand off, then dad would go to work & we would walk or ride our bikes to school. Those were the days! So carefree and simple! Each morning early, we used to wake up to the sound of dads big old wooden record player in the lounge room playing, Michael Jackson – Billie Jean and so many other great songs. It would wake us three kids up to get out of bed for school. I remember laying in bed thinking I'm so tired, but next minute I'd be singing to the song & thinking 'okay I'm awake and feeling good now. It's amazing how all those years of daily music shape your life, happiness and make you feel motivated. I'm grateful for those simple days. Like we didn't have the biggest house in the area, or a pool or even two cars for many years, but it's amazing how you learn to share, have patience, communicate more with family members, and help each other out to get shit done. Like five people in a three bedroom, one bathroom, one toilet home, with one car. I shared my bedroom with my younger sister, and we didn't have too much stuff or clutter in our rooms, certainly you'd never have a TV in your room like these days. You certainly learnt the art of negotiation, collaboration and patience. These were such freedom days. Loved it!

Mum was just always super loving; both my parents are very hard workers. My mum (Sandra) is the definition of a selfless woman, who will give all to you, despite her own tiredness, sadness or any pain she might be experiencing. She would never let you know if anything is wrong; she just gets on with life and gets shit done. Mum is always smiling and happy, uplifting the people around her with her laughter, just like her twin sister. Yes mum is an identical twin, and the stories they told me about their school days at Brighton, Sandgate growing up, well if you can just imagine switching classes with each other a lot … haha love that … and the teachers never knew any different. If I could give my parents the world, I would, but I know they already have *the world*, which is something that doesn't come from riches. We were never rich; we were middle-class to sometimes-struggling. I have two wonderful siblings, an older brother, who is always there 100% for his family, (he works himself to the bone sometimes), and my sister, who is a shining light of positivity, and the one all the family goes to for good advice. She is also a hard worker. Wonder why, hey? Ingrained from our parents.

Actually, when I was fourteen years old, we lost our family home, as my dad's travel agency went into liquidation and we declared bankruptcy. This was due to the pilot's strike, high interest rates, the cost of living and other factors. From that day on, we've rented houses and lived in quite a few different homes. This certainly put strain on all of us, but more so for mum and dad.

When I was in grade ten at high school, I decided to leave, and it suited all of us, as I didn't like the idea of grades eleven and twelve, with the subjects I thought, would be totally useless for my life. I knew I would be able to get a full time job and pay my parents board each week, so I wasn't costing them money. I actually loved this decision. I had a blast at full-time Tafe college business studies for twelve months, met new friends, got treated like an adult, and never stopped working from the age of fourteen.

I worked in travel for my dad, then a travel agency in the city, which I loved: Sunlover Holidays. I also met my first serious long-term boyfriend at the age of fourteen, who would soon become my husband and partner of thirty years. I met him through my brother when Dad grounded me for escaping out of home one night with my cousin. I used to escape out of the house at night, with my best friend from school too. We never did anything bad, we just rode our bikes around Redcliffe Peninsula, meeting up with friends, both boys and girls. We would sit in park playgrounds and chat for hours to our friends under the night stars; it was amazing and so carefree.

Anyway, my cousin and I were busted by my uncle for escaping out of the house and when Dad found out, he grounded me for three months. I was only allowed out with my older brother, as chaperone. He took me to a party at Rothwell, not far from our home, and that's where we met. We both had an amazing connection and chemistry. Long story short, we became boyfriend and girlfriend and years later, had our son, when I was twenty-one. We then had our daughter when I was twenty-six. We married in 1997, divorced in 2017. Twenty years married but thirty years together, from when we first met.

Life isn't always easy. I am the *Forever Spiritual Girl* because my absolute faith in spirituality never waivers. I am always feeling connected to the other side and that we are being constantly guided and watched over. My hope was to always be forever with the same man. Someone I love dearly. Someone I marry. Someone I have kids with, grow old with, have our grandkids with. Someone that shows me the same level of affection and love that I show them. It wasn't meant to be. Don't get me wrong; I loved the kids' father, and he loved me dearly too. But the battles of living with his depression and drinking, for so many years, got hard for me to bear in the end. He was such a hard worker, which I was as well, and this can sometimes put a strain on the whole family unit. I cannot fault him, for one single minute, on providing for his kids. He would sacrifice himself to work hard to pay for the family, to have a good home – and we did have that. We had an incredible beautiful Queenslander home, in Narangba, and beautiful things; the nice cars, boat, JetSki, caravan, pool, bar area, lots of camping, boating, fishing, holidays. We took the kids traveling around Australia in a caravan when my daughter was five and my son was nine. What an incredible holiday. One that was meant to be life changing for his depression, but it returned, not long after we got back.

I forever kept enduring the struggles that came with living, and loving, someone with depression. Suicidal depression impacts everyone involved. I used to think: *Why can't you see past yourself and be there for me sometimes?* Years later, I would find out through my own depression, that it's not always that easy to do.

We did have many incredible times as a family though. So much fun. We grew up together with our kids really, being such young parents.

I would talk with him a lot back then, about getting out of his overthinking head and into his heart. To trust in the law of attraction and universal guidance. To exercise, move your body, practice yoga and meditation. These can be life changing, especially when experiencing feelings of depression. He would sometimes try, but it felt too hard for him with where his mindset was at. He would deal with his feelings through alcohol, and that really doesn't help.

When you feel you are giving way more in a relationship than your partner is, it can be truly heartbreaking and draining.

Over the years, from child to teen to marriage, many things have happened that have been truly devastating. I lost my beloved dear Grandad Chesher (Robert) when he was just fifty-four years old, to motor neuron disease. I'll never forget his hands hanging down with no control. I would make him cups of tea in a huge special mug the family had made for him, so he could hold it himself by slipping his whole hands through the big handles on each side. Grandad drove me to the chemist, when I got my first period, as my parents were overseas at the time in America.

Super embarrassing but Grandma Chesher told him and she didn't drive. For a while, when he first got motor neuron disease, Grandma would hold the steering wheel to help him turn the car because his hands didn't have enough strength. Can you believe that even happened? It certainly wouldn't nowadays.

Grandad Chesher wasn't a big believer in psychic stuff, but supported his wife, my Grandma, every step of the way. Grandma Chesher was a psychic medium and started her own spiritual church in Redcliffe when I was just a child. *The Redcliffe Peninsula Spiritualist Church.* I remember him putting chairs and stuff in the back of a ute and taking it to the church to set up for her. Grandma was Reverend of her own church for so many years and dedicated her life to it. She had so many wonderful friends through her spiritual work. Grandad would sit in her spiritual church services every Sunday, without fail. After he passed away from motor neuron disease, I remember sitting in Grandma's church service and seeing Grandad's empty chair was still there. The same chair he sat in each week, was kept empty for him, out of respect. We all sang the hymn *Amazing Grace* for Grandad that day; it was one of his favourites. I teared up singing it; I felt so emotional seeing that empty chair.

I learnt so much from all the years of being in Grandma's church services, healing days, meditations and psychic fairs. I learnt about connection to spirit, trust and faith that things work out as they should. That what is meant for you shall not pass you. And about love, empathy, compassion, spirit guides and guardian angels. I also felt I had psychic ability, like Grandma.

I never intended to use it, until one day Grandma asked me to do psychic readings for her psychic fair day at Redcliffe Community Centre, to raise money for the church. I said *yes*, of course … how could I say no to Grandma? But I thought, *Wow! Grandma knows I have psychic ability*, even though I never told her I could see or hear things. Nervous as I was that Saturday, I raised the most money for the church that day, got great feedback for my readings, and people were saying 'go see Julie for a reading'. This was weird for me to hear. I felt like an imposter at times, even though I knew I wasn't.

Once I experienced what it was like to give the gift of channeling someone's loved one, or purely giving them messages that could help their life move forward, or have a sense of direction or closure, I realised it was something I wanted to do with my life and career, as it's a way of helping people. At heart, I love helping people and providing community service too.

I've been doing psychic mediumship readings now for almost twenty years … and love it. From approximately the age of thirty and turning fifty last year. Oh dear, that is a weird thought!

Losing Grandad Chesher to motor neuron disease was one of many losses of loved ones I have experienced. This one is close to me though, as I have so many memories of Grandad getting out of the car and him not able to walk very well; his legs were wobbly. Grandma and I would get either side of him, he would put his arms over our shoulders and the three of us would walk into the shops like that, to ensure Grandad wasn't going to fall. I remember feeling so much emotion for what he was going through. Even though I was a child of primary school age, I just wanted to help him as much as I could. It is a truly devastating disease that is awful for anyone to live with. Grandad was a butcher, and when me, my siblings and cousins would stay at our grandparent's house, it was always such a fun time. Grandad would bring us home Cherrios from the butcher shop. We would all run to the door when he got home from work to see him and eat the Cherrios immediately. Grandad often rode his motorbike too.

I lost my Grandma Phie, (Ruby) my dad's mum, on 4th May 1985 of a cerebral hemorrhage of the brain, when she too, was only fifty-four years old. I was so young, I didn't realise the profound impact of that until later in life, when as an adult, I would have loved to have her around to talk to. She seemed a lot like me … or me like her; the girly clothes, jewellery, makeup, perfume … and her spirituality also. She used to sing, which has been passed down to my daughter. When Mia was a baby, a psychic told me that Grandma Phie would be with her whenever she was singing on stage or to an audience. So many people on dad's side of the family can sing. It's amazing really. I love all our family music nights; they are truly something special. My mum and dad have kept these going for years! Nothing like a bit of karaoke fun, I say. Grandma and Grandad Phie got married when Grandma was 18 yrs old in Clermont, Queensland. Years later Grandma and Grandad would divorce. I loved Grandma Phie - she was such a gentle, kind, beautiful woman, who seemed to go through quite some struggles throughout her late 40s to 50s with mental health.

I realise now that I am age 50 and going through menopause, Grandma Phie could have been going through menopause at the time causing her mental health issues & along with a marriage separation that is truly devastating to a woman. I know as I have been through exactly the same, and without help it is so hard to cope with these things sometimes, and in those days those things weren't spoken about and women certainly got no help for the hectic ride that menopause causes, let alone a woman facing living alone with the cost of living and kids, and back then no government help. Sadly my dad was called to grandma when she passed out that day, and dad tried so hard to resuscitate his mother to no avail. It's no one's fault what happened to grandma Phie, those were just the times and the era. I couldn't imagine what that must have been like for my dad being in his 20's and trying to save your dying mother who is 54. It makes me realise what a strong person my father actually is & why he has such a big heart for all the things he's been through. Dad has been saved many times from near death experiences, if you talk to him, you could write a whole book just about those experiences. Maybe his mother is there each time making sure he is okay. I am sure Grandma Phie has a hand in that from the spirit world.

Grandad Phie, (Dawson) my dad's dad, passed away at 69 years of age of acute chronic renal failure. He loved his drinks and used to smoke. He also loved his music and worked hard. He would play the keyboard and I remember many parties at their house with lots of music. The music nights were always so fun, with all the Phies. Grandad Phie's favourite song was always *My Way* by Frank Sinatra. Grandad had a hard life and childhood. He was an orphan at the age of 12 and had to make his own way in life. It is believed that Dawson Lesley Phie, was working underground in the coal mines in Ipswich at the tender age of 13. Actual dates or age cannot be confirmed. My dad doesn't know anything about Grandad's parents other than their names are Daisy Beatrice Baggot, his mum, and his father's name was George Joseph Phie, he was a miner. Dawson's parents passed away when he was 12 years old. Grandad was in the Army post World War II, and he was in transport and posted to Papua New Guinea. At this point, my dad, Ray and his mum, Ruby (my grandma) were flown to Papua New Guinea by a Lancaster Bomber of the Australian Airforce, so that they could reconnect with their dad and husband. Grandad was such a strong-willed determined man to make shit happen for his life. He went from poverty to making his own riches, with his wholesale business. It was one of the biggest wholesale travel businesses around at the time for large scale school educational trips away. I have many fond memories of Grandad playing the organ, buying lots of lotto tickets and way too many ice blocks for the grandkids. I am proud of granddads achievements, having to make his way in life alone from the age of 12 as an orphan. Love all my grandparents.

Losing our nephew at the young age of 22, to a sudden leukemia diagnosis, was devastating. He was gone in the same week he was diagnosed. Saying goodbye to him in the hospital that day was truly heartbreaking. He was the son of my husband's eldest sister. Years later, their other son also passed away, at the age of forty-four. I can only imagine they must have some solace together in the spirit world now, reunited. I have many fond memories of our fun times together in the Sunshine Coast, with all the gang of us that were in our late teens, surfing, camping, fishing, boating, swimming and partying.

I'll never forget attending the funeral of our friend who suddenly passed away just a few days after attending my thirtieth birthday party at Narangba. He had complications from Crohn's disease. He and his wife were such a great couple and his funeral was packed out the door of the church with so many people; it was truly sad. A day I'll never forget.

Our dog, Simba, a gorgeous Labrador, was so loving and caring. He was our son's dog and we got him when our son was two years old. He died in his arms when our son was 14, at home alone, while his father and I were away for work. He had breathing problems. Simba loved swimming in the pool with our kids. They would play the crocodile game with him, where Simba would chase them in the water and the kids would scream and swim away from him; he loved that game so much.

There have been many heartaches and many challenges, but overall I have spent my lifetime raising my kids, even though I was just a kid myself. Well, I was twenty-one, but you don't realise at the time, just how young that is. Don't get me wrong - I have loved every minute of raising my son and daughter. Being their mother is something I'm truly grateful for, and I feel so blessed that God gave me such beautiful loving children. My children are my true loves, and I am so proud of both of them. I can't believe they are both well into their twenties now. Wow. My daughter (Mia) has massive singing talent, and my son (Jayden) has massive acting talent, but what they decide to do with that is their choice. Their life purpose and happiness will come to them over time. Overall, their happiness is pivotal to me, and for them to know they are dearly loved. My son was always my 'full-of-energy' entertaining child, who made everyone laugh, and my loving daughter, a calm child who entertained herself. Where did that time go? Being a young mum gives you a lot of advantages as well, including endurance, strength, patience, the ability to adapt and overcome adversities, resilience, empathy, compassion, selflessness, dedication, devotion and a never-quit attitude.

I am so proud of my son, who has recently become a pilot. Not an easy thing to achieve, and it was wonderful to be taken for a personal flight over Moreton Island for the first time with my son as pilot for my 50th birthday. Not something every mother gets to experience, and very proud my daughter for her unwavering love of animals, her independence, and ultimately both of them for their supportive friendship and love of each other as siblings.

Being a working mum throughout the whole time has been truly rewarding, as I have a hectic work ethic, like my parents, and I can't sit idle and just rest at home. It never felt like that was for me, even though that may be perfect for someone else. It comes with its challenges however, which was always the juggling of work, kids, school, homework, housework, social life and time for your own relationship and marriage too. With both parents hard working, it can take its toll.

Throughout the years, I always wanted to get out and do bigger things that are within my soul. It's hard to explain, but these things were not in alignment with my husband and I always felt like my dreams were diminished somewhat. That my passions would be put on the back burner. I felt the teamwork or reciprocation wasn't there for me, in return for what I was giving in the relationship. This becomes draining over the years. I tried my absolute hardest to make it work and to be a positive light of influence for both my husband and kids. In the end, if things aren't working and you've exhausted all avenues, you have to walk away from each other to save your souls. I'm sure he had his reasons, and I may have been annoying in many ways as well, it is never a one-way street. We were so young when we met.

One thing that got me through many challenging times was my faith. My unwavering faith in God, Jesus, Archangels, spirit guides, guardian angels, and my passed-over loved ones. I knew they would always have my back, guiding me, and that things happen for a reason. Even in my darkest, saddest days, I knew they were nudging me into the next phase of my life. I had somewhere else to be, something else to do. I knew it involved my spiritual work and wellness.

I was around 9 years old when I remember seeing my first spirit guide. I was staying at Grandma Chesher's house in Scarborough. I went up to the third level of the house into Grandma's room to get a hairbrush, and there she was, staring back at me in the mirror, but behind me. It was Grandma Butler, my mum's Grandma. I froze, but also felt relaxed, remembering that my Grandma always told me she saw spirit guides and never felt afraid. She knew they were there for a reason. Otherwise, if you don't know them, you can just ask them to move on. Grandma Butler was there, then she disappeared. I felt a little scared, but more supported than anything else.

I would spend so much time at Grandma's spiritual church, watching in awe at what she did as a reverend and how kind she was to everybody. Grandma Chesher was a truly humble, selfless and loving lady. A beautiful grandmother who nurtured and cared for everyone in her family and presence. I learnt so much from her. It's ingrained in me, and now that I've actually turned fifty, I realise just how impacting all those times were, spent with my grandparents and the church.

I felt I was *home* in Grandma's church, like it was a loving, safe space where I had complete faith that everything works out the way it should in life. *The Game of Life and How to Play It* by Florence Scovel Shinn, is a book Grandma told me to read years ago. Another is *Your Word Is Your Wand* by the same author. I have those two original books of Grandma's still with me now. They have amazing lessons and teachings in them about life and overcoming hardship. If everything was easy in life, we would never learn anything new or challenge ourselves.

Grandma would ask me to read from her poetry books on stage at the church, when I was a child. I loved it when she asked me to, even though

I felt nervous. I always felt it was a special privilege to be asked to get up and speak on a church platform to the congregation, as you could be changing someone's life while speaking. I felt that way back then when I was a child - I still feel that way now; through public speaking, being a radio host for the *All Abilities NO LIMITS* radio show, through my yoga class teachings, running guided meditations, when I train people for fitness, do psychic medium readings or when I run wellness retreats. I feel I am in a truly special place of making a positive impact on peoples' lives. It's something I don't take for granted, and it is something I truly love doing. I feel it is the essence of why I am here on this Earth. I have done a lot of work with people with disabilities over my years too, working at Woody Point special school through my twenties, to doing support work and marketing events in my forties. That drive, motivation and empathy of caring for people is innate within me.

Remembering to care for *me* now too, is something new, and has taken me forty-nine years to realise. The burnout I experienced last year when I left my salary job in the disability industry, was from not only doing too much for a company, but being hit with peri-menopause. Going through those hormonal changes sent me into a deep depression for a while.

I experienced anxiety and lows, where I could barely function. I wanted to escape the world. I didn't want to see anybody or do anything. I cried every day, so many times, that it got me thinking what that level of depression must have felt like for my ex-husband; getting to a point of not wanting to live. I felt very close to that point, which is a scary place to be. I think menopause for women is very underestimated by men and the public in general. It's not understood fully, even by women. I knew nothing about it, until I was hit with it. I didn't care if I was alive or dead. Ultimately, I cared about being around for my kids and family though. That never left me, and I knew I had to ask for help and remove myself from anything too toxic or overwhelming.

Resigning from my job was the best thing I ever did. Choosing to go fully back into my wellness business again has been such a healing for me. It's a reminder of why I called my business *Elixir For Life* all those years ago. The elixir is your potion for life, your reason to live, your why, your purpose, your passion that drives and motivates you to get up in the morning. Everyone thinks certain things make you happy in life, but overall, it's as simple as having something meaningful to do in a day; something that makes you feel alive and happy. Someone to love and someone to love you. No amount of money or fame can bring you that. It is only something you can bring within yourself. Go back to the basics of what you love. For me, that is my spirituality that I've had inside of me since I was a child back at Grandma's church. That is what my sense of purpose is; to show, teach and guide people to have positive beliefs that they can do, live and achieve anything they desire. That they are loved, valued, seen, heard. I love showing people compassion and helping them to feel like everything is going to be okay.

I know I have to check this in for myself now, but it's always going to be in my nature to take care of someone or something. I love it and I wish for all people that they use the tools I have used now for many years now, to take care of themselves through, yoga, meditation, fitness, adventure, the outdoors, wellness retreats, psychic reading connections, medical intuition, essential oils, journalling, writing or whatever it may be. These are some of my passions to live a happy, healthy life.

I am forever in love with love. A hopeless romantic, a loving, kind woman that just wants pure fun, adventure, happiness, positivity and someone to share my life with, eventually, if it feels right. To travel the world and enjoy the simple things, and show up for myself finally, other than putting me last. It doesn't need to be complicated, just pure loving – as my Grandma taught me as a young girl. My hope is that love conquers all … forever. Whether it is family, a lover, your children, your parents, your friends, your pets … just forever LOVE, and listen to SPIRIT, and be LOVED in return. Loving yourself first and foremost allows you to have true inner peace within your soul. Remember, your spirit guides are always with you, just ASK!

Oh, and I do have two dear pets; Chester my Boston terrier boy dog, and Daisy Maureen, my pPug girl. I adore them, they are truly little vulnerable, spiritual beings, with beautiful, kind, playful hearts. Take notice of your animals and nurture them – they teach us so much xxo

My hope is for you to find your true Elixir For Life FOREVER <3

Much Love in Spirit!

Julie M Phie xx

Excerpt from my Grandma Chesher's writings that she left me after she passed away in January 2023 …

Many Ascended Masters surround you in all ways, they come to assist you. Help with your missions and answer your prayers. Tune with them and ask questions you wish!

ABOUT JULIE

Julie M Phie is a multifaceted practitioner dedicated to supporting individuals on their journey of healing, self-discovery, and holistic well-being. With a passion for empowering others, Julie combines her expertise in Yoga, Medical Intuition, and Psychic Mediumship to offer transformative experiences through retreats, personal sessions, and workshops.

A skilled practitioner in a range of modalities, Julie's practice also incorporates the use of essential oils to promote balance and healing. Her approach is grounded in a deep understanding of the mind-body connection, and she integrates her training as a personal trainer (P.T.) with her intuitive and spiritual practices.

Julie's work extends to the airwaves, where she shares her wisdom and insights on her program on 99.7 Bridge FM, providing guidance, comfort, and inspiration to listeners. Her commitment to facilitating positive change in the lives of others is reflected in her online presence at Elixir for Life, where she offers resources, tools, and personalized services for healing and growth.

Whether through guided meditation, energy healing, or intuitive insights, Julie M. Phie is dedicated to helping individuals find peace, clarity, and empowerment on their unique life paths.

EMMA WEAVER
THE ROLL OF A DICE

Life can take you on many journeys, and one thing is for sure, it happens to us all and can come so unexpectedly. How you deal with change and new situations is what builds your resilience and becomes part of you. I have been faced with many challenges in my life. After many twists and turns along the way, each experience has changed me, making me stronger and raising my vibration in the world and showing me a higher purpose.

Becoming a young mum, I was grief stricken when my daughter's dad was killed in a traffic accident. As a mum already to two beautiful children when I met and fell in love again, I was living the dream. Everything was going so well. We decided to add to our family to bind it together.

We decided early on that we wanted to have a child. The yearning was there, the excitement was real and the hope filled our lives. With enthusiasm, passion and love we set about making magic happen. After one month went by I laughed that we thought it would happen straight away. We were both healthy people, my cycle was regular, and we could see no obstacles. Six months later and still we had no success, so conversations started. Perhaps we need to time this better, be more aware of fertile days. We purchased an ovulation kit, the first step on the road of the whole thing becoming less romantic and very clinical.

Every month I could feel the disappointment, the pain and the grief of not being successful. As the months added up and became a year, more action had to be taken. Two family members were now pregnant, and excitement had begun for their journeys, so we kept quiet about ours. It can be such a private matter and an internal battle of feelings. I wondered, *What is wrong with me that this is not happening for us?*

The realisation was now starting to set in that this was not happening. My internal voice shook with panic, and I started to question everything. We decided to do some research and take things a little further and try something different. We read books, watched podcasts and listened to ever-changing opinions on what was best to do and not do. Loose male underwear, herbal remedies, reflexology, acupuncture, legs in the air, positioning, waiting until the time of the month was just right, and lots more, we tried everything. The romance was taken out of the equation and it became a numbers game.

Days of ovulation, days of sperm, favourable days to conceive; all of this became part of our daily life.

We reached the twenty-month mark feeling vulnerable and at a complete loss. I contacted the GP, and we went to discuss our concerns. He referred us to a consultant. This was not an easy appointment, we had to discuss everything about ourselves, my cycles, how long we had been trying, our medical histories. We then had to go for every test imaginable, both internally and externally.

Another appointment to the fertility clinic revealed that this was just not going to happen naturally for us. We found this particularly hard to let sink in, even though we knew by now that we were unable to conceive on our own, that we would need assistance. Every emotion comes to the fore: shock, disbelief, sadness, grief, anger – our heads were spinning.

I decided to do some research and developed a sense of the enormity of fertility issues and how it can impact couples and individuals.

On the 25 July 1978 history was made, bringing hope and options for those who previously thought it was impossible. This was the day the first IVF baby was born – a healthy baby girl, Louise Brown.

Since then, over five million babies have been born through IVF.

Millions of people wanting to become parents but were unable to do so, whether it was due to male or female infertility, couples in same-sex relationships or being a single person, many have gone through this process to achieve their dream of having a baby, becoming a parent and feeling complete.

The dictionary describes the cycle of life as a series of changes in the life of an organism, including reproduction. One of the assumptions that people make about life is that we will reproduce, and if not all, at least most of us. People assume that they will become a parent, that the ability to reproduce defines us.

One-sixth of the human population – just under 15% – is faced with fertility challenges. The emotional and mental impact of this is profound. We had options, although we felt robbed of the chance to conceive on our own and had to mourn the choices that had been taken away. But it was out of our hands. our dreams were now in the hands of another.

There was a two-year wait for fertility treatment – imagine, this issue is so prevalent that there is a waiting list of two years! So many people are impacted and yet I had never heard anyone talk about it. This was all new to me. A two-year waiting list and only one health service available.

We decided this was our journey and we would not tell anyone what we were going through. We decided to go private and hopefully be successful within the two years, while waiting for our turn in the health care system. No-one knew we were trying for a baby, and when anyone was insensitive enough to ask when we would be adding to our family, we brushed it off, saying work was too busy. Little did anyone know what we were going through, these comments were so unhelpful.

The two-hour journey to the closest clinic was a strange one, we were nervous and excited as we spoke about what we thought was going to happen and ran away with ourselves thinking of outcomes and time scales. The feelings are real, and hope is what keeps you going.

More tests, bloods, examinations and deep conversations about my body. Conversations I have never had with myself, never mind others. I was now starting to feel like a vessel, not a human. It was very clinical and all about body parts.

After a while it was determined that we would have a procedure called ICSI. This is where they put the sperm directly into the retrieved egg to ensure contact, leaving nothing to chance.

A schedule was drafted, and we had to then pay in advance for all the injections and suppositories. Then we waited for my menstrual cycle that month, everything was meticulously planned around that. It's a numbers game after all.

Along came my period, it is strange this roller-coaster. Before this, I would pray every month for my period not to come. Now, I was praying that it would hurry up and come so that we could start our ICSI cycle.

This journey is full of paradoxes. What you think should happen is the one thing you do not want to happen, it's all about assisting nature to take its course. It can be hard to get your head around the process. A lot of people have an opinion on this process, however it is so personal that each person or couple should be allowed to make their own informed choice.

I embarked on the cycle of injections, finding them particularly hard, they stung and I had to dig very deep, once in the morning and once in the afternoon. My day revolved around these injections; they were constantly on my mind. I tried everything to make them sting less: ice cubes, pulling an elastic band to distract me and many other tactics before finding that chewing gum helped. Hey, whatever works!

I was now feeling more isolated, still deciding not to tell anyone, we decided to keep going it alone. I made several journeys up and down to the clinic – it was a four-hour round trip – to see if my ovaries have been stimulated by the injections to create follicles. The key is to create as many favourable ones as possible without over-stimulating, then waiting for them to trigger, which is, yes of course, another injection. All this was happening while I was working and attending family events, trying to suppress my emotions and feeling very vulnerable – which was a new feeling for me. You really must look after your wellbeing throughout this journey and that is not something that is spoken about. Perhaps you might read it in a leaflet.

The weight of all of this started to show within our relationship and tension was rising. Talking about it was painful; not talking about it is painful too. My tummy now felt like a pin cushion, skinny jeans were too uncomfortable to wear; dresses and skirts were my only option. Whilst this may seem trivial, in the grand scheme of things it was yet another option taken away from me.

Egg retrieval day came, and I was now over-stimulated. We retrieved lots of eggs which was a good thing, and my partner dispensed his offering so that ICSI could take place. All was well at that end. It's not all about the woman; men go through this too.

We had eighteen beautiful high-grade embryos. The aim was to grow them to blastocyst (day five). Each day we received a phone call to say how they were doing, and we really felt that our babies were alive. You become attached and get upset when the numbers go down a little.

Due to my over-stimulation they decided to freeze our blastocyst embryos. We were devastated as we had thought we were good to go. This is the roller-coaster of IVF; nothing is predictable, and you must let go of the controls as the decisions are ultimately out of your hands. The key is not to be so rigid about the process. I had it all worked out in my head, I even had the date of when the baby would possibly be due if all of this went to plan. This allowed me to hope and to dream of a positive outcome, which you need to keep going, however it is not helpful when things do not go exactly to plan – it can cause you more stress than you need. I learnt to let it go a bit, to trust the process and take it in stages.

Again, we waited for my menstrual cycle. When it arrived, we phoned in. The insemination procedure is strange, but you potentially get to see your baby conceived as they insert the embryo through a tube using an ultrasound as guidance. We watched the whole thing on a screen. Well, that was it, it was where it was meant to be. We must be pregnant!

The two-week wait is torture, you watch every part of your body, every twitch to see signs of pregnancy. I was going for walks and eating lots of pineapple because I read somewhere this helps the embryo to attach. I was determined to make sure I did everything right.

Two weeks later, the test was negative. We were absolutely devastated, and disbelieving, as we had seen the whole process. It is strange how we were so convinced, as after all, there is only a 20-35% chance of success after the first treatment. This increases with time until the chance of a successful pregnancy increases to 45-53% after three full cycles. Nonetheless, this news led to lots of disappointment and grief.

After a few months we decided to try again. I am not sure if it was better or worse knowing what lay ahead: injections, procedures and the two-week-wait. We became more familiar with the nurses and the consultants and saw the familiar faces of other clients. I remember one day we were sitting in the waiting room and a couple came in with a toddler. We all just smiled at each other and watched in amusement as he entertained us with his playfulness. The mother of the young boy looked at us apologetically and said they often felt bad bringing him in as they know why people were there, and that they were going through the process again. Their little boy was an IVF baby, providing proof that it could work. This gave us more hope. I am not sure if we have ever knowingly met a child born through IVF – not that it matters, but we truly felt he was a miracle.

We went through the whole process again, with another negative result.

At this stage things were becoming strained. Two failed attempts and the accompanying heartache, we were tired of it all and decided to stop and take stock. People had already noticed that we were under strain, they could tell something was going on, and we wanted to keep our pain private.

A few weeks later when the NHS letter came to call us forward for treatment, I actually could not believe it, it appeared in such a timely manner, yet we were still so raw. It was a little nudge saying, *Go on, one more try I know you can do this.*

After many lengthy discussions we decided that this would be our last go. I think it is important to discuss how long you will try. We decided to do things a little differently. For a greater chance of success, we identified and eliminated all stressors from our lives: people, extra work and situations that caused us unnecessary stress.

Down the same road we had to go, back to the start of the whole process. Even though we had embryos, we went through everything all over again.

I learnt to be kinder to myself, I rewarded myself every day for taking the injections. I would go to appointments on my own in the early hours of the morning and blast music for the whole four-hour journey, surrounding myself with good things. The waiting rooms were full, even at 7am, full of people on the same journey, with the same look on their faces; and still no-one talking.

Understanding how this all works, though, you do have to leave it to the professionals and hand over the power to them to get you pregnant. Faith, I think it is called. This helped me a lot as I was so methodical with the whole process and thinking things would go a certain way. I became very upset at times when they didn't. A life lesson learnt there I feel.

On that day in August 2015, I was nervous. This was it for us, the strain was taking its toll and we were all in. It was a lovely drive up to the city, no problem getting parked we walked in to the all too familiar, packed waiting room, with new faces every time we took our seat and waited to be called. I remember we took a picture of us sitting in the waiting room, not sure why, but we always wanted to keep memories of our journey regardless of the outcome.

When we were called, I was brought to a separate room to get gowned up in a not-so-flattering blue medical gown. Lying on the bed, legs high in the air, breathing in through my nose and out through my mouth, having general chit chat, the nurse confirmed my name and checked the catheter to ensure the proper embryos were waiting.

The doctor came in, didn't speak. We watched the screen as before and saw the line of the tube, and just like that, we saw a flash of white light. An unmistakable white flash. We looked at each other and laugh acknowledging what we had just seen.

The doctor got up and said, 'Well that's that. Good luck.' Up I got and we headed home. The dreaded two weeks wait was upon us …

After ten days I sneaked off to take a test. It was positive! I get goosebumps every time I say that. In 2016 our beautiful baby was born, all 9lb 6oz …

Looking back, I have learned so much. The experience has changed me as a person. How could it not? Be kind to everyone you meet as you truly do not know what people are going through.

I learned to show up for myself, not for others.

Sharing our stories and being true to who we are changes things. It allows us to connect with ourselves and with others going through similar situations. We all have many sides to us and different life experiences. We are evolving, changing and learning all the time. It is our experiences that shape us and make us who we are. So, embrace it all, learn who you are, take time to know your values, your inner voice – and love all the colours of you.

ABOUT EMMA

Emma Weaver is the founder of Mental Wealth International, an organisation supporting businesses to achieve better mental health and wellbeing within the workplace.

Emma is also an international bestselling author with her debut novel, *The Blue Line*.

An international speaker, Emma uses her voice to champion causes close to her heart. Her purpose in life is to support people to have a voice and to create a safe platform where this can happen.

Emma has over twenty-two years' experience working in the mental health and wellbeing sector. Motivated by her purpose, Emma provides hope and expertise to people through both her personal and professional skills and experiences.

Emma currently resides in County Fermanagh, a beautiful rural county in Ireland. A native of Clones, Emma lives very close to her family homestead. She is a mother of three beautiful children, who are her world and her inspiration every day.

KAREN WEAVER
THE YEAR I DIDN'T ROAR

There will always be times in any journey where we have to pause. That for me was 2024. I'd had a few tumultuous years, personally, in the lead up to it and I believe 2024 was the year where everything hit the peripheral fan. I was, I suppose, processing the trauma of my daughter being ill over the last few years. I had to pour into her, but I was also trying to keep the business afloat and keep my magic happening … but the magic wasn't there, and I had to surrender to it.

It was also supposed to be a HUGE year where we roared into the world with *HEAR US ROAR*. We had launched the *LION* edition in Crom Castle in Ireland in November 2023, and I continued tapping along with it doing some filming days and keeping us on track with whatever revealed itself, but I had expected more for the project in 2024. However, my energy was not fully aligned, and I am a great believer in *not* showing up whenever your energy is not aligned with what you need to deliver, because people can see it in your eyes and feel it from your heart. When I'm connected, I'm a person that will usually glow – but not last year. I even attended an event where someone said to me, 'Goodness, Karen, who's this? Who is this person that's here?' They felt like it wasn't really me 'showing up'. I knew it, but I felt it was an event I had to show up for, even though I now wish I hadn't. That's why I believe with all of my heart and knowing, that 2024 was the year of the pause.

Importantly, 2024 was also the year I didn't give up. I stuck with it. I rode it out – and now I can build upon it.

On reflection, I now look back at 2024 as a year when 'nothing happened'. It was a year where everything stood still. I know I wasn't the only one this happened to in 2024. We had such high hopes, after a couple of rough years, and it brought a lot of things to the forefront. This has given me so much strength for 2025, because I'm back and I can feel it. The stars have now aligned and energetically, things are changing.

It was a year for me to recalibrate and for me to see what really mattered. It was a year for me to build the foundations for a transition; a transition year into coaching with NHI, and to getting the *HEAR US ROAR* stories out into the world. And I absolutely kept the faith with *HEAR US ROAR*. Every time I put even a small amount of energy into it, it just soared. Now, my stealth and faith are paying off because it's all coming together.

But how did I keep it all together – how did I do that? Well, by incorporating the wonderful principles of Napoleon Hill and doing the self-discipline camp. They are what have helped me through my transition. My health had started to decline, but during our heart meditation, we put healing to wherever needs it, and I did it consistently for three months. When I went to get results for my tests, where the doctors thought I may have had something seriously wrong with my womb (possibly womb cancer), we discovered that I didn't – there was nothing wrong. That was just amazing. I *know* it was because I placed my healing there. I know that focusing on gratitude and really getting clear on my thoughts helped with all the doubts and the transition I was going through.

As well as being a year of pause, 2024 was also a year of extremes; there were some amazing things happened, and then also some terrible things. I'm still clearing things and making things right because that's very important to me. I lost a friend I thought I would have forever, and it broke my heart. I had to heal from that. I also went through a divorce.

Now, 2025 is an opportunity to really learn from any mistakes I've made, which I identify with and know what they are. I can now take steps towards the greatness that I've experienced before, and it's all to do with the power of story, as well as sharing the Napoleon Hill principles through the power of story. I live it every day now. I can't see myself ever doing anything else. It balances in with my family and just makes everything *right*, so I will never compromise any of myself anymore.

That's one of the things that came to the forefront, that I give my all and more, and it can be difficult to stay focused on what's important when others don't always see or value what you do in the same way. I had to get clear on what is truly important – and that is *the power of story.*

Say yes to the things that you would do, whether you are getting paid or not. Say yes to the people around you who are aligned with your values. And just say yes to yourself because it's you that shows up every day, for you and for others.

I just love to serve and make good things happen in the lives of others and I feel blessed and excited that everything is aligning once again.

And so in 2025, writing this stealth and faith chapter marks a monumental time in my life and in the life of my family. And yes, there's going to be bumps in the road, and there's going to be things that need to be overcome, but I have a new-found appreciation for life. Ambition will always be there, but it's more of a wholesome ambition. I love to achieve things, and I will achieve things, but I will do it aligned with my core values, because when I compromise any of myself, it doesn't feel fulfilling to celebrate the wins. I hope that through reading this story you will feel inspired and have the courage to be stealthy and take the moves towards the big change you want to see in the world … because it does take courage.

And it does take faith. If I hadn't had faith that everything is happening for my greater good, I don't know if I could have gotten through last year. It was tough. Every time I thought I had conquered something, something else would come and slap me in the face. I also discovered that if I was down, people were kicking me when I was down. It's the universal law of attraction. But I like to hang out in positive. I realised that I was feeding into that feeling and facilitating it; allowing it to happen. When you choose to be the eagle, and the crow comes and bites, you need to rise to a higher altitude because the crows can't reach you there. You're too high and you're soaring. That's where the frequency is that I choose to hang out in. That's the frequency of the Napoleon Hill Institute. That's where we hang out. That's where things happen, where the flow is, where the movers and shakers are. I choose to be the eagle, to soar above and let the crows do their worst, but they will never reach me at my high altitude.

So, what does stealth and faith mean to you? Are you making moves and not telling anyone about it? Have you set a goal? And are you committing to that and taking the stealthy steps towards it coming to being? Do you have faith that you are going to achieve what your heart desires? If not, it's time to choose you, choose your dreams, and start taking action for yourself. Have faith that every step you take that feels aligned, and that you say yes to, is a step closer to your dreams.

ABOUT KAREN

Karen is an award-winning publisher, author, TEDx Speaker and advanced law of attraction practitioner.

Author of numerous books across many genres – fiction, motivational, children's and journals – she chooses to lead the way in her authorship generously sharing her philosophies through her writing.

Karen is also a sought-after speaker who shares her knowledge and wisdom on building publishing empires, establishing yourself as a successful author-publisher and book writing.

Having built a highly successful publishing business from scratch, signing major authors, writing over forty books herself and establishing her own credible brand in the market, Karen has developed strategies and techniques based on tapping into the power of knowing to create your dreams.

Karen is a gifted teacher who inspires others to make magic happen in their lives through her seven life principles that have been integral in her success.

When time and circumstance align, magic happens.

Website: kpwofficial.com